THE AMERICAN SPORTSMAN TREASURY

A Ridge Press Book

SE SHOOTING.

RTSMAN TREASURY

Alfred A. Knopf|New York

Editor-in-Chief: Jerry Mason
Editor: Adolph Suehsdorf
Executive Art Director: Albert Squillace
Art Director: Harry Brocke
Managing Editor: Robert Elman
Associate Editor: Moira Duggan
Associate Editor: Barbara Hoffbeck
Art Associate: Mark Liebergall
Art Associate: David Namias
Art Production: Doris Mullane

ACKNOWLEDGEMENTS
Cover: Photograph by Barry O'Rourke
Pages 2-3: Photograph by Arie deZanger
Sporting equipment in above two pictures courtesy Abercrombie & Fitch.

Page 141: Lithograph courtesy Library of Congress.
Pages 174-175, 177 bottom, 178, 179, 181, 182, 183:
Fly rods courtesy The Orvis Company, Inc., and the
Museum of American Fly Fishing, Manchester, Vermont.
Page 176: Fishing equipment courtesy Abercrombie & Fitch, New York.
Page 177 top: Fly rod courtesy Harry Darbee, Roscoe, New York.
Page 186: "In Search of Trout" reprinted by permission of Harold Ober Associates, Inc.
Pages 218-219, 222-223: Photographs courtesy "Sports Illustrated."
Pages 228-229: "Bugling Elk" courtesy Glenbow Foundation.
Page 230: "Caribou on the Smokey" courtesy Kennedy
Galleries, "Mule Deer" courtesy Glenbow Foundation.
Page 231: "Lake Louise" courtesy Kennedy Galleries.
Page 232: "Dall's Sheep" courtesy Glenbow Foundation.
Pages 232-233: "Moose in Water" courtesy Glenbow Foundation.
Page 234: "A Woodland Stag" courtesy Glenbow Foundation.
Pages 234-235: "Rocky Mountain Goats" courtesy Glenbow Foundation.
Page 235: "Bear in Landscape" courtesy Kennedy Galleries.
Page 236: Sketch of moose courtesy Kennedy Galleries.
Page 244: Lithograph courtesy Library of Congress.

CONTENTS

PREFACE

The American Sportsman Treasury is a loving tribute to the natural world. It is truly a treasury, bringing together twenty of the extraordinary features on North American hunting and fishing from *The American Sportsman*, which, in the short time it existed, opened new windows on the outdoors.

Each chapter has been chosen for its pertinence, for style, for wisdom, or for the validity and beauty of its associated photography —sometimes for all of these at once. Pictures, as you will see, are valued equally with words. It is never the intention simply to illustrate an article, but to make photography a major story-telling technique which integrates powerfully with the expertise of the text. In a number of instances, months were spent by photographers not only in solving the technical problems of photographing fish under water or capturing wary game with long lenses, but in earnest and patient effort to show the miracle of a creature's seasonal cycle of life. It is not too much to say that there are picture sequences here that have never been tried, and certainly never achieved, before.

For the experienced outdoorsman, few of the contributors to this volume will be strangers. Their authority is acknowledged wherever men and women find it important to analyze wing shooting, the taking of fish, the pursuit of game.

Lee Wulff, innovator and sportsman of impeccably high standards, is represented by a definitive article on hunting whitetails; Marvin E. Newman accompanies it with remarkable photographs of eastern deer in action.

Roderick Haig-Brown, the gentlemanly magistrate of Campbell River, offers a gracious insight to the mysteries of taking trout.

Charles F. Waterman, the ambidextrous hunter-fisherman of the South and Far West, writes beautifully on brown trout, and his friend, Bill Browning, the superb wildlife photographer from Montana, shows how the brown lives. This is only one of four amazing picture stories by Browning. The others blend with fascinating articles on bighorn sheep by Andy Russell, elk by Bob Hagel, and rainbows by David Shetzline.

Leonard M. Wright, Jr., contributes three enormously erudite articles on custom fly rods, the deadliest lures (flies, of course), and Florida bonefishing—the last of these portrayed with considerable skill by Bob Gelberg.

It is likely that few men, if any, know more about grouse, or describe more sensitively the acute relationship of man, bird, and gun dog, than George Bird Evans, know more about surf-casting for stripers in salt air than Frank Woolner, know more about the mystical woodcock than William G. Sheldon, or know more about wrestling bass than Grits Gresham; all of them are here.

Walter D. Osborne has a striking portfolio of ducks and geese, at rest and in flight. There is hunting art by the great Carl Rungius, and the diary of a pioneer trail guide about hardships and hunting on the Way West in the 1850's. And more.

The American Sportsman Treasury belongs with every memory of a day in the open.   *Jerry Mason*

THE B

Wariest

BY CHARLES F. WATERMAN PHO

ROWN:
of Trouts

TOGRAPHY BY BILL BROWNING

The brown trout holds his hallowed niche by cautiously choosing the classic dry fly and the master angler's upstream nymph. True brown-trout fishermen, building their own traditions, are a little like spawning salmon, climbing back up the same creeks to stand on the same rocks and cast for the same trout year after year. Most thoughtful of the trouts, the brown appeals to thinking fishermen who are likely to be successful in many fields, and it may be said that *all* dedicated brown-trout fishermen are successful people, if not in worldly goods, at least as anglers, for the fish is not for everyone and his pursuit is not a frivolous thing.

These fishermen are from nearly the same mold as Atlantic salmon seekers and are often the same people. Although there is nothing financially or socially exclusive about fly casting for brown trout, the skills and attitudes required are as selective as any membership committee.

Most of the famous streams that filled angling literature thirty years ago have been

Best brown-trout fly may vary with conditions, from tiny match-hatching dry pattern to big bucktail.

lost to progress, but newer brown trout traditions are coming on, and a world-traveled angler chiseled his initials unobtrusively on a rock near an unknown creek of the West fifteen years ago. He is not the kind to initial public places but he had released two three-pound browns there, caught on a small dry fly, and felt some celebration was in order. Each July he pulls back the willows a little and looks at his mark.

In the first week of September every year, a retired insurance executive from Pittsburgh stands in the same bend of the same creek near Bozeman, Montana. An investment banker from New York will be two pools down, although they haven't seen each other since last September, and a famous surgeon will be on a favorite ripple in Wyoming two hundred miles away. About the third week of September they'll be eating steak together in Livingston, Montana, with others of their kind, and in October they'll be scattered all over the world, some of them meeting in Scotland or Argentina—where

Large wet fly elicits pleasing action in Montana pool after natural presentation to good-sized fish.

each again wades his own little swatch of water for brown trout.

This migration goes largely unnoticed and is only an undercurrent of the flow of ordinary tourists, many of whom are fishermen but of a different breed. The trout regulars are frequently unknown near their favorite haunts, sometimes schooling up in motels and leaving no rooms for other travelers, sometimes renting disreputable shacks, and occasionally buying streamside property for "fishing cabins" which may turn into showplaces. Torn between their favorite streams, one of their favorite recurring topics is where to live, and they are constantly looking at property and contacting real estate dealers.

Their object of catching brown trout on a fly rod is the same for all, but the approach and reasons are very different.

A Chicago executive who makes his own annual circuit of trout waters and who runs his business by telephone, carries with him an immense chest which opens into innumerable, catalogued drawers of fly-tying materials. His brown trout urge comes from a constant desire to fashion different and exquisitely made flies and nymphs that will catch more and more brown trout to be carefully released. And, strangely, his creations are unnamed and have little relationship to standard patterns. Even more unusual is the fact that he has little knowledge of traditional flies, and seldom recognizes them.

His opposite number on a neighboring

Netting is often a delicate scooping operation which must be nicely timed, deftly executed.

creek is bound stiffly to traditional fly patterns and methods and would as soon use a worm as an unnamed nymph built of synthetic materials.

Even he is a fishing liberal compared to the successful young geologist who uses antique greenheart rods and nineteenth-century reels, and grumbles at the necessity for modern floating lines.

A real estate executive goes deep for most of his trout fishing, believing that seeing the floating fly and the rising trout makes fishing too simple, a doctrine he religiously avoids mentioning among his associates, some of whom fish only with the dry.

The brown trout is a native European and, because original American plantings were from Germany, it is often known as the German brown, or sometimes as the Loch Leven because later plantings came from Scotland. Scottish and German strains are intermingled in the United States, and the brown is found in most of the world where habitat is acceptable, as far north as Iceland. South America and New Zealand attract anglers because they have big fish and light fishing pressure and, within the United States, the best brown trout fishing is now in the West.

But for most brown trouters, size is relative and a twelve-inch fish from a hard-fished eastern stream is as much a prize as a four-pounder from a thundering western river—and possibly harder to catch.

Big browns are less sleek than smaller trout, but their rich colors can hardly be equaled.

American trouting mores came mainly from the British Isles, and British tackle and literature are still prized by the serious fisherman. It is mainly the dry-fly lovers who still use bamboo rods, although glass has taken over most of the fishing world.

Rods have become lighter and generally shorter, down to five-foot gestures for some experts, but most settle for seven or 7½-foot rods on small streams and eight or 8½-footers on bigger water. The classic reel is a single-action to match the rod's size, and although an automatic would work the lesser streams few perfectionists would consider it.

Science has blunted the game a little by producing monofilament leader material so much stronger for its diameter than silkworm gut that the latter is hardly ever seen now. Trout fishermen have always classified leader tippets by diameter instead of strength, and 6X gut required a master's touch to land a sizable fish, while the beginner snapped off his fly before a fish saw it. The same diameter in nylon monofilament is so strong that even an ordinary mortal has a chance with a two-pound trout. Dry-fly leaders are tapered and from nine to twenty feet long.

Any dry-fly fishing for brown trout is a study of water movements and casting delicacy, even if the prey is an unsophisticated bumpkin in a wilderness river. The natural float of a fly is the product of careful casting and wading, the cast pushed up and a little across stream with the line mended or slacked over intervening currents of different speeds. If fly selection is unimportant, as it is on some waters, these skills alone will take fish, but when the fly must match a hatch of natural insects, as on most hard-fished waters, the problem is multiplied. And if the insect to be matched is very small, calling for flies of #16 size or smaller, and the water is very clear, the true brown

trouter cinches up his waders and is willing to miss his lunch.

Maneuvering into position for fly presentation is an art in itself, and a veteran stalker can wade almost imperceptibly with the patience of a heron. Even when the best possible casting station is reached there will be the intriguing problems of varying current speed, and the perfect cast must show the fly to the fish before he sees the leader or the line. False casting must be done so that no shadow strikes the fish's lie; he must see the fly long enough to intercept it, but he should not be permitted to study it too long or too minutely.

The artist prefers to cast to a specific fish, selected before he approaches closely, and if the fish is visible on its feeding station the contest is that much more exciting. A splashy upstart who comes from an unseen hold and takes the fly before the chosen target reacts is gratifying evidence the fly is attractive, but the triumph is incomplete and the chosen victim may be scared.

Visible or not to the caster, the trout is concerned with two locations: his lie where he awaits his food, and his taking area where he actually intercepts it on its downstream path. In his feeding lie he holds comfortably near bottom, in a pocket protected from hard current by obstructions or bottom conformation, with his head upstream.

A sizable fish generally takes small natural flies gently and, if the hatch is fairly heavy, the flies coming by regularly, he establishes a feeding rhythm, intercepting his fragile quarry at a point requiring the least physical exertion, sometimes sipping several from the surface before sinking smoothly to his station to hold for a time before rising again. His routine is duly noted by a studious caster and the artificial fly is applied at the logical moment.

If all goes perfectly, the artificial comes drifting downstream at the exact speed of the translucent naturals and the riser takes it with the same gentle sucking, the rod tip moves up gently and the tiny hook is placed. So deft is the perfect presentation that a heavy fish may take another natural fly before he feels the point. If such a sequence develops as prescribed, this single event will make a fishing day complete.

It is primarily the smaller fish that feed on flies, and as the brown trout grows he loses his dainty manners and becomes a deep-going ruffian for the most part, striking huge streamers and gleaming hardware to the guarded dismay of those with delicate gear. Still, through some memory of his youth, a great fish will sometimes rise to a #18 dry, therewith burning more energy than any tiny insect body could replace, and find himself opposing the tackle only his truest admirers would use.

Matching a hatch of insects, usually one of dozens of forms of mayflies, is part of the brown trout formula, and although exact duplication may be impossible, success depends on at least approaching size and color of the naturals, whether with conventional pattern or special creation.

At least the dry-fly fisher can watch his successes and failures take form and can make corrections. Dedicated nymph anglers say this fishing is oversimplified and that true proficiency comes only in showing unseen patterns to unseen fish. The nymph, a stage of the water-reared insect in which it is preparing to shed a husk and appear as a fly, is represented by subsurface patterns, possibly moving slightly as though through their own energies but generally drifting free, and the presentation is both the deadliest and most difficult of fly approaches, as potential drag is invisible to the caster. It is almost wet-fly fishing, but not quite, and the plucking strike after a slightly upstream cast is detected only through practice and concentration. When near the bottom, busily

nymphing fish often leave no surface sign.

There is yet another delicate form, surface-film fishing, which requires tiny flies in the #20 to 22 range, not truly dry flies but suspended after a careful cast by surface tension, and used when fish feed on really tiny things, generally with little bulges, not quite the same as the dorsal and tail rise of the nympher and not quite the plop or gurgle of the dry-fly taker.

Attractions of bigger and bigger fish have coarsened the methods of many fine anglers who know that a four- or five-pounder is more drawn by a hellgrammite or minnow than by a frothy insect, and their descent to big streamers and gargantuan woolly worms is understandable.

Big-fish methods for most of these anglers have developed only in the past ten years. The basic technique began on big rivers in the fall when heavy, brightly colored browns feed freely in preparation for spawning in late autumn, winter, or early spring. With the summer fly hatches over, the streamers became bigger and bigger to copy bigger and bigger sculpins or shiners. At first the rods used were just the slightly longer and stiffer tools reserved for normal, windy-day operation, but there was a quick concession to the weight-forward, tapered line formerly used only for black bass and salt water.

Once turned from tradition, the big-fish seeker became almost completely practical. At first he was content to cast a big streamer across current and let it swing down on a slow retrieve, leaving a trace of wake on the surface. The storied muddler minnow, a burr-headed, neutral-shaded imitation of nothing in particular, but hinting of sculpins, grasshoppers, and huge nymphs, did this well and some of the surface strikers slashed like dolphins.

But the biggest fish in the bigger rivers hang deep, and it was only a step to sinking lines and then to the shooting head, a short section of heavy line backed by monofilament running material to make long casts easy. The leader was shortened to keep a fly almost constantly within inches of the bottom, possibly even rolling on the scoured gravel, and now the casts neared a hundred feet, propelled by saltwater fly rods and the double haul.

The muddler stayed on, getting bigger, and receiving special touches of color or conformation to please its individual employers, and since natural bucktail grows only so long the double tie was employed in other patterns to make larger streamers.

The tiny, upstream nymph was replaced by strange, fuzzy worms, almost hellgrammites, and the final heresy was a fleck of lead on the leader and possibly on the hook, too. At that point some diehards commented that the only relation to fly fishing remaining was the presence of the reel at the end of the rod rather than its location near the thumb as in surf-casting, but some lovers of the Loch can switch smoothly from dry flies and cobweb leaders to the steelhead format in a single day and enjoy both equally.

In a spring creek, my wife, with woman's patience and a trout lover's stealth, slipped her felt-soled waders through a fringe of watercress and to the dark sand bottom of an exceptionally wide pool. At the head of the pool the flow was only moderate, but it was deep there and the current's deposits had fanned out until the pool's tail, seventy feet wide, was less than a foot deep and barren of fish during most of the day, running so slowly that the dark sand had settled, forming gentle, sculptured designs on the more solid bottom structure. It was dusk and the cottonwood leaves hardly moved above the pool. There was no identifiable fly hatch, but a delicate drone of scattered land insects and an occasional surface ring, too small for any catchable fish.

The featured actor appeared first as a broad, gentle bulge where the bottom shelved up from the pool's head. More pronounced as the water shallowed, the bulge finally became a bow wave, very slow and hesitating at irregular intervals, marking the progress of a foraging fish.

There was no tricky current to cast across but a big brown trout in ten inches of clear, still water is easily flushed and I nervously watched my wife appraise the situation. The line or leader must not fall across the fish, false casting must be kept out of his range of vision, and a poorly presented fly would strike like a grenade on so still a surface.

Instead of advancing to the fish, now sixty feet away, Debie gently retreated to the watercress again and backed to solid ground. There she could work out line over land with no danger of being seen. The cruiser moved haphazardly and Debie chose to cast when he was quartering slightly away from her, laying the #16 Blue Dun three feet beyond his bulge. The bow wave stopped dead and for one moment it appeared something had gone wrong, but the fish had simply been attracted to something on the bottom, the edge of his tail showing lazily as he tipped down slowly and then moved off at another angle. The touchy cast must be repeated. The next try landed only a foot from where the fish's head must have been, but it drew no attention until Debie twitched it—so slightly it might have been a fly adjusting its wings. The fish turned a little and took solidly.

The fight began slowly. The fish was uncertain what was wrong and moved with a single shove of his tail toward the deeper head of the pool, coming to a stop when he felt the positive pull of the rod. He then rushed on into deeper water and made his only jump among the current bubbles there.

Once, when teased by a dogged series of tugs in the deep end, he squirted almost the length of the pool and came nearest to freedom as he raked along a fallen downstream tree. Probably never seeing his captor in the gloom among indistinct shoreline bushes, he uselessly wore himself down in the open water and was persuaded toward the watercress fringe, finally to turn on his side and flounder awkwardly under the rod tip. Debie then came back into the water and somehow scooped him to the grass without a net. As in all good fishing stories, the 6X tippet broke as she landed him, and he was only a little shy of four pounds.

On another evening, this time in late fall, I fished for bigger trout in a wide mountain river, heavy water where the thrust of current moved gravel disturbingly under my feet as I sidled uncertainly to a cásting position as near as possible to the main current where no fisherman could have stood. Even with the steelhead rod I carried, I needed all the distance I could get, for well out in the crowding torrent of midstream there were holding areas formed by huge boulders, probably rolled down centuries ago from bordering bluffs, most of them now invisible except for traces of diversion in surface currents. Some of them pushed out of the water, obvious targets for the caster who knows heavy fish may lie in the downstream eddy, as well as in the bulge of delayed water above the obstruction.

The water was cold. A chilling mountain shadow suddenly reached me from the opposite bank as I waded in, and there was a skift of snow among scattered pines only a little way up the slopes.

It took time for the fly to work down. Cast straight across, it sliced the surface as the full rush of water whipped the line downstream and then the big streamer, a nameless plagiarism of the Silver Doctor, dug down toward the bottom, only to swing shallow again as it fetched up directly downriver. A little manipulation of it there and

I would pick up and make sawing false casts before reaching for midstream again. My big fish took below a boulder where he had held in the gravel pocket, twenty feet across. The streamer simply stopped and I struck; if he'd taken in direct current he would have set the hook himself.

Such big males may lose the sleek contours of their youth, but they are never grotesque to the fly fisherman, who counts these richly colored trout the most beautiful of all fish and does not see the hooked jaw and reptilian grimace. This one, wearing his bright spawning colors, came out immediately, going high and sailing horizontally for an instant, showing his long, toothy jaw, and then ran hard against the current.

Later jumps were flounderings as the heavy leader snubbed him short and I looked furtively for a place to beach him, sidling downstream. I knew that when he tired he would swing below me. He made the big trout's plunging and dogged fight. He would hold in one spot and give headshaking tugs that meant he had his head down behind a boulder and out of the current, a place you wouldn't want him resting for long, with the hook wearing a constantly larger hole.

I worked him back into the current several times and finally there was the slower tug and the abrupt sweep downstream as he lost his power and went with the river, one of the bad moments because he had to be stopped and swung toward the bank.

I gave a little line but he swung, slowly at first, and then rapidly toward my side of the river and I led him into shallow and nearly dead water where, with careful guidance, he nearly beached himself. A friend scooped him to the bank. He was more than eight and a half pounds. He was a size to match his roaring river and a fine catch, but no better than a smaller brown trout that matches its own tinkling stream. ◉

The Best Way to

Hunt Whitetail

by Lee Wulff

Alone and silent, the deer hunter who stalks his quarry, without aid of dogs or drivers, becomes part of the forest and thus gains a sharp awareness of the wild world, an awareness denied most men.

photography by **Marvin E. Newman**

A butternut tree, tired with the weight of a hundred and fifty years, lost its grip on the rocky ledge and lay stretched out with its broken moorings and half-rotted branches making a dark and ragged pattern against the brown leaves. Below, on the gentle slope, the hardwood mixture of the Vermont hillside stretched away until all the beyond was screened from sight. Behind was a gentle dip and then the land rose steeply for fifty yards to reach a ridge that sloped gently, both right and left, as far as the eye could penetrate.

Clad in green plaid, nestled against the butternut stump in such a manner that no human outline was visible, and moving little but his eyes, a hunter waited. He had been there since dawn. He watched a pair of squirrels, busily working in the dry leaves a hundred feet off, unhurrying and unconcerned. Other than the squirrels and a few nuthatches and jays, he'd seen no living thing. It was the fifth day of deer season.

In Vermont, roughly one licensed deer hunter in ten gets his buck. Fully a quarter of the deer killed are taken on the opening day of the fifteen-day season. The chances of a hunter's getting a deer on any single day after the first weekend is something like one in two hundred. There were probably three bucks somewhere on the long ridge—and twice as many hunters.

Our particular hunter had chosen his hideout with care. He had selected the kind of place a deer would choose to hide on such a day, then settled himself in it to wait. The bucks that had survived to this point had already settled into the many similar places open to them, but if one were disturbed he might then move to this one. A deer, resting or feeding where the hunter sat, would be pretty safe. If a hunter tried to approach from behind, the gentle wind curling up over the ridge would carry his scent hundreds of yards ahead of him. The deer's keen eyes watching the slope below would see the first telltale movement. His ears would hear the special sound of human

Eight-point buck, in full retreat, leaps high to clear brushy tangle.

*These whitetail deer,
all photographed in New York,
are typical of what any
solitary hunter may
encounter if he is sufficiently
quiet and watchful.
Small buck, upper right, and
larger one, above,
are alert to hunter's
presence but have
not panicked. Two fine
bucks in the lower
pictures have raised their
flags in alarm and are
bounding away, but both are still
within easy range. Note
how well does and young, center
right, are camouflaged
by their natural surroundings.*

Top: Two immature does clear stone
wall at edge of orchard. Above: Forkhorn,
suddenly aware of presence of human,
leaps for safety of thicker cover. Right:
Fine whitetail buck is surprised by
approach of hunter and stands fast for a
moment—torn between curiosity and alarm.

26

footsteps in the dead, dry leaves at a distance greater than the eye could see. Should a hunter approach him in such a spot, he would move off slowly—a brown shadow, barely rustling the brown leaves. Where would he go? Perhaps just across the ridge, out of sight and listening, then back to the same spot once the hunter had passed from view. Perhaps to another similar spot where he could feel secure. But once a deer starts moving, he must look ahead and listen. He has little fear of the moving hunter, for the sound of human movements in the stillness of the forest is a dead giveaway. As easily as he breathes, he scents the forest air and with it reads the presence of the things upwind. He moves tentatively, a few steps at a time.

Shortly after ten, the waiting hunter saw just the briefest movement of a brown shape past a distant white birch trunk, a moving shadow where no motion should have been, over a hundred yards away at the same level on the slope. Slowly he raised the binoculars to his eyes. He carefully scanned the spot, but found no patch of hair, no flash of brown. Had that distant movement been an illusion? He studied hard. A whole deer, standing lengthwise, can be hidden by the trunk of a tree. Half a deer, showing at an angle, can look like a rotting stump or a cluster of dead leaves. Suddenly the deer materialized—sprang into being in the autumnal pattern like the dotted numbers that show up suddenly in tests for color blindness. The deer was lying down. The

lifted head faced down the slope, dimly seen at that distance through blurred twigs. If there were horns on that head they were hard to see, and the hunter had to be sure. He waited and he watched. Minutes later when the deer's head turned to look uphill, a splash of sunlight flashed on slender horns for an instant. He centered the crosshairs on the neck where it merged into the rounded mound of the body. Death came to the deer more swiftly than the sound of the rifle shot.

The whitetailed deer may well be the finest big-game animal of all. He provides an annual crop of fine wild meat that may run as high as a hundred-million pounds, which hunters pay an estimated dollar per pound to harvest. Hunting is spread from Florida and Texas to Nova Scotia and British Columbia. Perhaps no other big-game animal has learned to live so well with man and survive such heavy hunting pressure. The whitetail is a trophy in the oldest tradition of western European civilization, paralleling such horned animals as the roebuck and red deer, long hunted in reality and story. The species fits the pattern of majesty and grace in a manner that such an equally edible and possibly as sporting an animal as the tapir does not.

Whitetail range in size at maturity from under fifty pounds in the Florida Keys to more than three hundred in some of the most suitable northeastern habitat. Normally heavier and larger than the doe, the buck is big enough to be a major trophy, yet small enough on the average for a lone hunter to drag or carry home. He can be, and most often is, a trophy that one man seeks alone, in single-minded endeavor. Originally few in numbers and limited to the eastern coast, the whitetail has taken on a continental range.

Every year in most of this range, when snow covers the ground, the deer must browse in order to survive. To fortify himself against the lean, cold months, a deer must gorge himself during the fall on the forest's nut crop and the vegetation of its slopes and meadows. When his annual test of survival comes, he is able to browse and digest the young growth, the tip ends, of trees and shrubs. The food is poor, but it will carry a deer through the cold months if he can find enough of it. Then, if the snow is not too deep to forbid movement for too long a time, he will come out in the spring—with a thirty percent weight loss— to seek the first tender shoots in the fields and meadows. When there is a heavy, immobilizing snow that prevents deer from reaching the needed browse, they starve and die. Last winter was such a year for southwestern Vermont. We found thirteen deer carcasses within three-hundred yards of my hunting camp. It was sad, indeed, to find them, sadder still to see on that day's tour of the property the track of but one lone, living deer and to know that for several years to come deer hunting would be very, very poor.

This was a disastrous setback to an already dwindling local population. It was so far down in the previous hunting season because of heavy winter-kill that only one hunter took a buck on a two-hundred-and-fifty-acre area that usually produces more than half a dozen. All living things must die, and man, the supreme predator, takes his toll. But he must also guarantee the seed that means survival. By law we limit ourselves to a hunting season that may vary in number from one day to a hundred. In most areas we do not hunt with dogs; in some we hunt bucks only; in others we limit the number of hunters who may work in concert. When dogs run deer, they trail the animals and keep them moving. The hunters take stands where they hope the deer will pass. This is the time-honored and

Fine whitetail buck was intercepted late in day as it moved from bedding ground to feeding area.

universally legal method of taking rabbits, but it has been found to be too deadly for deer hunting save in the swampy ground of our southeastern seaboard. In many places, a favored method is that of driving deer: A group of hunters surrounds a section of woodland and, while part of the group drives through to move the deer, others "stand" to shoot them as they pass. These methods are not for us on these pages. Our interest lies in the challenge of outsmarting, by hunting skill and good fortune, a revered animal.

Nature knows no sentiment, but man, of a certainty, does. Having learned that deer are polygamous and that a fair share of males may be taken without disturbing the recuperative potential of the entire herd, we tend, in some cases, to carry the bucks-only concept too far. For a long time we have practiced a chivalry that accords special protection to the weaker female of the species, and some states, in spite of heavy hunting pressure, go all the way with bucks-only laws. When more than the "fair share"

of males is taken, the result is a reduction of the reproductive capabilities of the herd and the strength and stamina of its individuals. The "kindness" of a law that permitted only one buck to be killed by rifle on my property in Vermont last year, while thirteen deer, only two of which were male, died the same year by starvation may stand in question.

How does a sportsman hunt the whitetail? He may wait in a place where he thinks a deer will come to hide or feed, or a place along a deer run where the animal is likely to pass when moving from one area to another. He may move quietly through the woods, trying to see a deer before it hears, smells, or sees him. Or he may simply walk along casually, hoping to see a deer that feels it is so well-camouflaged it need not move out of sight.

The wild-country deer that sees few hunters may simply run away from danger. When frightened, he can head into the wild area surrounding him and travel fast and far. If there's snow on the ground and the swamps are frozen, a hunter can follow him readily enough by tracking, but if the ground is dry, hard, and leaf-covered, that deer is pretty safe. Even if a deer is followed, he'll be waiting, having eventually swung back to a spot where he can watch the last loop of the path he took. By contrast, when the country is hunted hard, a deer that rushes madly away from one danger is almost certain to encounter a silent hunter like our friend upon the hill. The harder the pressure, the more certain it is that a deer will simply bound swiftly into the nearest cover and pause right there to watch and wait. From that position of safety he can determine by sight, sound, or smell whether the hunter has decided to follow him or to look for another buck. If the deer feels that his position is safe, he may wait there to see. If not, he will move off carefully to some other position.

Can a hunter walk up to a deer, see him without being seen, and shoot him? Sometimes. When the woods are damp and quiet, a man may do it by the rare skill that lets him travel so silently the deer neither sees nor hears him. When the woods are dry and noisy, he can do it only by trickery. Or he may combine trickery and skill. Deer know full well that they blend into their woodland background, and they often stand motionless while hunters pass within their vision. A hunter may make a lot of noise as he travels, but if he constantly looks to the sides he may see a deer that has chosen to remain immobile and to rely on its protective coloring to hide it. Such a hunter must not only have sharp eyes but must be able to recognize the deer when he sees it. A deer standing in the open and perfectly outlined is rarely encountered. The animal is usually half-hidden and must be recognized by minor things, like the flick of his white tail, the white patch on his throat,

the brightness of his eye, or the fact that his legs—in contrast to the trees among which he stands—grow thicker as they rise from the ground. To reach a deer over soft, wet, silent ground, the hunter still must worry about snapping a branch or rubbing his clothing against something that will make a sound. More than that, he must make sure the varying winds do not carry his scent to the deer he hunts. And he must stay out of sight until he is ready to shoot.

Naturally, a hunter needs to know where deer will most likely be in order to hunt the right area. If he knows where deer hide and feed, he can conduct his hunting as a continuous stalk to those places, and, if wise, he'll try to approach deer from a position of vantage. Ideally, he can work down a mountain notched with benches, approaching from above, peering quietly over each ledge to the bench below.

It pays to find out where deer feed by walking the woods before the season starts. Generally speaking, they feed where there are beechnuts, acorns, or apples, green meadows or good browse. They feed early and late and at night during hunting season, and they know when the season opens. They are alerted to opening day by the sounds of the cars on the roads the night before and by the unusual early morning sounds. If they are very young, they may be a little careless that first day, but once the shooting starts they learn very quickly.

When there is snow, the hunter can easily see tracks and follow deer. He can track for hours to see where the animal went. He can pick up the same track the next day to learn where the deer fed and where he bedded down. Eventually he can recognize a pattern and try to ambush the deer as he travels a familiar route, or approach him during one of his periods of waiting, coming in on him from an unexpected direction.

Favorite hiding places are ridges and side

hills where a few steps can take a whitetail out of sight to anyone approaching, or open areas where anyone approaching may be seen and heard at a distance.

A hiding deer will plan on some safe avenue of escape from an approach in any direction. If the animal cannot simply fade away into invisibility, he has one final resource—his speed and maneuverability. It has been estimated that only three out of a hundred shots fired at running deer ever draw blood. Shooting a running whitetail as he streaks through the timber calls for rare skill. The wisest hunters usually pick a lane between branches, hold there, and shoot when the deer shows in their sights.

When the forest consists largely of conifers, the hunter's vision is especially limited. Hunting becomes rather a game of hide and seek. Snow is almost imperative for tracking and a man can then pick up a deer's track, estimate how far ahead he is, and, circling, try to approach for a glimpse of the animal.

If snow has fallen, but melted on sunny slopes, the deer will follow the sun, knowing they are less conspicuous against the bare ground than against the stark whiteness of the snow.

Rainy days in the woods are noisy. The splatter of drops from sky and branches makes a rough blanket of sound that drowns out the hunter's footsteps, and the dry branches that snap so readily are water-soaked and soft and break with a muted sound. When it rains, deer may be found feeding where they can watch for an approaching hunter, or resting where the driving rain will bother them least. At the end of one rainy day when I was slogging home, tired and discouraged, I glanced over at a huge maple, then glanced away. Doing a double-take, I looked again. Standing tightly against the gray-brown trunk was a gray-brown buck and, at my second look, he lit

out, white flag flying. In three jumps he was safely out of sight.

Deer, like most animals that know a territory, have daily patterns, although most rules are off soon after hunting season starts. Their approach to a feeding ground from a resting area (they normally rest when it's warmest and feed when it's cool) can almost be timed to the minute. If it's in their mind to go to a certain place and a hunter's presence blocks them, look for them to detour but to continue to the original goal. If a wise hunter sees a deer and can guess where it is headed, he may be able to get there first and wait in ambush.

Hunting for only bucks is quite different from hunting deer of both sexes. Where bucks alone are legal game, they become wary in the extreme, and they tend to be loners, hiding out during the day. When it becomes important not merely to see deer but to see bucks, a hunter looks for the marks on the saplings where they've rubbed their antlers, or where they've pawed the ground during rutting season. A poor hunter may see two dozen does in a single day and never see a buck.

One of the biggest whitetail racks I ever saw was on a head that moved into my vision briefly as I sat, rock still, some sixty yards away. The buck was wise enough to know what a man looks like, even when that man was leaning quietly back in a cluster of small oaks. I didn't move and my clothing was an inconspicuous green. His doe, a big silver-gray animal with all the grace of a woodland queen, had crossed ahead of him. When she moved on, I was waiting for the buck behind her, alert and ready. Yet I didn't have a chance. That big buck moved his head into sight as if to follow her and then, just as I saw him, he saw me, motionless and camouflaged though I was, and he vanished in an instant.

All too often, when the bucks-only hunter

has finally made himself so much a part of the forest that the other animals have forgotten he is there and the deer come, the does come first. Immobilized where he sits or stands, the hunter dares to move only his eyes. He cannot turn his head to see if a buck is in sight behind him, or anywhere beyond the angle of his vision. He can only watch the does and wait, unless, feeling sure there is a buck in sight behind him, he takes a chance. I did it once, after five does had been feeding within fifty yards of me for more than ten minutes. The buck had stayed on the higher level, but when I turned he was in sight and within range, and seconds later he was mine.

Whitetail country is usually woodland and it is rare for a hunter to get a long shot. Most shots at whitetails are made at less than a hundred yards. Open sights are adequate, and they have the advantage of not being affected by rain or snow, which can interfere with vision through a scope sight. However, scope sights do give a hunter better placement of his bullets and thus mean cleaner kills, especially on the longer shots. The best deer gun has a scope sight which can be easily detached and replaced with an open sight when the rain is heavy or when snow, barely melting on the branches in the sun, will splatter lens faces and then freeze on them.

Binoculars are a great asset, especially where the law permits only bucks to be shot. Spikehorns are difficult to see at a distance, especially if there are any branches to break up a clear vision of the head. Although a scope sight can magnify to a similar power, bringing a gun up to look through a scope is a much more visible motion than the simple lifting of binoculars to the eyes. Furthermore, lifting a rifle and aiming it to find out whether something you see is a deer or not may be effective, but it isn't particularly courteous if the ob-

ject of your interest turns out to be another hunter. Magnification can be valuable, too, close in as well as far out. Dozens of times, a close study of a thicket, with glasses, has suddenly shown a deer's eye, or the bend of a leg, or the patch of white on the throat.

The best cartridge is probably the .308. It is a short cartridge for its power, making for a shorter action and a lighter gun. Any caliber from the .243 to the .300 Magnum is effective on deer, but too fast a bullet will deflect more readily if it strikes a branch. The pioneer .30/30 is still one of the finest deer loads. The best gun is one which combines accuracy and wallop—with accuracy by far the more important factor of the two.

Most of the deer killed are fatally wounded on the first shot. Repeat firepower is a delusion. Five fast shots at a running deer are usually less effective than a single carefully made shot.

One contemplated change in today's hunting methods I think should be considered. That is, all deer rifles should be plugged to permit only a single shot without reloading. Such a regulation would save a good many humans. No hunter would want to waste his single bullet unless he was sure he would be making a lethal shot at a deer.

It is not unrealistic to hope for restrictions of this type. After all, many laws have already been passed for the sake of preserving our deer populations. True, some of these laws—like the bucks-only restriction—have failed to achieve their goals in certain areas. But limitations as to the number of deer that may be killed and the season when they may be taken have achieved gratifying results. The whitetail has learned to survive in proximity to man by his increased awareness, and we have learned to let the species survive by balancing our hunting pressure with the animal's need to multiply. May the whitetail continue to grow in numbers and his range increase. ◉

Shorebird
of the
Uplands

*The woodcock is a bizarre recluse
with a bill nearly as long as
its body, an explosive, unpredictable
manner of flight, and an
elite following among gunners.
by William G. Sheldon*

Photography by The American Sportsman-ABC

As twilight descended on an open slope fringing the Green Mountains of Vermont on an early May evening many years ago, spring peepers set up their chorus in a marshy fen a few hundred yards below, bats darted by in their evening foraging for insects, and a whippoorwill began to sing at the meadow's edge. There I watched one of the most colorful courtship performances in the avian world, the sky dance of the male American woodcock. Accompanied by a veteran hunter and naturalist, this was my introduction to a remarkable and curious game bird. Leaping aloft in a spiral flight to three hundred feet, where he appeared no bigger than a moth, he descended to his courtship field like a crippled plane zigzagging to earth. This descent was punctuated at intervals by his chirp-like, liquid song. On the ground he uttered a queer insect-like "peent" at intervals. Little did I realize when I saw that performance what an important part this bird would play in my life.

As a woodcock hunter since 1935, I have long been fascinated by this shorebird of the uplands. In the early days I was as baffled and curious as my fellow sportsmen when, seated before a fire on an October evening, we discussed the many mysteries of such a singular bird, each of us expounding his theories. I became aware of how little was known about this popular little game bird which we depended on for sport in the years when ruffed grouse were scarce.

During the war, when I often dreamed of woodcock while crouched in a foxhole under fire with fellow commando troops, I made up my mind to devote the rest of my life to a career in wildlife conservation. I returned to Massachusetts to train other young men in this rewarding profession and to conduct wildlife research. Located in an area with abundant breeding woodcock, I had the chance to turn an avocation into a serious investigation of the elusive timberdoodle. Sportsmen usually are familiar with the quarry only during the fall, but, of course, game abundance and behavior in the fall often hinge on what happens during the other nine months of the year.

The woodcock is so colorful and unusual that it has many aliases, among them timberdoodle, bog sucker, wood snipe, bec (for the French, *bécasse*), night partridge, mud snipe, blind snipe, wall snipe, bog borer, siphon snipe, and owl snipe.

The European woodcock, which is much like ours but almost twice as large, has been famed as a game bird and table delicacy for centuries, even being incorporated into the English language. ("Cockshut time" referred to netting woodcock in England and became a synonym for twilight.)

The bizarre woodcock is a recluse by nature, abroad at dusk and night, unique in physical adaptations, and a test to the gunner's eye. Unrecognized by many laymen, its mystery challenges the scientist who strives to discover some of its secrets.

A woodcock's body is as large as a man's fist, with brown, black, and gray plumage which blends with the forest floor. Large black shoe-button eyes set well back on a head which is the size of a golf ball, a long bill, and spindly short legs are at once

apparent. Its ear patches are below and in front of the eyes. Because so much of the skull is occupied by the large eye sockets, the brain, in the course of evolution, rotated so that now it is literally upside down. The most conspicious feature is the bill, which averages two and three-quarters inches long. When probed to the hilt in mud, the sensitive nerves at the tip act as antennae which detect the movement of earthworms. It is hinged near the tip, enabling the woodcock to grasp worms underground or pick up ants or catch flying moths aboveground. These curious and extraordinary features are unique to the woodcock. Woodcock spring from a shorebird ancestry, but in the course of time have moved into the uplands.

Unlike the fast-running grouse or the scuttling pheasant, the woodcock lies well in front of a dog. This bird has gained a devoted following among upland gunners; it elicits the highest ethics of sportsmanship and holds little appeal for the meat hunter. Often, hunting woodcock goes hand in hand with ruffed-grouse shooting, but there is a dedicated coterie of sportsmen who prefer hunting woodcock above all other birds.

I have a favorite woodcock covert in central Vermont, which I discovered in 1948, the site of a farm abandoned forty years earlier. Once prosperous with crops of hay, potatoes, apples, and corn, its topsoil was washed away by a thousand rains and the crops began to fail. Today only an old cellar hole, tumbled stone walls, and abandoned orchards bear witness to its former occupancy.

Fields grew up to hardhack with patches of aspen, knolls became covered with small birches, and damp swales with willow, alder, and other assorted shrubs. It was dotted with small open fields. To a bird shooter's eye it spelled woodcock cover.

One early October, the first hunting day

of the fall, I was hunting there with an old gunning partner. I cast off my female setter, a fast-going, fairly wide-ranging dog but absolutely staunch and dependable on woodcock. My friend was accompanied by a highly intelligent and effective pointer.

As we struggled up the steep hillside, the pointer drifted into an edge of birches, slowed his pace, finally crept forward a few steps, and stiffened in a classic point. I moved in on the left, gun ready. My friend guarded the other side. For a few seconds the tableau was frozen, then the picture shattered in a flurry of action. With a metallic "whirr," a long-billed woodcock broke for the edge. My friend missed the twisting target with his first barrel but connected with his second at about twenty yards. The bird dropped, leaving a puff of russet feathers drifting in the air. At the command "Fetch," the old pointer romped forward and brought the bird to his master.

As we continued our hunt we found lots of woodcock sign—the characteristic chalk-colored droppings about the size of a quarter. For the amount of sign, we were very puzzled by the scarcity of birds. I shot another woodcock over my setter on the edge of a field, and later we shot a grouse and woodcock which flushed almost simultaneously from the same spot.

This was the end of our sport for the morning, although we carefully combed over a hundred acres of this prime covert. The temperature, which had been frosty at dawn, approached eighty degrees at noon, and we decided to leave. As we trudged down an old road on the way out, our dogs ranged under a dense stand of spruces. The dogs pointed, and woodcock exploded from the forest floor. The spruces were much too thick to afford shots, and we determined to return late in the afternoon to try our luck again. In hot weather it is typical of woodcock to seek the clean forest floor under dense stands of conifers where they rest in the cool shade during the day.

We returned half an hour before sundown. Woodcock began to fly from the spruces at low altitudes, dropping into the hardhack of the open fields. We enjoyed some excellent shooting, easily filling our bag limit of four woodcock apiece. At sunset we descended from the cover. Woodcock buzzed by in the dusk, lighting in the feeding coverts on the hillside. Many hunters have described seeing woodcock drop into coverts like falling leaves during twilight. They often mistakenly interpret this as a group of "flight" birds. They return in the morning but find only a few, thus confirming in their minds that many have moved south. I have found that twilight feeding flights occur at all times of year except spring. I have counted fifty lighting in one small field in July. They feed and usually leave about a half hour before sunrise, scattering to upland retreats and often to dense shade if the weather is warm.

In Michigan and other Lake States, most of the virgin timber was cut, and second-growth forests took its place. Successive fires resulted in dense growths of aspens. In more recent times in Michigan the chain saw has replaced the axe to cut large aspen for pulp, and dense stands of aspen suckers ten to fifteen feet high have replaced the old trees. Here is an environment attractive to timberdoodles.

I will never forget a late afternoon in September, 1968, when I accompanied a veteran woodcock hunter to a covert in Michigan. It was a beautiful, clear evening. An added thrill was the occasional bugle of elk, which have been successfully reintroduced to that state. We released our setters and set forth. For the next two hours the two dogs spent more time on point than hunting! The cover was thick and when the bells of the dogs stopped tinkling, it was a problem not only to find the dog but to get into position for a shot. Once my companion dropped a bird my dog was pointing, and the timberdoodle fell into a beaver flowage. Although my excited setter was an inexperienced retriever, she plunged into the water and brought the bird back. In that one afternoon she came of age and began to hunt like a veteran.

The next morning we released our setters in a stand of large aspens. Early autumn had turned the leaves yellow, and tinged the dogwood shrubs with red. Up to this point in my hunt in Michigan, my setter had paid little attention to me, ranging out on long excursions of self-directed hunting. Stepping into the edge of the first dogwood thicket I flushed a woodcock with neither dog near. The bird was very close but dodged out of sight on the other side of the bush before I could even get my gun up. Woodcock seldom flush straight for any distance. They often circle and have an amazing capacity for sudden changes of speed and direction.

After twenty minutes my companion's fine little tricolored setter stiffened in a point. Andy stepped forward and I positioned myself where I thought the bird might flush. I heard it start with the characteristic wing twitter. It came out low and circled around a spruce tree as I fired. Investigating, we found the bird with a broken wing. A few minutes later, after crossing a dirt road, my companion shot another woodcock over his dog.

Then came the moment I had been waiting for. My dog went on point, and I could see the woodcock a few feet in front, frozen to the ground. Andy came over and his setter backed mine. I saw the woodcock take a step, flashing the white of his under-tail feathers. He flushed and two guns fired simultaneously. The bird fell as the day's first prize for my dog.

For the rest of the afternoon we averaged a flush every ten minutes even though it was too early in the fall for the arrival of any migrants.

A large variety of hunting dogs may be used for woodcock—the pointing breeds such as the English setters and pointers, the Gordon and field-bred Irish setters, Weimaraners, the German pointer, the Brittany spaniel. Some prefer the flushing breeds, which include various other spaniels and often retrievers. I favor a pointing breed as it adds anticipation to every shot. I confess to a liking for classic style, so often seen in English setters and pointers. If a dog is intelligent and very staunch on point, some speed and range are acceptable though many hunters prefer very close-working slow dogs.

Guns for woodcock should be open-bored, and they may be any gauge from .410 to 12. The finer the shot used, the better. Most hunters use #9's. A woodcock is not difficult to kill, as the average shot seldom exceeds twenty yards, but they can survive amazing injury. Their habit of dropping their legs when they flush exposes these limbs to shot injury. One-legged woodcock are not uncommon; many have been netted on the wintering grounds. Last fall a friend bagged a healthy, strong, flying woodcock with *both* feet gone.

The inexperienced hunter may find difficulty in knowing where to find woodcock. There are certain characteristics of habitat that should be sought. The bird needs clear space six inches above the earth so it can forage at will. Thick, heavy grass, for example, is to be avoided. But even though a stand of bracken fern may look dense it will be clear six inches above the ground where woodcock walk to and fro under the fronds. Another general feature is that the covert may contain mostly alder or aspen, yet the best coverts are not homogeneous in vegetation but include trees or shrubs of

Woodcock is upland game species that sometimes seeks damp areas. Here, bird forages in marshland.

different varieties. Young forests or brushy cover is the most attractive to woodcock.

I have found these birds in strange places. Most of us usually hunt aspen, alder, or birch coverts interspersed with low brush of various kinds and near the edge of forest land, although this may vary with the region—on islands in northern Michigan, woodcock are sought among red osier dogwood. One time I flushed a dozen woodcock from a cornfield which had withered, uncut stalks. And I've found them under crab apple trees in a high Vermont pasture and in a cattail marsh in Ithaca, New York.

To the uninitiated, my advice is to go with an experienced woodcock hunter, but don't expect him to take you to his best covert. The woodcock-hunting fraternity is often secretive.

Woodcock hunters have been increasing each year. More than a million birds are shot annually, and in some states such as Michigan there are more hunters of woodcock than waterfowl. Those of us who are charged with the responsibility of managing this bird constantly strive to make regulations which hold no threat to a game bird that offers so much to so many.

When I started work on woodcock in 1949, I realized that I must learn how to capture birds for banding in order to determine migration routes, find how many return each year to the breeding grounds, estimate annual mortality and population trends. The more I learned, the more fascinated I became with the natural history of these birds.

The adult male woodcock, in contrast to the jacksnipe, is a polygamous creature, accepting no responsibility in rearing his offspring. Woodcock hens lay one clutch of four eggs and are reluctant to move from the clutch. I have often stroked them with my hand before they flushed. The hatched chicks are very precocious. They can fly short distances when two weeks old, and at four weeks are virtually indistinguishable from adults.

After their molt and with the first frost of fall, the birds become restless. Assimilating a layer of fat and developing flying strength, they depart for the South in mid- or late October from the northern breeding grounds, which stretch from Minnesota to Nova Scotia. Those from Ontario and the Lake States follow the Mississippi Valley to Louisiana. The migrants from Nova Scotia, Maine, and New England usually migrate close to the Atlantic Coast. Two of my banded birds from New England were killed in winter in Florida. Migrating in loose flocks at low altitudes, they reach their wintering grounds along the Atlantic and Gulf coasts by December. These hardy migrants return north behind the snowline in the spring, and most hens start incubating when patches of snow still remain.

In the fall, every woodcock hunter hopes he will stumble into a flight of migrants. Woodcock migrate southward at a leisurely pace unless an extreme cold wave causes a mass exodus from the north. Generally the birds migrate in loose bunches not unlike robins, and finding abundant birds in one cover doesn't mean the next cover also will contain migrants.

Years ago my shooting companion Dick and I awoke on an October morning and heard light rain beating on the window-panes. It was miserable weather for bird hunting, and we knew the grouse would be in the pines and spruces well under cover. But we were young and restless enough to try anyway, as woodcock rather relish such wet conditions.

On a high hill where our vision was cut by fog and mist mixed with rain, we climbed over a bank beside a dirt road, Dick with his pointer and I with an old setter. No sooner had we passed through a fringe of spruces into a stand of sapling birch than action erupted. Both dogs pointed and three woodcock flushed into the fog. We fired, but saw only one bird fall. As we waded through the cover, already drenched, two more birds flushed. One flew directly at me and disappeared before I could swing and pull the trigger. Dick apparently wounded the other as we saw feathers fly. A bird flushed which I fired at quickly— and was totally surprised when my dog retrieved a jacksnipe.

We drifted down the slope to an edge of willows and alders. Two startled deer bounded away but our dogs ignored them. Woodcock were everywhere, though I don't believe we ever used so many shells to get bag limits. The dogs were almost continu-ally on point as we shot holes in the fog where only faint silhouettes were seen.

We cut into one edge of heavy spruces. Dick's pointer made game, and Dick got off a difficult shot at a grouse flushing from the top of a spruce. My setter did not dis-tinguish himself when he made a half-hearted point of a porcupine ambling ahead. We hunted the ridge for three hours, and were thoroughly drenched when we reached

home. After a change of clothes, we sat before a roaring fire, elated to have had such a successful hunt under such trying conditions. Yet I would advise most hunters to stay at home when there is stormy, wet weather, as it is rare to hit into a flight of woodcock as we did. Most game birds seek heavy cover and are difficult to start.

Many sportsmen are particularly inter-ested in "flight" birds, some claiming they can recognize these migrants by size. The only way I know to distinguish migrants from "natives" is by visiting a covert and finding it empty one day, but full of birds the next. I had such an experience in Vermont when flight birds had arrived after a rainy, cold night. Some were so exhausted I was able to touch them with a gun barrel in front of my pointing dog. Occasionally there is a congregation of hen birds, which are larger than the cocks. When hunters hold that flight birds are bigger than natives, I suspect they have stumbled onto a group of hens. Evidence indicates that small males may be the latest to migrate south.

There are several ways to capture birds for study. I designed a trap which I baited with the stuffed decoy of a hen woodcock and placed on a breeding field. Over eight hundred males were lured to the trap in subsequent springs. Pointing dogs are in-valuable during all of the seasons. Many re-search men find and band hundreds of chicks annually. One worker in Michigan banded a hundred broods (three hundred to four hundred chicks) in ninety-five man-dog hours. Hand-netting, using lights, has been practiced for many years in Louisiana, where birds congregate in hundreds in large feeding fields at night. The birds are spotted by the reflected red glow of their eyes. Today most captures in spring and summer are made with virtually invisible Japanese "mist" nets. My discovery that woodcock congregate in fields in summer led to widespread banding throughout the breeding grounds.

From these studies, we learned how to determine the sex and age of any woodcock from an examination of its wings. Thus wings can be used to measure annual breeding success. This led to a nationwide campaign to encourage hunters to mail wings to wildlife agencies for census purposes. It is one way the hunter can help the welfare of his favorite game birds. (Postage-paid envelopes can be obtained from the Bureau of Sport Fisheries and Wildlife, Patuxent Wildlife Research Station, Laurel, Maryland; this agency manages woodcock on a national basis and supports research.)

An account of woodcock hunting in 1839 by Frank Forester may well amaze the modern hunter. His experience seems remarkable in view of the relative inefficiency of the muzzle-loading shotguns then used:

"On no ground, however, have I ever seen, or shall I—I much fear--ever again see this bird in such multitudes as on what are called the 'Drowned Loads' in Orange County, New York. In 1838, I shot over it accompanied by my friend, Mr. Ward, who then weighed over 300 pounds and shot a single barreled Westley Richards gun. In the successive days we bagged 57, 59 and 98 cock over a single brace of dogs, not beginning to shoot until late in the morning. In the following year we shot on the same ground all day the first, until noon on the second, bagging on the first 125 birds and on the second 70."

Only at certain migration points do we have anything remotely approaching such concentrations of birds today. In seven nights in late November, 1968, woodcock banders hand-netted and banded over six hundred woodcock in a relatively small area on Cape May, New Jersey.

Regulations rescued the woodcock from virtual extermination at the beginning of this century. The last years of the nineteenth century were the heyday of market hunting, which began in July and extended through March or April. In 1874, woodcock were selling at a dollar and a half a pair; eighteen hundred birds were sold by markets in New York City in a single week. Particularly heavy bags were made on the wintering grounds, where woodcock concentrate in large numbers on open fields at night and can be easily caught and killed by using a bright light. In fact, in 1904 an eminent ornithologist marked the woodcock as a species on the road to extinction. Fortunately, it responded rapidly to stringent regulations which limited the bag and restricted the season, and today it does not appear to be threatened. Using rough census methods, no significant changes in populations have been detected in the last twenty-five years. Although this is encouraging, we have no reason to be complacent. Hungry bulldozers invade the land, destroying many fine coverts; chemical pesticides cloak the landscape, infecting most woodcock.

However, I believe heavy freezes on woodcock wintering grounds, and unfavorable weather during migration are the chief factors causing mortality at this time. Man cannot control the weather but he can, of course, set shooting regulations. Of even greater importance today in the face of burgeoning human populations is the care man takes of his entire environment. Reducing pollution of all kinds, preserving open areas, and developing a conscience regarding land and water husbandry will benefit the woodcock as well as all other living creatures.

The woodcock is a treasure in the natural world and has long elicited the wonder of laymen and naturalists. In short, this remarkable game bird is a natural resource of rare quality, offering recreation and esthetic pleasure to thousands. It is a resource we should forever be vigilant to preserve. ◉

The Deadliest Lures

The colorful history of angling flies has produced a host of patterns—some with barnyard simplicity, others composed of wondrously exotic frippery— which can entice fish when naturals and other artificials fail.
by Leonard M. Wright, Jr.
photography
by Robert Stahman

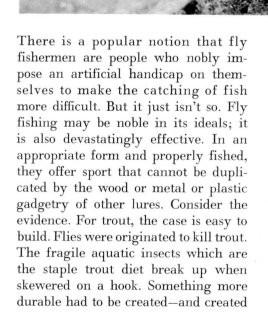

Preceding pages:
Wet fly is Royal
Coachman (shown
with materials used
to tie it), dry
is Light Cahill,
and streamer
is Badger. Four more
wet patterns
are Leadwing Coachman
(above), Coachman
and March Brown (top
right), and Quill
Gordon (right).

There is a popular notion that fly fishermen are people who nobly impose an artificial handicap on themselves to make the catching of fish more difficult. But it just isn't so. Fly fishing may be noble in its ideals; it is also devastatingly effective. In an appropriate form and properly fished, they offer sport that cannot be duplicated by the wood or metal or plastic gadgetry of other lures. Consider the evidence. For trout, the case is easy to build. Flies were originated to kill trout. The fragile aquatic insects which are the staple trout diet break up when skewered on a hook. Something more durable had to be created—and created

it was, some two thousand years ago according to surviving records, and perhaps artificial flies were no novelty even then. The worm and the minnow may have their innings under certain conditions, but the fly is the most consistent trout killer and has been for centuries.

No less an authority than Edward R. Hewitt stated that the skillful nymph fisherman was the only man who could clean a stream of sophisticated brown trout by legal angling. And the nymph, though a fairly recent refinement, is very much a fly and in the classic tradition of close imitation.

Further proof is provided by the fact

Above, streamers display variety of colors, materials, and shapes. Clockwise, beginning with large wet fly, they are White Maribou, Nine-Three, Art-Neu Special, Rogers-Knight, Supervisor, and Alott. Though Alott is meant for salmon, such flies are quite versatile. At left are three bucktails: black-and-white pattern for salt or fresh water, pink bonefish lure, and tandem bucktail for trolling.

that professional fishermen use flies, perhaps not exclusively but very regularly. In France, anglers who make a living by supplying restaurants with wild trout taken from heavily fished public streams use flies most of the time. In high water or when they're after a specific large fish, they may turn to the spun minnow, but they earn their daily French bread during most of the season with the fly. And I might add that the best of them may be the finest trout fishermen in the world.

The same is true in Spain. Men who fish the few public salmon rivers in the north use flies regularly when the water is neither too roily nor too deep. And when you consider that the average Spanish salmon can be sold for as much as a laborer earns in two months of hard work, you can be sure that the fly is no affectation there.

Trout and salmon may be the traditional victims of the fly, but all game fish, except perhaps those which live in unreachable depths, are highly susceptible to fur and feathers. Spinners, plugs, and naturals are not so universally effective, regardless of what their adherents may claim. New York State employs an expert fisherman to check populations of lakes, ponds, and streams and to catch fish for scale samples. His quarry are mainly smallmouth and

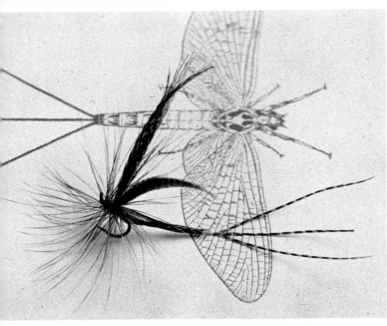

*Top, far left:
Impressionistic dry
flies tied by
Theodore Gordon.
Left: Experimental
Brown Drake,
modern dry pattern
which imitates
big mayfly. Other
flies pictured
are standard dry
patterns as tied today.
Top: Hendrickson.
Center left: Tup's
Indispensable.
Center right:
Irresistible. Above
left: Mallard
Quill; above right:
Quill Gordon.*

largemouth bass, yet he uses a fly rod exclusively and claims that an orange streamer is his most effective lure.

Even commercial tuna fishermen in the Pacific use flies. For on the end of those two- and three-pole rigs with which they yank tuna into the boat there is a special quick-release hook covered with white feathers. And large white-feathered jigs have been used for decades by sport fishermen and commercial trollers.

Of course, the flies just described wouldn't be recognized as such under a New England covered bridge. Are, then, these large minnow and squid imitations really flies? In one sense yes, and in another no. The Spanish say no. They make a clear distinction that is surprising for a country not noted for its sport fishing. There, a fly that imitates an insect is properly called a *mosca*, while a streamer or salmon fly is a *pluma*. I think they are right in calling one the fly and the other the feathers, but our own language has no such nicety.

However, the English definition has its merits, too. Both the dainty insect imitation and the large feather squid owe their effectiveness to the same qualities—qualities that separate them from live bait, spinners, or solid wobbling plugs. First and foremost of these

These flies are all nymphs. Near left, from top: Long-Tailed March Brown, Isonychia, and Bailey's Mossback. Large photo, clockwise from bottom left: Blue Quill, Breadcrust, Flick's Hendrickson, Zug Bug, and Atherton No. 2.

is the action of feather, fur, and hair. They breathe, wiggle, and kick in a unique manner when drawn through the water. And perhaps equally important, all these materials are translucent in the water, as are the insects, minnows, elvers, or squid that they counterfeit.

In the beginning, of course, was the wet trout fly. In fact, until about a hundred years ago it was *the* fly. The great blossoming into many styles for many types of fishing is a rather recent development, and testifies to the high quality of the materials that flies are made of.

The artificial nymph, for instance,

is merely a refinement of the basic wet fly, and it came out of England at the turn of the century. Probably the great Frederick Halford of dry-fly fame was indirectly responsible for its development, although he was to fight till his dying day against the use of nymphs. It was Halford who established the doctrine of exact mimicry in dry-fly fishing. So successful was he in implanting this ideal that wet-fly fishermen took to more exact imitation of the underwater, or nymphal, forms of aquatic insects. Under the leadership of G. E. M. Skues, the nymph fishermen fought the Halfordians for over a quarter of a century. While neither

Materials for salmon flies, including silver pheasant, bucktail, blue kingfisher, golden pheasant, jungle cock, macaw, and European jay.

side ever won a clear-cut victory, the literature that resulted is some of the most spirited in the entire angling library. Since the turn of the century, the nymph has appeared in a wide variety of patterns. It is not only a recent invention but an extremely important one, for Hewitt was right in his estimate of its efficiency on wary fish such as the brown trout.

The streamer fly and its cousin the bucktail are purely American in origin. One story has it that a man was fishing with a large wet fly when the throat hackle broke, unwound, and streamed out behind the fly. This accidental lure was an immediate success and an idea

was born. After all, big trout and land-locked salmon feed heavily on min-nows, and a hackle feather of suitable color, undulating along the hook-shank, makes a very likely imitation, as we now know. However, the story is considered apocryphal. Officially, the streamer is credited to Maine fly tier Herb Welsh, and the date is recorded as 1901.

The bass fly was also developed in this country. In its older, purer forms, it is basically a huge trout-type wet fly, usually in one of the brighter patterns and dressed as fully as possible to make it a chunky mouthful. You don't see this type of fly around much any more, though. The big streamer fly has largely replaced it. And the exciting surface lures of clipped deer hair are becoming more popular each season. They mimic such delicacies of the bass menu as frogs, dragon flies, crayfish, and even mice. If hair-and-feather minnows and squid are to be considered flies, then these hair-bodied counterfeits would also seem to fit the category. And they do catch fish with gratifying regularity.

But unquestionably the most important fly development in recorded history is the dry fly. Here, too, there has been progress in recent years but, surprisingly, not because of any great advances in the science of entomology. Ronalds' *The Fly-fisher's Entomology* was published in England in 1836 and is still widely quoted. While it may be a taxonomist's horror (it avoids Latin names, preferring terms like Pale Watery Dun), it speaks the angler's language. In America we have no such single standard work. There have been valiant attempts like Ernest Schwiebert's *Matching the Hatch* and Art Flick's *Streamside Guide to Naturals and Their Imitations*. Schwiebert dealt with the entire United States, while Flick limited himself to New York's Catskills. Both books are often very useful. Yet I know a stream ecologically similar to Flick's Scoharie, and not forty miles from it, where half of the important insects bear no resemblance to Flick's favored dozen. Apparently, America is too huge, too rich, and too diverse a habitat for any one man to entomologize. This may be an argument in favor of the slight leaning toward impressionism discernible in many modern American flies.

There has also been a trend toward drabness, simply because drab flies seem to work well on our streams. No longer are flies designed primarily for brook trout in ponds, as they once were, because the ecological picture has changed. The colorful artificials which were used for that purpose evolved into bass flies.

Finally, there has been a trend toward chunky, less delicate dry flies on both sides of the Atlantic, and this has a simple explanation. Trout streams in most well-populated countries have a higher percentage of newly stocked fish each year. These trout must remember the hatchery mouthful better than the mayfly. They simply go for something which looks like an insect and is fat enough to rivet their attention. The highly selective wild brown trout of Halford's day are now hard to find, and today's flies reflect this change in conditions.

Furthermore, many more fish are considered game species now than in the late nineteenth century, and many more sportsmen have learned to use the fly rod. This has resulted in an incredible proliferation of both classic patterns and relatively new ones. Even if a fisherman finds himself on strange water with nothing to match the hatch precisely, he can switch from fly to fly until he finds a good one, or he can shop for local patterns. Being inexpensive, flies encourage experimentation.

Of course, certain of the oldest classic patterns are still with us in pretty much their original form—dries like the famous Blue Dun, wets like the Wickham's Fancy, Coachman, Leadwing Coachman, and Royal Coachman. They are far too effective to be forsaken. But excellence has not hindered experimentation. For instance, it was discovered quite early that some dry flies could be tied as wet patterns to imitate drowned insects. Hence, we have both wet and dry versions of the great Quill Gordon, Light Cahill, Greenwell's Glory, Gold-Ribbed Hare's Ear, plus many newer patterns.

Through experimentation by anglers and professional fly tiers, the list is constantly lengthened. Among the relatively new and vastly popular wets are the Fledermaus, the

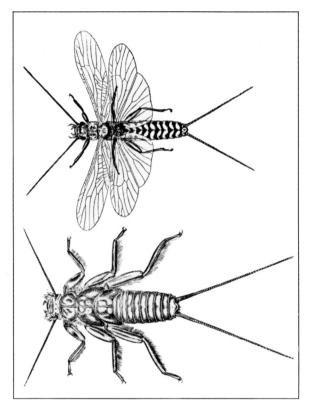

Drawings from 1897 British volume on dry-fly entomology: stone fly adult (top) and nymph.

Muddler Minnow streamers, and the woven-hair-bodied nymphs which are now being used extensively in the Rockies. And recent years have brought fame to such dry patterns as the Rat-Faced Macdougal, Gray Wulff (and other Wulff variations), Jassid, Irresistible, and a whole batch of small midges and terrestrial insects, such as beetles and ants. These little terrestrials, which originated with the "Pennsylvania school" of fly tiers, have provided still further possibilities for dry-fly experimentation.

The name of the actual inventor of dry flies has been lost—if, indeed, one person was the inventor. Late in the nineteenth century a number of factors made the development of the dry fly almost inevitable. One was the introduction of the split-cane fly rod. Here was an instrument that could not only reach out to shy fish in clear, low water, but could also flick the droplets off a

fly and dry it on the false cast. Then came the vacuum-dressed silk line that brought out the potential of the bamboo as the older braided horsehair and linen lines never could. And perhaps most important of all was Henry Sinclair Hall's perfection of the mass-produced, eyed trout hook. Before it appeared on the market in 1879, trout hooks were "blind." Their tapered shanks were whipped to a piece of gut or to a single strand of horsehair. Changing a sodden fly for a fresh one under those circumstances meant changing the leader, or at least part of it. Without the eyed hook, dry-fly fishing would have been too tedious to become popular. And it was with the rising popularity of the dry fly late in the last half of the nineteenth century that the hackle feather became the rightful center of fly-tying attention. For a dry fly must float on its hackle tips, and most of its effectiveness depends on hackle quality and color.

Halford and his crew of dry-fly zealots had little difficulty obtaining their feathers. Since their numbers were small, their demands were not large. As a matter of doctrine, they cast only to rising fish; this meant that even mediocre hackle could be used, because the fly had long periods of inactivity in which to dry off. Lastly, cock fighting had been abolished as recently as 1849, and many a stiff-hackled cock still strutted the British barnyards.

The dry fly was launched in America in 1885, when Halford sent a set of his dry flies to Theodore Gordon in New York State. Gordon was an inventive and observant sportsman. He realized that Halford's flies imitated British insects and that insects on this side of the Atlantic were quite different. He originated many impressionistic imitations of the naturals he found on his own favorite streams—the Quill Gordon being perhaps the most famous of his patterns. His flies seem a bit large-winged to us today, and the style of winging has changed slightly, but the present-day master tiers of the Catskills carry on his basic tradition.

The first American book on dry-fly fishing didn't appear until some twenty years after Gordon began his experiments, and by the time the dry fly became really popular here, a bit after World War I, the materials situation was becoming acute. First, American demands on hackle were far more severe than Britain's. Our streams are more turbulent than Halford's stately chalk streams. Only the very stiffest hackle would do. Then, too, our insects are larger, and a bigger, heavier hook has to be supported. And, finally, casting only to the rise doesn't work well here. An angler must prospect likely water in our mountain streams, rise or no rise. So the fly must float, cast after cast, with only a false cast or two to dry it.

Even today, there is no synthetic dry-fly hackle on the market, nor any miracle chemical that can transform soft hackle into needle-sharp barbs. Superb hackle can float a fly unaided, but the pioneer dry-fly anglers in England often resorted to coating the hackle with paraffin solutions. Theodore Gordon frequently used kerosene. Until a few years ago, standard fly-line dressing was dissolved in gasoline or the less flammable carbon tet. Now we have the superior silicone preparations, which represent another advance in fly fishing, but this is not to say the problem has been solved. Poor hackle still floats poorly.

By the time the dry fly gained wide acceptance in America, the source of hackle supply was diminishing. Not only had cock fighting long been outlawed here, but the agricultural revolution had transformed chicken-raising into a mass-production industry, to the detriment of the hackle supply. Birds were now bred for fast growth and plump breasts, or for greater egg production. Certainly not for first-class hackles.

And to top it all off, most cockerels were killed for fryers when only months old.

To see the full implications of this fly tier's nightmare, you must understand a few facts about the nature of the bird that bears the indispensable hackle. All of our current breeds of chickens are descendants of a wild bird from India called the Bankiva fowl. The males of the species are extremely polygamous and, hence, highly combative. While the females have unimposing neck feathers, the males have long, stiff, glossy hackles, which protect the vulnerable neck and throat area from the leg spurs and beaks of rivals. Since the bird that survives the fight gets the hens and begets the chicks, birds with the stiffest neck feathers prospered. The process of natural selection toward stiff neck feathers was started in the wild and continued until cock fighting was outlawed. Then the purveyors of eggs and white meat stepped in, and the tier had to scout the ever-decreasing subsistence farms for a source of supply.

How then, you may ask, is the current army of several million fly fishermen supplied? The answer is, poorly—except for the anglers who deal with top custom tiers. General stores, hardware stores, and even sports shops have to take what they can get.

Most of the hackle is soft, and half of it has been dyed—a process that further reduces the quality of already indifferent hackle. The necks are bought in bulk from importers who buy them by the hundreds of thousands in India. Most of these necks are ginger, red, or white—useful colors, but not the full spectrum a tier would like. A few of the necks are first-rate, and you're fortunate if you can pick and choose from a boxful. But commercial houses can't afford such sorting and discarding. Surprisingly, top-notch flies can still be obtained if you know the right professional tier. There are a few of these men left, yet very few

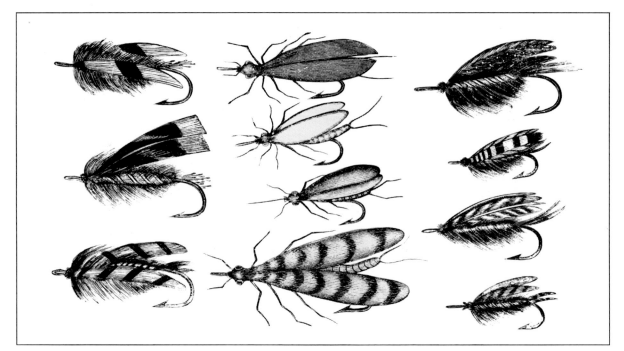

Antique flies tend toward specific realism. Hook eyes are probably loops of gut, popular prior to introduction of mass-produced eyed hooks. Another method was to whip leader directly to hook.

young tiers are coming up. The reason is that there's no money in producing quality flies.

A tier must raise most of his own roosters. True, some necks in the more common colors can be picked up from a friendly importer, but none is likely to be found in the all-important shades called natural duns. These are a slaty blue-gray color, and fly tiers have made their reputations on their dun hackles. To get such hackles, birds must be bred, crossbred, pampered, and plucked, and the price of doing this is almost confiscatory. Yet nearly half of the most popular dry flies call for this shade, and a dyed feather always shows a bogus blue or purplish tinge when held up to the light—which is precisely how a trout sees it.

To get the natural duns, you have to raise a lot of birds. About fifty percent of the eggs hatched will produce cocks, but only a few of them will have top-quality hackle. Then, too, the blue-dun color is recessive. No matter how you breed, you'll end up with lots of badger (white with black center), black, and white hackles. Only a small percentage will be true duns.

Most of the superb modern flies pictured with this article were tied by an acknowledged master, Harry Darbee of Livingston Manor, New York. I once asked Harry how he bred his magnificent dun roosters. He was a bit guarded about just how he has built up a superior strain after some thirty years of continuous breeding, but he did tell me that he has to breed back in a Cochin strain from time to time to keep the feathers in the small, usable sizes and to keep up the steely quality. But what is his ratio of duns to the less useful colors? His answer was, "Man, do we eat a lot of chicken!"

Since I myself have raised birds for hackles, I can readily understand the economic plight of the professional tier. It cost me $10 a year per rooster just for the special small-grain feed that hackle-producing birds are supposed to have. It takes two years for birds to reach full maturity, so a bird has eaten $20 worth of feed before he starts producing.

With luck, a bird should produce excellent hackle for several years. A prize rooster is seldom killed; he is plucked with tender, loving care three or four times a year.

Curiously, despite the costs and risks of trying to raise excellent hackle, flies tied with these superior materials by the finest artists of the day cost only pennies more than run-of-the-mill shop-tied flies. I once asked Walt Dette, the master fly tier of Roscoe, New York, why this should be so. "It's all the traffic will bear," he explained. "After all, trout flies are expendable. The average guy leaves several of them in trees during a day's fishing. Who'd pay a buck for a fly?"

There is only one factor that sweetens the pot for independent, custom tiers like Darbee and Dette. There's no middleman. The feathers go straight from rooster to fisherman, and fly tier takes all. Even so, most fly tiers drive old cars. And the finest craftsman that I ever knew gave it all up to work in a barbershop a few years back. Once a man has paid for the hooks, thread, wax, and other purchasable materials—not to mention the costs of rooster-raising—he can't tie much more than $5 or $6 worth of flies in an hour. If machines were available, the economic picture might be brighter. But every fly must be tied from start to finish by hand.

What, then, keeps the few remaining perfectionists in the business? Pride, certainly. The good life, probably, too. Tiers live near good fishing and shooting. But there seems to be more to it than that. They are celebrities in the eyes of dedicated fishermen. Their advice is sought by presidents and board chairmen. You stand in line to get their flies and you don't dare annoy them even if your order doesn't arrive by opening day.

Since the basic materials of most flies have always come from the barnyard, it's natural that there's a touch of barnyard earthiness in some of the flies themselves. One all-time favorite is named the Cow Dung because it imitates a green-bodied fly that is usually found on meadow muffins. Another classic is the Tup's Indispensable, invented by R. S. Austin of Tiverton in Devon. The exact dressing of this killing fly was a closely kept secret for years. Sound business was one reason. Victorian prudery another. For how would you explain to a nineteenth-century gentlewoman that the beautifully translucent yellow body was dubbed with urine-stained hair taken from the indispensable portion of a ram, or tup?

The famous Hendrickson dry fly originated by Roy Steenrod, an early pupil of Theodore Gordon's, has a similar origin. The body is dubbed with fur from the crotch of a red fox vixen, which has a permanent pink stain.

Those are some of the more esoteric materials—including a few of the most expensive ones. Feathers, and particularly hackles, are still pivotal to fly tying and to fly fishing, but long evenings at the tying vice produce a lot of experimentation. In streamer flies, maribou stork feathers with their octopus-like action are rivaling bucktail and saddle hackles. Silk floss and similar body materials have always had their place, but newer materials are now finding other uses. For instance, tarnish-proof strips of Mylar tinsel are showing up more and more in the wings of these flies.

Bucktail flies obviously get their name from the deer tail of which they're made, and this material has always been plentiful. Because of its texture, consistency, and length, it is valuable for many wet-fly effects. In a way, its versatility makes it more valuable than that special hair from a vixen. The deer hair that's being displaced nowadays in streamers is popping up in, of all

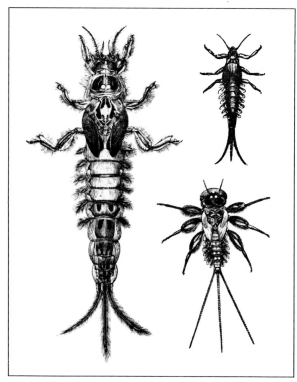
Turn-of-century studies of ephemeridae nymphs show three different types common in England.

places, dry-fly dressing. Many of the shaggy but effective Wulff flies have bucktail tails and wings. Harry Darbee's inspired Rat-Faced Macdougal and the series of variations that have followed it sport bodies of clipped deer hair.

These flies may be a bit chunky for delicate mayfly imitations, but they are the only flies that will float in a downpour. And since a pelting rain can knock enough insects out of the bushes to make a pool boil, such flies represent another deadly set of lures.

In wet flies, flourescent flosses are also appearing these days—particularly in the bodies of salmon flies. They give off a glow on dark days or in the depths, causing many anglers to swear by them. Synthetics aren't really new; J. W. Dunne of England popularized them back in the Twenties. In *Sunshine and the Dry-Fly*, he advocated a series of artificials with bodies of cellulite floss over white-painted hook shanks. When an-

nointed with oil, these bodies had a succulent translucency. They haven't been on the market since World War II, but new types of brightly glowing synthetics are being tied into wet patterns.

These changes in materials and in flies tell a lot about trends in fishing. Most of Halford's original split-wing floaters were winged with dun-colored starling primary feathers and epitomized the ultrarealistic approach. Theodore Gordon leaned toward bunched wood-duck flank feathers glimpsed through the hackle. He was an impressionist. Darbee's Rat-Face and the Wulff flies are highly utilitarian and offer a good mouthful. Experimenting with shapes can probably go just so far, but experimenting with materials, from the dullest to the most garishly fluorescent will probably never end.

Happily, the materials used for wet flies, nymphs, and streamers, whether new or old in dressing style, remain in good supply. A Royal Coachman, for instance, utilizes golden-pheasant tippet, peacock herl, red silk floss, red-brown cock or hen hackle, and white primary goose or duck quill. A fly tier has little trouble obtaining these items.

Salmon-fly materials felt the pinch early in this century when many feathers were proscribed by international treaties. Indian crow, cock of the rock, toucan, and bustard disappeared from the salmon-fly repertory, but suitable and effective substitutes have been found, and the fully dressed fly of today is hard to distinguish from its nineteenth-century prototype (though smaller, less fully dressed salmon flies have also gained wide acceptance).

Fortunately, the banned feathers were used mainly as color accents. The most widely used exotics—golden pheasant, jungle cock, English jay, summer duck, florican, European kingfisher, blue-and-yellow and red-and-yellow macaw, silver pheasant, and the rest—are still available to fly tiers even though they can be quite expensive.

The demand for these materials is not increasing, because salmon-fishing tactics have changed considerably. In the good old days, it was mainly an early spring and late fall sport. Salmon were considered uncatchable in low water and warm weather. The British now use smaller, less colorful, more sparsely dressed flies during the summer and have opened up a whole new season for the sport. And in Canada the fishing is mostly from late June through September, and the same small, relatively drab flies are now most popular there, too.

Most of these flies are winged with hair or with the natural plumage of various ducks like widgeon, teal, and mallard. Usually such feathers are relatively easy to obtain from hunting friends, but bulk shipments from overseas are under continuous attack by the National Audubon Society. While the Society's main objection is to the use of the feathers by the millinery trade, tiers feel threatened, too.

The Audubon people are worthy opponents. A few years ago an Audubon friend of mine told me with some satisfaction that a member of his chapter was head inspector of feathers for the New York customs department. "You fly tiers can't fool him," he claimed. "Why, he can tell what kind of bird almost any feather comes from, and you can bet he catches lots of contraband shipments." I had the last word, though. I told him that a fifth-generation salmon-fly tier I knew who came from Ireland could do that dead drunk. And, when sober, this man could tell which square inch of the bird the feather came from and estimate the bird's age accurately! He really could, too.

Of course, these economic and legal tugs of war that plague the fly tier are little noticed by the world at large. Only once, to my knowledge, did fly tying hit the headlines. Late in the last century, a man was killed in northern Ireland following a heated discussion about the precise shade of dyed seal's fur that should be used in dubbing the body of Michael Rogan's Fiery Brown salmon fly. However, one has to suspect that some fiery brown liquid may have been more to blame for this crime of passion than the fly itself.

When fly tiers and fly fishermen do make news, it is generally conservation news which appears in publications devoted to the subject or is, unfortunately, relegated to the back pages of the papers. For these men are extremely active in conservation groups that fight pollution, wanton industrial development of wild areas, and similar threats to wildlife. And even though flies are so deadly in expert hands that they may, as Hewitt stated, take every trout in a stream, the fly fisherman is the trout's best friend. He may catch ninety percent of the trout that are netted on our hard-fished streams, but he understands that running water will support only so many fish, and he knows of the scarcity of running water itself. He releases most of the fish he catches, to avoid depleting a limited population.

His sport allows him to do so, and this is another angling advance that is virtually unique to the fly. A fly-caught fish is almost always lip-hooked and easy to release. Treble-hook plugs and spoons and bait hooks which are easily swallowed are another matter. Studies have shown that nearly half of all worm-hooked, undersized trout soon die. The comparative figure for fly-hooked fish is three percent, and this estimate is not restricted just to barbless flies; the figure would be much lower for the many fly fishermen who carefully remove the barbs from their hooks.

So, even though the lure may be deadly, the man may be merciful. And there's wisdom in this. It's better to enjoy golden eggs than to eat goose. ◉

Salmon and Caribou of the Ungava

by
Jerome B. Robinson
In Quebec's
wild northland, where
mornings are for
trophy hunting,
afternoons
for trophy fishing, a
man soon learns to
expect the unexpected
and to keep
both rifle and rod
always at hand.
photography
by
Hanson Carroll

*Soon after taking two fine
salmon (below), author felled caribou near
river's edge; he and guide brought
trophy to camp in canoe (preceding pages).
Photographer Hanson Carroll (right) caught
several good fish in same large pool.*

In the far northern reaches of Quebec, halfway between Hudson Bay and the southern tip of Greenland, is a sportsmen's mecca known as the Ungava region. Until a few years ago the vast area where pure rivers flow north to Ungava Bay was familiar mainly to nomadic Indian and Eskimo hunters and to geologists in the employ of mining companies. Today the name Ungava is murmured reverently by knowing outdoorsmen.

The mining companies opened up this subarctic region, and scheduled airlines now stop regularly at places previously seen by few white men. The airport at Schefferville on the Quebec-Labrador border has become a crossroads for caribou hunters and Atlantic salmon fishermen.

Failure to catch fish is unthinkable on Ungava salmon waters, such as the George, Whale, Koksoak, Leaf, and DePas rivers. Wealthy sportsmen who have sought the Atlantic salmon throughout its European and American range have reported that the angling in the Ungava region in July and again in September is the best they've ever experienced. In the seven years that the Ungava

60

Caribou are frequently seen swimming DePas River (left) during early morning and again in late afternoon. When prime bull pauses atop nearby ridge (below), clear silhouette offers hunter ideal shot.

has been open to hunters, ninety-four percent of those seeking caribou have come out with trophies.

The typical pattern in an Ungava sporting camp is to hunt caribou in the morning when frost whitens the tundra and fishing is prevented by icing of rod guides. By noon, when the weather warms, the caribou are bedded down in gullies of deep willow bush and spruce, and insects stir from the moss and lichens on the hillsides. You move down to the river and cast for salmon during the early afternoon hours. With the chill of dusk, the insect hordes are stilled and the caribou come down to the rivers to drink. It is time to hunt again. Conversely, salmon are notoriously late risers, usually ignoring flies before late morning. Since the fish are most active when the game is least active, caribou hunting and salmon fishing make an ideal combination.

The airport in Schefferville is strangely modern. The building is of metal and glass, and four-engined aircraft keep the muddy runway busy. It is when you step inside the air terminal that you know you are in the North. Nearly everyone in the waiting room is a sportsman. The baggage area is crowded with gun cases and fishing rods, boxes of caribou quarters and freshly caught salmon. Antlers are piled high and tagged for flight back to Montreal; most of the racks measure more than three feet high. The sportsmen coming in meet the sportsmen going out. Racks are examined and advice to the newcomers flows in torrents: fly patterns are recommended, water levels on various rivers are compared, and hunting tips are offered. "Don't shoot the first big rack you see," they tell you. "They all look big at first, but the biggest racks are often spotted after you've shot a smaller trophy."

We flew by float plane from Schefferville to Fritz Gregor's DePas River camp, eighty-eight miles to the northeast. Fritz operates the Montagnais Hunting and Fishing Club which has eight comfortable camps in the Ungava. The little bush planes that ferry sportsmen to the Ungava camps are kept busiest in July and September, for in July the salmon fishing is almost matched by the trout fishing, and in September, when the caribou season is open, the summer salmon run is still in progress and a later run has also begun.

Our flight took us over rugged terrain. Barren rock mountains hunched up amid thousands of long lakes. In the valleys, spruces grow in black profusion, but from the mountain shoulders to the summits growth is limited to ankle height. The bare mountaintops are covered with the light gray-green caribou moss and lichens, which are the primary foods of the big deer of the North.

From the air you see the game trails. An endless tracery of black lines carves the tundra into a million pieces like a puzzle that has been loosely put together. These trails scar the hillsides for years after they are created. The huge cloven hoofs of the caribou, as large across as those of a moose, cut through the lichens and mosses to the rock below. The extremely slow growth rate of these plants in northern latitudes requires ten to twelve years before the tracks are obliterated. This is true also of the plants upon which caribou have browsed. If a large herd feeds over an area, it can trample and eat enough of the lichens and mosses to limit that area's grazing potential for years to come. Thus caribou must keep on the move almost constantly.

Our camp was a comfortable two-room wooden building—a bunk room and a large kitchen with dining area presided over by a camp cook. Overlooking a wide sweep of the DePas River below barren hills, the camp is an outpost of civilization in an awesome, wild landscape. On the beach in front of the camp were tracks of caribou, made the day before. Nearby in the wet sand was the track of a hunting wolf.

On our first morning, photographer Hanson Carroll and I boarded a 22-foot freight canoe with our guide, Leo Poitras, and were taken three miles upstream. The river, two hundred yards wide in most places, was low and the sun was bright. Such conditions, pleasant though they were, did not indicate good salmon fishing. Usually the weather is cold and the skies are gray. Water levels fluctuate and conditions change day by day. This was, however, an ideal day to hunt, and it was possible that I might see a trophy before midday.

Leo poled, paddled, and motored us up long stretches of rapids where the tundra-covered hills swoop down to the spruce-heavy river valley. We stopped at a bend in the river where the hills above us looked like high New England sheep pastures. Skirting through a fringe of spruces, we climbed through dwarf willow and berry bushes for a few hundred yards and emerged on the barren but mossy uplands. As we followed a deeply cut caribou trail to the summit, we scanned the rocky outcroppings for movement. At the top we crouched in the sweet, spicy-smelling caribou moss and began searching the hillsides which stretched away to the horizon.

"We will see many caribou from here," Leo told us. We had climbed only fifteen minutes from the river bank.

In a moment the first caribou appeared. At one instant there had been only a rocky summit on the hill ahead of us, but at the next a caribou was framed against the sky. It was a cow, chocolate-coated, with short jutting antlers poking above her head like pieces of jagged driftwood; caribou cows are the only female members of the deer family that grow antlers. Behind her came a young bull, and I saw at once why we had been warned against shooting the first bull we spotted. The guide shook his head negatively, although the animal had a rack easily three feet high, with a broad shovel sweeping out vertically from his forehead. To one accustomed to looking at whitetail deer, he seemed gigantic.

"Small one," Leo muttered disdainfully. "Wait, we'll see the rest of the herd now." Then, after a long pause, he said, "Look, here comes a good one for sure."

Above the summit of the hill, the top of a rack was emerging. The antlers looked at first like a wind-twisted willow bush with its leaves turned up and over by the wind. But this was no willow bush. The rack rose higher and higher over the summit, revealing a wide bow. The top tines were long, jutting up with a forward curl; halfway down the main beam, another branch appeared. Then the big bull's head popped over the top, revealing a heavy brow shovel and the whitened face of an old campaigner. This was a herd bull. He mounted the

summit, silhouetting himself against the sky, and raised his muzzle so that the long antlers lay back along his flanks as he tested the wind. His coat was whitened by age and the sun, and his powerful neck bulged with a hump of muscle.

We were hardly more than a hundred yards from the old bull, in plain sight but downwind of him. He looked directly at us and began to circle to get our scent. This is a common maneuver in regions where caribou have not developed the intense fear of man that marks other members of the deer family. The caribou's enemy is the wolf, and even the wolf is dangerous only to very young animals or old, weak ones. The bull showed only curiosity and caution, not fear. He bounded along the slope parallel to us with the graceful high-kneed trot of his clan, muzzle outstretched, antlers back along his sides. His fluid rhythm took him over the broken, rocky ground as if he were floating in slow motion across a movie screen.

He stopped perhaps a hundred and fifty yards away, still unable to get our scent. Throughout his display, I had held my rifle on him, studying him through the scope, but I had no desire to shoot a caribou the first morning, regardless of how fine a bull he was.

"His antlers are good but not a real trophy," Leo said. "He has only the single shovel. And his meat will be very strong."

Caribou venison is excellent—tender, well-covered with fat, and mild-tasting. It can substitute for beef in any recipe. But the old bulls have a strong flavor which some people would call gamy. I had decided to hunt for a good bull with nice antlers, but I also wanted fine venison to take home. A fat four- or five-year-old bull with an impressive head was what I wanted.

The old bull dashed over the top of a hill and disappeared, but then his curiosity drove him back and we spotted him sneaking in on us from another angle. Several times he reared on his hind legs and whirled and dashed away, only to come trotting back in his high-kneed prance.

"He is almost in the rut," Leo said. "He begins to act crazy for the females."

Like all the caribou we saw in Ungava during early September, he was still in velvet. But already he was feeling the urge which, by the end of the month, would cause him to gather a harem and to fight viciously with any rival bulls. By September, caribou antlers have reached full growth, and the thin hairy membrane which covers them is ready to slough off in long strips when the animal engages in mock battles with the twisted branches of dwarf willows. October is the rutting month, and by then the shooting season has passed. For about six weeks, the bulls engage in a continual orgy of battling other bulls and breeding the dozen or so cows in their harems. During the breeding season, the males have little time or inclination to eat. By the end of the month, they are gouged and torn, weakened and wasted.

In September, however, just before the rut begins, the animals are prime; sleek and fat after a summer of easy living and abundant feed. The hindquarters are covered with layers of fat up to three inches thick, the ribs filled out and round as the barrel of a horse. The caribou of this region range from two hundred to four hundred pounds, and the best hunting arms are therefore rifles of .270 caliber or larger, using bullets of at least 150 grains. Shotguns are not permitted in caribou camps.

We found bands of the animals each day on the DePas River. They were always cautious, but seemed to feel safe enough so long as they could keep a couple of hundred yards away from us. No day went by without our spotting good bulls. A hunter can never know what problems he may en-counter, but with a scope-sighted rifle in the open tundra, a kill is often fairly easy—once you have found the trophy you want.

Mine appeared late one afternoon while I was fishing a smooth piece of water a mile below our camp. I saw the bull come down to the water half a mile upstream, and a quick check through 8x30 binoculars showed him to be fat. He had a tall, symmetrical rack and his coat was brownish-gray. Deciding to try for him, I ran to the canoe as the bull stepped into the water and began swimming across. While we were speeding upstream, I exchanged my fly rod for a sporterized Springfield .30/06 and pressed four 180-grain cartridges into the magazine. When the bull neared shore, Leo turned the canoe and ran it aground. The caribou was galloping up the shoreline seventy-five yards away. I chambered a shell and put the cross hairs on the back of his upraised neck. The boom of the shot combined with a walloping thud as the 375-pound bull fell dead at the edge of the willows.

Dressing the bull and dragging him back to the water's edge was done with such ease that we didn't realize how difficult this chore can be under other circumstances. We learned about that the next day when Hanson Carroll collected a similar bull on the backside of a ridge two steep miles from the river.

We had hunted along the ridge where the old herd bull had been spotted on our first morning. From the summit of the barren rock mountain, the tundra stretched away into a valley where the early-morning light sparkled on a small lake rimmed with spruces. White frost glistened on the dwarf willows, and shrouds of mist rose from the eastern sides of the sun-washed hills. In the distance stood regiments of black mountains. We swept the valley with binoculars and finally spotted a caribou calf grazing on the slope of the next mountain.

"That calf will be near to a herd," Leo said. "We'll go over there and look in the next valley."

We walked down the long slope, slipping on the spongy, sweet-smelling tundra, wading through a swamp where the twisted willows tangled our feet and caught at our clothes. Emerging from the bush, we found the calf grazing near a hilltop a quarter-mile ahead. Quickly we climbed above the brushy draws and came into the rolling tundra. We followed a low gully across the face of the hill, keeping out of sight of the calf.

When we were barely a hundred yards from her, we glassed the valley again, but still saw no other caribou. The calf, about the size of a whitetail doe, now saw us but her curiosity overcame her caution and she bounded a few yards toward us. She then cut downhill, circled, disappeared into the gully, reappeared several hundred yards away, and bounded away over the ridge.

"She'll spook the herd for sure," Leo commented. "They'll watch for us now."

We reached the summit in time to see eight or nine caribou trot into the bush in the next valley. Ten minutes later we spotted them again, swinging along in a brushy draw. Then they broke out onto the tundra on the slope of a mountain about half a mile from us. Several had tall racks but they were too far away for us to assess them accurately. Once more we headed down a long slope, clawed our way through the boggy, brush-choked lowlands, and climbed into the open where we could glass the herd. There were three bulls, and all of them had the combination of handsome rack and well-fattened young body we sought. The calf had alerted the herd, but they had not seen or scented us yet. After a minute's rest, Hanson slung the Springfield over his shoulder and we circled toward a ridge that rose above the animals. The stalk continued like that for over an hour as we worked back into the hills more than two miles from the river.

Finally Hans bellied ahead of us toward a summit, raised his head over a rock, and looked into the face of a caribou cow only thirty yards away. She plunged downhill, sending the rest of the herd into a panic, and they raced across a hillside. At nearly two hundred yards, the fat double-shoveled bull that Hans had chosen separated himself from the herd and offered a clean though difficult shot as he trotted up the slope alone. Sitting, Hans braced the rifle across his knees, put the cross hairs on the front of the bull's chest, and fired. The bull toppled, crashing into the low brush.

It was a fine, heavy bull of four or five years, with handsome antlers and twin vertical brow shovels. Leo dressed the animal, skinned out the hindquarters, and cut them away at the loin. Now the job was to get our prize back to the canoe. Leo carried the 120-pound hind section on his shoulders while Hans and I dragged the rest of the animal. Going downhill, we pulled on the antlers and the carcass skated along behind. But when we got to the swampy, flat bottoms and into the tangling bush, perspiration began to pour. The antlers caught in brush and we stumbled frequently. The uphill drags were tougher still, even after we attached a leather tumpline to the antlers. The sun was high now and the early-morning frost had melted away. Our smashing through the bush seemed to awaken hordes of black flies and mosquitoes, and the heat of our bodies drew them to us. It was afternoon when we got the carcass to the river bank and sprawled on the rocks.

"Now," said Leo, grinning, "you see what caribou hunting is like. One day you shoot the bull at the river's edge. Another day you kill him but you almost kill yourself, too."

Because of the caribou's unpredictable

grazing pattern, the herd you see one morning may be miles away the next morning. On the other hand, a hillside that's rich in deep caribou moss may hold a herd for several days. To scout for a record head, the hunter will usually have to spend much time combing the slopes and slogging through the swamps between the upland stretches. Caribou are daylight feeders, grazing from dawn until late morning and again from about four in the afternoon until dark. More caribou are seen at the river's edge late in the afternoon than at any other time. It is also well to remember that a hillside which shows very fresh tracks and droppings is likely to be a grazing spot again the following morning.

When frightened, a caribou can move with amazing speed. They have been clocked at thirty miles an hour over rough terrain. But once a bull has put a couple of ridges between himself and a hunter, he resumes grazing. Thus, a trophy caribou that has been spooked can generally be followed up half an hour later, but of course the stalk becomes much more difficult when the quarry is nervous. We had learned that lesson well by the time Hans got his shot.

After returning to camp with our meat, we sat down to a dinner of fried caribou liver and onions. We were jubilant. Our hunt had been successful, and the next day we would be on the salmon waters.

I don't know why I put off for so long my personal introduction to the stately Atlantic salmon. I had taken my share of hefty brown trout on tiny flies in New England. I'd landed big Maine squaretails on June evenings when the brown drakes pop through the surface film of mountain lakes and a quietly presented Wulff-tied dry is potent. I knew the stealth that brings success on mountain streams where brook trout feed at dawn. My schooling had been arduous on landlocked salmon streams and lakes.

I'd even ventured north and taken arctic char and monster speckled trout on bright flies under the tutelage of Eskimos. In short, I considered myself a fisherman of fair experience. Yet I'd never met the grandest fish of all.

My introduction to *Salmo salar* came on the DePas River, a few hundred yards from where I'd shot my caribou. Nothing can surpass the thrill I felt the first time I saw a hook-jawed old cock salmon, resplendent in spawning colors, rise to my fly and then sink slowly back upon his lie. It wasn't just his size or the color of him that made my breath come short; it was the slow, deliberate way in which he came for the fly—pushing a bow wave across the slow glide of the current, thrusting up to within a foot of my bright bucktail, his beaked lower jaw slanting down in a white line—and the way he settled back toward the bottom with a dignified air of refusal. There was no splash, no frenzied rush, only calculated curiosity.

"Hey, he's a good one for sure," Leo shouted from the bank. To Leo, everything positive is "for sure."

"What now?" I asked, afraid of making a mistake and spoiling this august ceremony we were conducting to tempt a salmon to take hold.

Leo shrugged. "Maybe you try a smaller fly."

"Bright or dark?" I was nervous. Everything I had learned about taking fish seemed to have escaped me. Any pattern Leo suggested I would use. He had caught salmon by the thousands, and this was the first I'd ever seen. Leo would know what to do.

"Probably one either of dark color or bright maybe will work," Leo ventured. He wasn't saying "for sure" anymore.

Books had taught me that when a salmon rises but does not take, the angler should change flies and try again. For the moment, however, this booklearning was ignored since I had no idea what fly to change to. Excitedly I rolled out a cast, lifted it high in back of me, and sent the same bucktail sailing over the water. I let it sink for a few seconds in the current and then began a slow retrieve that would swim the Tri-Color past the same spot.

The sweep of my line showed that the fly was nearing the spot where the salmon had risen. He came again. A black bulge of water pushed up behind the fly and I saw the salmon coming. I saw him open his big white mouth—open it wide enough to take a muskrat—and I struck! Everything in me reacted and I yanked back on the rod and pulled the bucktail skittering across the surface two feet ahead of the sedate fish.

"You scare him for sure that way," Leo observed.

I never saw that salmon again. During the course of the afternoon I learned three basic ways to scare salmon without hurting them. I had already put one fish down by yanking the fly away from a rise. The next one departed with a fly in his jaw when I struck to set the hook. You don't strike salmon. You tighten up when they hit and let them hook themselves as they turn away.

"You give him too much the horse," Leo remarked.

The third fish never got a look at the fly. I sent him flashing off in terror by wading directly into his lie before covering the water ahead of me with careful casts.

"First you fish in the water," said Leo. "Later you walk in it."

Late that afternoon, when the shadows of the jagged spruces lengthened on the water and the breeze came down from the hills with a feeling of snow, I got another chance. The water was a long, smooth glide a hundred yards below a shallow rapids. About four feet of water slid over a dark bottom covered with rocks the size of a man's fist and littered with heavy boulders. The current moved at a half-walk speed. The surface was almost glassy, with just a little turbulence around boulders.

I began with short casts and gradually lengthened them. Three dozen times I swam the fly past the tail of a boulder that caught my eye across the current and just a bit below me. I had learned one thing for all of my mistakes that afternoon. A salmon isn't like a trout. Sometimes a salmon will watch a fly go past countless times and refuse it and then, for no apparent reason, rise and take, long after you have convinced yourself that casting is useless and the only reason to continue is that your guide expects you to.

That was how it was. I'd shown my fly to every inch of water within casting range dozens of times over. Then, as the fly drifted past the back of the boulder for perhaps the fortieth time, there was a slight disturbance and the curve of my line straightened and pulled up out of the water with little droplets springing from it.

Pinching the line against the cork grip with my forefinger, I raised the rod tip steadily and felt the big fish embed the hook deeply into his jaw as he turned against the tightening pull. For a moment he seemed confused by the restraint of the hook. I felt him throbbing and moving slowly away across the current. I gave a small amount of line and kept moderate pressure on the fish. Then he made up his mind to rid himself of the irritating hook, and took off. He smashed through the surface and leaped, shining silver, heaving spray as he wrenched his heavy body into the air and fell back with a crash upon the surface. Five times he jumped, arcing three feet into the air, carrying his fight out toward the middle of the wide river.

Mentally I prepared myself for the long downstream run guaranteed in the angling books. My reel was loaded with a hundred and fifty yards of backing for this eventuality. Later I would learn that there are no certainties in salmon fishing. No two fish behave alike. This one never made the long run. He counted on high jumps and bulldozer dives to the bottom to free himself. Gradually I worked him closer to the rock on which I stood. When he saw me, the fish made a short dash upstream and thrashed on top. But I had an advantage, for in the faster water upstream the salmon had to fight the current as well as the rod. Slowly he exhausted himself, and finally his rolls on the surface were tired ones and the danger was only that he would roll himself in the leader and twist the hook free. In ten minutes I drew the spent fish into the wide mouth of Leo's waiting net.

Such was my first Atlantic salmon. Thirty inches long, he weighed an ounce or two below nine pounds. Not big as salmon go, he was nonetheless my first. On his cheeks a heavy blush of red broke through in crimson freckles. His sides were dark with vivid red spots. His tail, wide as a shovel, had a pink flare; his hooked lower jaw was almost sinister.

"He is bright now," Leo said, "and he is strong but not fat. He first comes to the mouth of the river in July. Through the summer he moves upstream each time the rains come and the water rises. He does not eat but lives on his fat—like a hibernating bear in winter. His colors keep changing and getting brighter.

"The July fish have been in the river all summer and now commence the spawning," Leo explained. "Through September and early October the spawning continues. Many of the fish are already here, but with the next rains should come more salmon fresh from the ocean."

The DePas River is a tributary of northern Quebec's famous George River. It runs from a point northeast of Schefferville for nearly a hundred and fifty miles north to Indian House Lake and joins the George just below the lake. The DePas is a new salmon river. When we were there in September, it had been fished by only two parties before us. Its full potential is still to be explored. All that is known is that it gets a heavy run of salmon in July and another heavy run in September. The fish rarely weigh less than eight pounds, and anglers have now taken them in excess of fifteen pounds. The average is between nine and eleven pounds, and there are plenty of these salmon.

Where Fritz Gregor's camp is located, the river is wide—two hundred yards on the average. Within five miles upstream and down are stretches of water that would delight any salmon fisherman. Near the camp are three sets of rapids separated by slow, flat places half a mile long. Below the rapids are pools studded with boulders where the current eases and a salmon can rest before making its next onslaught against the rushing current. It is in such places that salmon are most often caught.

One can stand on the dock and see salmon jump, but Leo Poitras does not fish his parties there. "The fish are only moving through that stretch," he says. "They will not take the fly. Me, I'll take you where they bite."

As a trout fisherman, I would have passed the best lies by and fished the faster water or floated a dry fly over the deeper pools, just those places where Leo said salmon would not hit. At one productive spot, a single rock jutted from the shore inside the curve of the river where it flattened out below a rapids and swooped into a long, deep curve. The water for a hundred yards was three or four feet deep, with a soft current and no particular place where a trout fisherman would say, "There, by that rock, the water forms a channel where the fish will feed on morsels carried by the flow."

The hardest thing to remember on salmon waters is that the fish are there to breed and not to feed. Although salmon can often be observed taking natural flies and nymphs, the food is rarely swallowed. The fish evidently takes the insect because of a response that has lingered since the salmon was a small parr. Now back in the river of its heritage, it responds to the old urge and rises to an insect, sucks it in—then spits it out. The stomachs of salmon in fresh water are usually empty. I had no luck at any spot that looked like a feeding station, and Leo taught me to search for places where the salmon could lie on their pectoral fins along the bottom.

When the sun was bright on the water, we took a couple of fish, but real success came whenever the weather turned. When the sky was heavy with looming snow clouds, and white flakes pelted us and a stiff wind riffled the surface, we had the best fishing. The day before we left, the river rose a foot and a half following a heavy rain. Despite mixed rain and sleet, we went out on the broad river on our last day and in two hours took two bright salmon—8½ and 10¼ pounds—harbingers of the late run which was just beginning on that high water.

For the most part, we took fish on #4 long-shanked Tri-Color bucktails. Although these orange, green, and white creations are not typical salmon flies, the brilliant colors seemed to attract fish consistently. However, Leo's favorite fly is a red and white bucktail, or a red and yellow Mickey Finn. Number 4 bucktails are big beside the average salmon fly, but on the DePas a big fly works best. We tried salmon patterns such as the Rusty Rat, Black Dose, Durham Ranger, Thunder and Lightning, Jock Scott —all good producers on the nearby George River—without success. The big bright bucktails were apparently just right for local conditions.

For general fishing, the best month on the DePas is probably July. Then the first salmon run is new in the river, and the big speckled trout and lake trout feed voraciously in the rapids. Late in August the speckled trout move up into smaller brooks to spawn and the lakers head for deep holes along the river's course. In September, the DePas is strictly a salmon river, loaded with fish which have grown colorful and just begun to spawn. And as the water rises each night, new salmon move up the river.

At this time of year, the weather is uncertain, and your bush pilot may inform you that you will have to delay as much as a day in Schefferville. You must nevertheless pay for the time you have booked at the camp, but if bad weather delays the flight *out* of camp, the extra time on the river is free. Like most aspects of fishing, it's a gamble.

The camp operators do not believe in making guests rough it in the wilderness. There is even plenty of fresh domestic meat on the menu, but few sportsmen will choose beef when the meat rack is hung with caribou and the moss pit holds newly caught salmon. Our camp cook delighted in serving caribou and salmon dinners. There's nothing like fresh salmon steaks broiled over a spruce-knot fire at the river's edge in the middle of the day when you are questing after adventure in a northern wild land. And adventure is the proper word. Even though a man may schedule his hunting in the early morning and his fishing in the afternoon, he must be prepared for the unexpected at all times. It is wise to keep both fishing tackle and a rifle handy, for in this genuine wilderness there is no way to tell when the salmon may become ravenous or a trophy caribou may wander to the water's edge. ◉

REMEMBRANCES OF SPRINGTIMES PAST

Springtime is not only a season of renewed activity, when an angler grows restless contemplating his first cast; it is also an interlude of nostalgia. The sight of a crystalline freshet can stir a yearning for an unremembered era, a lifetime or so past, when the air must have been sweeter, the waters purer, the trophy fish more plentiful. In celebration of this spring, as well as springs gone by, here is an album of angling art dating from the mid-nineteenth century to the opening of the twentieth. The total concentration of the bass fisherman on the facing page, no less than his gear, evokes the spirit of the 1880's. This painting typifies the style of Sherman Foote Denton (1856-1937), an American wildlife artist who was noted for his outstanding illustrations of fish in the annually published reports of the State of New York Forest, Fish, and Game Commission. Further examples of Denton's work appear on pages 78 and 79, while the other pages of this album are devoted to paintings by equally gifted American artists who produced books, portfolios, prints for framing, and even advertisements in those earlier years when springtime was reverently dedicated to the angler's avocation.

Preceding pages:
Leaping trout was painted by
Samuel A. Kilbourne
(1836-1881), whose studies of
game fish were lauded by
sportsmen and naturalists for
their lifelike detail.
Near right: Not many anglers
will recall when each
package of Virginia Brights
cigarettes contained a
picture card showing a fish;
old advertisement features
miniatures of fifty freshwater
and saltwater game species
and shellfish. Opposite page:
Hand-colored 1859 lithograph
published by Thomas Kelly
is from series called,
paradoxically, "American
Hunting Scene."

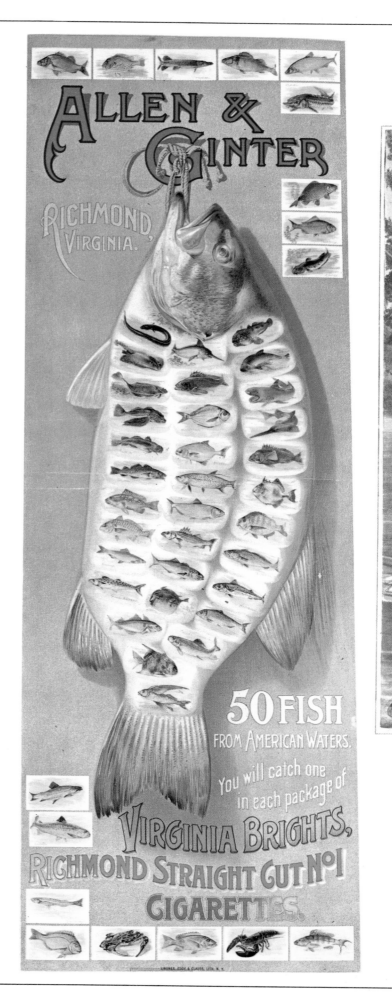

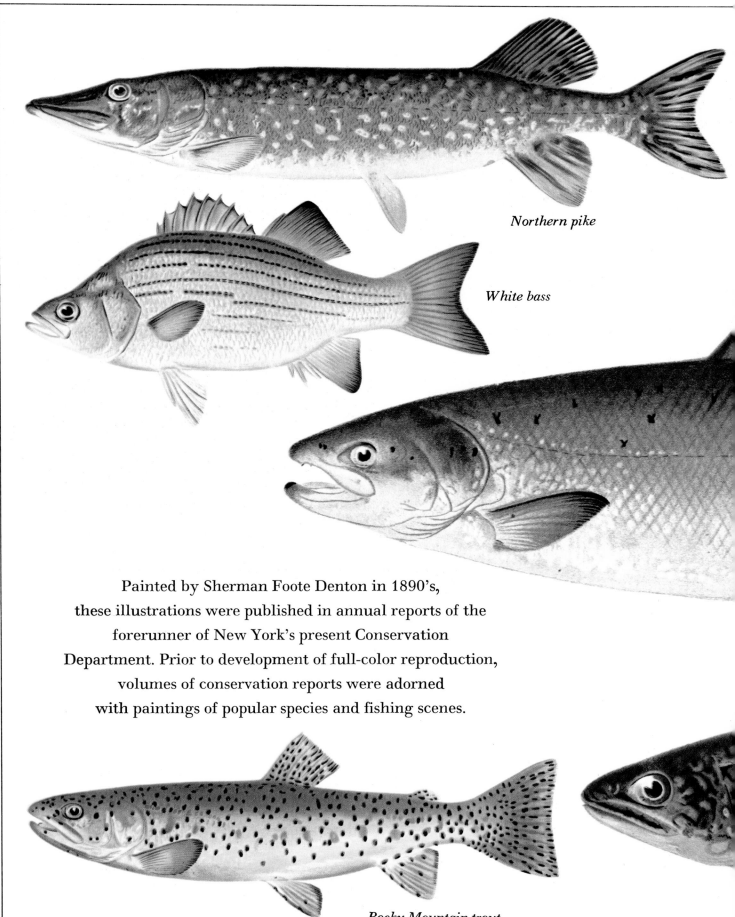

Northern pike

White bass

Painted by Sherman Foote Denton in 1890's,
these illustrations were published in annual reports of the
forerunner of New York's present Conservation
Department. Prior to development of full-color reproduction,
volumes of conservation reports were adorned
with paintings of popular species and fishing scenes.

Rocky Mountain trout

Landlocked salmon

Atlantic salmon

Lake trout

Left: 1862 lithograph, entitled
"Brook Trout Fishing," is among finest
examples of art that earned fame
for Currier & Ives. Below: Another
Currier & Ives print, dated
1859, bears simple title, "Hooked!"

Fox
of
the
Tidal
Flats

*by
Leonard M.
Wright, Jr.
Bonefishing
turns.
anglers into
hunters,
stalking
waters where
an
undetected
approach seems
impossible.*

*Photography
by
Bob
Gelberg*

Preceding pages:
Guide spots school of
tailing bonefish
for angler on flats
off Chub Key in Bahamas.
Right: Fish cruises
the shallows in constant
search for food.

Probably bonefishing has more in common with mountain-sheep hunting than it does with conventional types of fishing. The searching and the stalking are the high moments. The actual kill is often anti-climactic. The best guide I've ever fished with adds to the hunting atmosphere as he poles the boat toward a school of fish. "I see three, four of them," he whispers.

"Where?" He has the sharpest eyes I've ever encountered and always sees fish before his client does.

"Two o'clock. You ready?"

I make a quick visual check of the loose coils of fat fly line in the bottom of the boat to make sure there are no snarls and that I haven't shifted my feet onto them in the excitement. I nod.

"Not yet. They comin' this way."

I glance at him, expectantly.

"Not yet."

Now I see them. Not the fish, really, but the shadows under them—dark blurs, ever-changing in shape, distorted by the short, choppy waves. But the dark patches are moving and that means bonefish.

"Start getting line out."

I begin casting, keeping the line in the air, feeding out the coils as fast as the rod can take them. Once. Twice.

"Three o'clock. Now. Shoot! Shoot!"

I aim my final cast at right angles to the boat and release the last two coils of line, feel them shoot through the guides, and see the fly drop lightly forty-five feet away—three feet our side of the shadows.

Whether the fish now take the fly or not is important, but not critical. For on some days they'll savage anything you present. On others they'll follow a bit and turn away, time after time. You can't control that. But the team execution of a perfect stalk and presentation is a joy in itself.

Of course, everyone wants to catch the fish. But one or two a day is enough. As I've said, the hunt's the thing. And it is this hunting-fishing quality that draws men hundreds—even thousands—of miles each winter. Here, in the tropics and semitropics, they pit their cunning and skill against a fish that doesn't jump, is virtually inedible, and isn't big enough to cause much talk if it were caught in an overfished local lake. And come men do, their numbers increasing geometrically, it seems, each year. This is a new sport and still catching on. While the first record of a bonefish landed on rod and reel dates back to 1891, it wasn't till the late Forties that much was known about where and how to catch these fish.

Most of today's famous fishing authors played a part in the early pioneering and popularizing: Joe Brooks, Lee Wulff, A. J. McClane to name a few. But bonefishing has drawn all types of well-known men. Baseball's Ted Williams and golf's Sam Snead are addicts. So was Herbert Hoover. And George La Branche of trout and salmon immortality devoted his last few fish-

ing years to bonefish. He confided to friends that he had learned all he ever would about trout and salmon, but here was a whole new world to explore. Unfortunately, he left us no book on the subject. In fact, to date there is only one book that is devoted to bonefish exclusively. Stanley M. Babson's excellent *Bonefishing* stands alone at this writing.

And yet, *Albula vulpes* is one of the most talked-about fish wherever anglers gather. And no wonder. He may well be the perfect game fish. Even his name is perfect, "white fox." White he is—like polished aluminum when he shows his side underwater. And "fox" may be an understated epithet, considering his cunning and wiles.

The key to this fish, his behavior, and his temperament is his habitat. He lives and feeds on the vast, shallow tidal flats wherever they occur in warm-water areas. (Most sport fishing takes place in Florida, the Bahamas, Bermuda, the Caribbean, Mexico, and Central America, but the bonefish is distributed all around the globe.)

The tidal flats are as different ecologically from the craggy coastlines, reefs, and deeps of the ocean as a duck marsh is from the mountains. There's no hiding place here. It is a vast expanse of desert, thinly covered by water and exposed to a merciless sun. Here, except where there is a pasturage of turtle grass, there are no nooks and crannies in which forage fish can hide. But there is one little-harvested crop of food: the sea worms and small mollusks that inhabit the sand. Nature evolved a specialized fish to exploit this stark environment, one avoided by most oceanic carnivores.

For the bonefish is strictly one-of-a-kind.

Some fish species may have an undershot mouth for bottom feeding, others a bony mouth and throat for crushing shells, still others a tough, pointed snout for rooting and digging. But none has all three plus blinding speed for escape and the nerves of an opening-night actor. Bonefish live out their lives on the brink of nervous exhaustion. A few tiny sandpipers wheeling overhead can stampede them. A running outboard will spook them a quarter-mile away. And a cigarette lighter carelessly dropped on the bottom of a wooden skiff is enough to scatter them even when they are at a distance of more than two hundred feet.

Then, too, these fish can learn. There are still a few places where the fish have never been tried or have lived unmolested for several years. A reasonably cautious angler can rack up quite a score here. For a day or two. After that, the fish get very wary indeed. In fact, the more they're harried, the spookier they get. I have often fished a small flat that's right at the edge of a good-sized Bahamian town. These few acres of sand are flooded only at high tide and there's an hour or so of fishing, at most, each day. No more than four or five fish

Underwater view
shows fish's
pointed snout and
undershot jaw
—adaptations for
bottom feeding.
These two pictures
and scene on
preceding pages
show bonefish
at start of second
strong run.

will come up on a tide and they are the most sophisticated ones I have ever met. The reason for this is that they spend the rest of their hours on an adjacent, slightly deeper flat where the natives anchor their small boats. Here the turtle grass is so thick you can't spot them—much less fish for them. Yet I'm sure this daily contact with people has educated them. Of the hundreds of casts I've made to these fish (and that's counting only the casts that didn't flush the fish) I have had only seven follow my fly. Only two took it in their mouths. And those two nibbled the feathers so gingerly that they weren't even pricked by the hook. Mind you, these weren't large fish. Four or five pounds, perhaps. Yet I think I'd get more satisfaction in finally catching one of them than I would from hooking into the real monster I once encountered on the big flats across the bay.

Fortunately, most bonefish aren't uncatchable—even though they may seem so on some days. But you have to have the right equipment and a lot of skill or a good guide or all three. And a little luck never hurts.

Let's take a look at equipment. A good freshwater spinning outfit with two hundred yards of 8-pound test line will suffice. So will a nine-foot bass bugging or salmon fly rod and a salmon reel that will hold one hundred and fifty yards of backing. This reserve of line is important. Don't be misled by the size of the fish. They'll average three to five pounds. Five to eight is distinctly good. Over that is big. The world record may stand at a shade over nineteen pounds, yet I know an expert angler who's fished one of the best areas for at least a month each winter for the past twenty years and is still hoping to boat his first twelve-pounder. And yet, these fish will run off a staggering amount of line. A smallish fish may take off a hundred yards in a few

seconds. A six-pounder can peel off one hundred and fifty.

Eight-pound test seems about minimal for practical fishing. Six-pound test often breaks under its own weight if a fish changes direction more than a hundred yards out. Fly fishing calls for nine feet of tapered nylon ending in 8- or 10-pound test. But even in remote areas where you can get away with a heavier line or leader, you can't hold a fish that wants to run. I know. I once hooked into an estimated four-pounder when a loop of fly line was snagged around a finger. That fish broke a 12-pound leader as if it were thread. And this from a standing start!

Your selection of lures can be modest. Bonefish aren't selective or finicky. They'll take almost anything that's moving at the right speed and seems to be of reasonable size—when they're taking. They feed on a wide range of natural foods and have developed a catholicity of taste. Jigs and flies should be two to three inches long, and every shade from jet black to pure white seems to work.

If you're going to fish bait, your guide will provide. Shrimp, lobster, land crab, and conch are the standards. You'll need some good sturdy hooks about size 1/0. No sinkers. You can't risk the splash.

You'll also need a top-notch pair of polaroid glasses. Seeing is eighty percent of the game. And don't forget your favorite suntan lotion and lots of it. Bonefishing is sunny-weather fishing. The rays not only hit you from above, they bounce off the water and off the sand beneath the water.

Now that you're rigged and ready, how do you begin the stalk? Should you hire a guide or go it alone? Use bait or a lure? Spinning or fly rod?

First things first. If you're new to an area, by all means hire a guide. They're fairly expensive—about thirty dollars for half a day. But they'll put you into fish where you'd be lost alone. Even a run-of-the-mill guide will provide a good, flat-bottomed wood or fiberglass boat (never noisy metal) with a twenty-five-plus-horse-power motor to speed you out to the hunting area. Then he'll pole you for hours upwind and down without knocking the side of the boat. He'll spot the fish before you will, nine times out of ten. And he'll know the most likely areas as only a native can.

Fishing with a top-notch guide is an experience in itself—but you'll usually have to book him months in advance or take a chance on a last-minute cancellation. For, as executive recruiters can tell you, a good man is hard to find and even harder to get.

The average guide relies on local knowledge and this is his great asset. But the exceptional guide goes far beyond this. He observes acutely. He abstracts theories from his observations. And he tests each new hypothesis again and again. For example, even when the flats are cold and windy, the first-rate guide can probably put you into some fish. He'll know of a sheltered cove or a tidal creek that a few fish will frequent even when conditions are considered impossible.

Then, too, a man like this can read the flats. As he poles along, he'll continually scan the bottom for signs of feeding—craters about six inches in diameter which look like underwater anthills. These tell him how long ago the fish were rooting here by the color of the sand and by the sharpness of the crater edges. Often the shapes of these feeding holes will even reveal to him the direction in which the fish were moving and point the way to the current location of the school.

There are other subtle signs of bonefish activity that only the expert's radar can detect. Where the bottom is muddy or marly, some of the sediment stirred up by feeding fish will stay in suspension for quite a while. The man who knows his terrain and tides may say to you, "See that slight milkiness in the water? They were here about fifteen minutes ago. We should hit them about two hundred yards farther up this creek."

Once you've fished an area a few times, you can go it alone. Wading. You can't handle a boat and fish at the same time. Yet this is undoubtedly the most rewarding fishing you'll ever do. Not that you'll catch or see as many fish as you will with a guide. But think what you will have accomplished. You'll have estimated the location of fish through your own knowledge of their habits. You will have exercised your own judgment in making the stalk and presentation. And then perhaps you will hook a bonefish securely and play it properly without any advice. You can't top that.

The bait or lure choice seems to vary more with local custom than it does with the fish. Both are effective. But there's a bit of extra satisfaction in having coaxed them into accepting an artificial.

Probably ninety-five percent of all bonefish taken are landed on spinning tackle. The fly rod is just beginning to become popular. The reason for this is that the fly rod poses certain problems. How many fishermen can cast a fly to a precise spot at least forty-five feet away in a fifteen-knot wind? And without any warm-up tries? On days when the trade winds drop, the game is not so demanding, but those days are rare indeed. On the other hand, the fly rod in the hands of a man who's mastered it may well be the deadlier weapon. It delivers with a whisper instead of a plop; in shallow water this edge can be decisive. And fish will be in extremely shallow water day after day at times. Here you can spot the fish hundreds of feet away as they "tail" —feed head down with their tails waving above water and flashing in the sun. This is the most exciting fishing of all. But the lure must be dropped within a foot or two of the fish or he won't see it in that position. A fly here is murderous. A shrimp or an eighth-of-an-ounce jig, chancey.

Shallow, grassy areas are fly-rod territory, too. A jig or piece of live bait will quickly hang up in the weeds. A fly on a light-wire hook can be jerked along enticingly—an inch or two below the surface. This shallow-water feeding characteristic is what makes the bonefish so exciting. And yet, this is not an absolute rule. A few years ago, I was outboarding toward a flat in fifteen to twenty feet of water when I saw a cloudy patch ahead. The guide cut the motor and handed me the spinning rod. "Mon, we cotch 'em now," he said with a grin. And catch them we did. Four in the next half-hour until the school moved on. Yet it wasn't much of a show. The fish didn't make the long fast runs. They were already in the safest territory they could find.

How often bonefish inhabit the atypical deeps, I don't know. Gil Drake, owner of the Deep Water Key operation on Grand Bahama, once told me an interesting tale. He was casting for barracuda from his dock one day with a four-inch plug when he got a backlash. The plug just sat there, motionless on the surface in twenty feet of water while Gil picked out the tangles. Just as he was about to retrieve the lure a bonefish smacked the plug, was hooked, and duly landed.

We know that bonefish hang out in moderately deep water at certain times. When water temperatures on the flats sink below sixty-five degrees the fish usually disappear. And at dead low tide, they'll often congregate in holes five to ten feet deep if there's a channel cutting through the flat. It's a cinch to take them on bait when they're holed up like this. Not the peak of the sport. But then, the only bad bonefishing is no bonefishing.

Most devotees will agree, however, that the very best of it is wading alone with a fly rod, searching the shallows for tailing fish. And here, sometimes, there's an extra thrill thrown in. One day on the back side of Chub Key I was trailed by a three-foot barracuda. He never made a threatening move. He just followed like a dog some forty feet away and he followed no matter which direction I walked. After half an hour of this he had the flat to himself.

Another time on the North shore of Eleuthera Island I was prospecting afoot in deeper than usual water, trying to find some fish at dead low tide. All I found was a five-foot hammerhead shark. As I moved back toward shallower water he started to circle me. Then he pulled up a few feet away and just stared. I poked him smartly on the nose, fencing-style, with the tip of my nine-foot fly rod. That sent him on his way for a time, but I had to repeat the operation three more times before I made it to shallow water.

Looking back on it, I don't think I was in danger in either case. I believe I was being viewed as an object of curiosity rather than as a chunk of delicatessen. But, I repeat, there's an extra thrill in wading for bonefish.

While it is true that the hunt's the thing, bonefishing has another quality that sets it apart from more usual types of angling. With bonefish, luck is at a minimum. No unseen leviathan will suddenly take your hook. You catch what you cast for. You get what you deserve. For, remember, the whole game is played out in clear view. All cards are on the table, face up. Perhaps only the fabled trout fishing on the chalk streams in Hampshire, England, takes place from stalk to finish in such clear, continuous view of the angler. Any fishing with all this to offer has to rate right at the very top. ◉

Voices
Over
Gardner's
Marsh

by Dudley Cammett Lunt

PHOTOGRAPH BY ERWIN A. BAUER

On a day in the blind,
two hunters listen
for the music of ducks and geese,
familiar yet always
new as the false dawn.

I never voyaged so far in all my life. You shall see men you never heard of before, whose names you don't know, going away down through the meadows with long ducking-guns, with water-tight boots wading through the fowl-meadow grass, on bleak, wintry, distant shores, with guns at half-cock; and they shall see teal—blue-winged, green-winged,—sheldrakes, whistlers, black ducks, ospreys and many other wild and noble sights before night, such as they who sit in parlors never dream of.

Henry David Thoreau

To the seasoned wildfowler, high adventure begins when he steps from the fast land and his hip boots sink into the viscous black muck of a marsh. He stops, pulls his boots up over his thighs, and attaches them to the shoulder harness that he wears. It is dark, and the stars are sparks that glint in the black sky. Gun and gear laden, he plods steadily along a well-beaten path.

What is that?

It is a whispering overhead—*swi-wi-wi*—that waxes and wanes. This is the whistling in the still air of swiftly beating wings. The wildfowler looks up and glimpses two dark forms with flittering wings.

This is good. The birds are moving.

The wildfowler plods on through a stand of tall reeds. Feather grass he calls it. Phragmites is what it actually is. Upon emerging from this dark jungle the wildfowler suddenly stops short in his tracks.

There has been an explosion, an eruption into flight, and now ahead of him a large duck is spinning out over the marsh, emitting a series of startled quacks that diminish in the distance. This alarms another duck and yet a third. Black ducks or mallards, the wildfowler opines. It is too dark to be sure. Anyhow, they are big ducks. Another good omen.

Glaw, glaw, glaw!

The wildfowler chuckles softly to himself. This distant call is unmistakable. It is the plaintive cry of a lone Canada. Having strayed from his companions, he has lost his bearings, and somewhere in the dark murky sky above the wide-stretching marsh, he is cruising about calling for his fellows. Suddenly his wild calls are answered. Then they cease altogether. The stray has found a safe haven.

These sounds and flights are intermittent. Otherwise there is a vast silence.

The path leads straight across the open marsh to a ditch. Here a boat hugs the shore, and in short order the wildfowler, his partner, and George, the big black Labrador, clamber aboard.

The experienced wildfowler almost always goes ducking or goosing with a companion, a partner, one who will share the tasks of the day, the beauty of the flights, and the supreme excitement of the tolling of the waterfowl. He is a man verging on years, a bit grizzled but at the height of his powers. The relationship between these two has been tested and cemented by the days they have shared on a marsh, in fair weather and foul.

The boat moves slowly against the incoming tide. One of the two wildfowlers is rowing, pushing the oars away from his chest, fisherman-style, while in the bow the other one is setting out the duck decoys, dropping one first on one side of the boat, then another on the other side. Three decoys are saved, to be set at the mouth of a small ditch that debouches from the marsh in back of the blind.

This blind fronts on Quarter Gut, one of the myriad watercourses that with each tide fill and drain the Delaware marshes. It is situated near the downstream end of a narrow island where the Gut trends in a long, lazy curve from north to east. The shore opposite the blind marks the northern edge of the Bombay Hook Wildlife Refuge.

Ashore on the island the two men swap jobs. The decoy setter tends to the guns and gear, stowing them in the blind, shoves the boat into its blind, closes a reed-covered gate after it, and installs George in his blind. His companion meanwhile, following a well-beaten path to the east end of the island, sets up a dozen odd goose decoys broadside to the gut. These are oversized silhouettes, known in gunner's parlance as stick-ups. At length, with all these tasks accomplished, the men join each other in the blind.

They are in good time. They had arrived on the marsh in the dark of the night. Now there is light—the rare and lovely light of the false dawn. Twice a day the beams of the hidden sun strike the sphere and tangentially assault the upper ether. Then a reflected light bathes the earth for a short and precious interval. In the morning this is the light of the false dawn; in the evening, that of the afterglow. These are times for silence, observation, and enjoyment.

The two wildfowlers stand in their blind and take in the scene around them. The droplets of dew on the grasses that mask the blind are liquid moonstones, for a purple shows in their refracted light. The marsh is a great span of glowing gold. At its distant edges, the limbs and branches of the trees stand out in fretted black lines. The large hawk that every morning takes a stance in an oak on the refuge, again this morning is a dark prescience of predation. Along the eastern horizon a glow of red foretells the swift approach of daylight.

The ducks are in high flight. In small groups, in close order, they are seen etching their swift passages, now against the blue sky, now against the pink underbelly of a cloud. Despite the distance there comes to ear faintly the curious guttural rattle that is known to wildfowlers as the black duck's feeding call—*kuta-kuta-kut*. They are leaving for the river, but they will be back.

With the suddenness of an apparition seven green-winged teal appear in the kind of close-order flight that distinguishes a small flock of shorebirds. Sweeping down, they pass over the decoys, then, rising, make a climbing turn to circle out over the marsh and then return and pitch ahead of the decoys in a succession of little splashes. The two hunters watch silently.

These teal are nervous. For a few seconds they swim idly about. Suddenly, one leaps aloft. Then another and another, until in ragged succession all of them are airborne, and are seen spinning away in bouncing flight out over the marsh, where they suddenly dip out of sight into a distant ditch.

"Nice flight, that."

"Right. Maybe they'll be back."

The next event of the day is dawn, heralded by the glint of a slice of gold above the skyline in the east. This ushers in another kind of flight that is familiar to all wildfowlers, the dawn flight of the blackbirds. Over the entire marsh they are now seen, slipping out of the stands of phragmites where they have spent the night. They are heard, too, as a large but soft volume of *tchuck-chees* sounds in every quarter. Rising above the marsh, they soon assemble in the air, forming a great round cylinder of small black bodies in undulating flight. In this fashion they move steadily out across the marsh toward the cornfields of the upland. Wildfowlers watching for latecomers in the predawn flights of ducks have witnessed collisions when a duck passed in swifter flight through these vast, ragged flocks of blackbirds. This spectacle of the blackbirds is of short duration and, when it is over, a spell of quiet descends on the marsh. The two wildfowlers make it the occasion for a coffee break.

Their technique of handling the flights of waterfowl is a simple one. Facing Quarter Gut out in front, Bob occupies the left, and Jack the right end of the blind. When ducks are seen on a course toward the blind, wildfowlers use the device of an imaginary clockface, with noon straight ahead, to show their location. Like this: "Watch yourself! A pair of blacks at nine o'clock."

They start calling. On this salt marsh, wildfowlers use a steady staccato of sharp calls without cessation until the birds are clearly seen to be coming in over the decoys. But in this instance when the two blacks are over the marsh across the gut, the blaring of quacks suddenly ceases. In the disgusted tone of a man who has been through it before, Bob gives the verdict: "They're headed for Duck Heaven."

By this he means they will pitch on the refuge. And so they do, winding down in wide circles of flight while reconnoitering the marsh from aloft, until at length they are seen fluttering just above the grass, a prelude to their landing when, still fluttering, they disappear from sight.

The sun is now half an hour high. The sky is empty. There are no waterfowl to be seen, and the usual hiatus between flights ensues. The two gunners are used to this. They have long since learned that in duck shooting, patience is of the essence. They discuss the flight of the two black ducks. Perhaps it was the harbinger of more to come, perhaps not. In any event, the ducks will fly on the turn of the tide, and a quick glance at its level in the gut convinces Jack that this is an hour distant. A small breeze has sprung up out of the southwest and the possible effects of this small event are thoroughly canvassed. Then they take a good look around the marsh with binoculars, pausing to scrutinize the several blind sites, and, since no shooting has been heard, they conclude that they are lucky. On this November day they have Gardner's Marsh to themselves. No doubt this is due to the fact it is Monday. On Saturdays the place is alive with skybusters.

"Watch it! Here come those teal again."

"Where?"

"Four o'clock."

This is on Jack's side of the blind. He whispers again: "They're coming right up the gut."

On the wing, teal perform miracles of maneuver. Only rarely are they seen in level flight. Approaching in a compact group their course is erratic and unpredictable, now rising, now flaring, now turning, now dipping earthward.

The two wildfowlers crouch, guns in hand. Over the marsh across the gut, the seven teal are wheeling into a turn to the left that will bring them over the first of the line of decoys. On they come. When they arrive abreast of the three decoys behind the blind, they start shaking their wings. This is it. They are going to pitch, teal-style, just beyond the decoys. Up rise the wildfowlers. Simultaneous shots sound.

Two teal fall, and land on their backs in the water.

This is George's moment; Jack releases the catch on the gate to his blind and he bounds to the back of the gut. For an instant he stands poised, his head moving almost imperceptibly from side to side. Seeing the birds he plunges in, making a prodigious splash, and starts swimming toward the far bird. Upon reaching it, his lower jaw thrusts forward under the duck and his upper jaw closes just enough to secure it. Then he turns about, swims for the shore, delivers the dead bird to Jack, turns, and is off in pursuit of the other teal which has drifted quite a distance with the tide.

A professional performance, this. George's reward, after he has so thoroughly shaken himself as almost to throw himself to the ground, is a rubdown with an old towel.

The morning flight of ducks is now underway. At the height of the tide, they leave the river and come in over the marsh, flying high and spotting the sky.

"It's a good thing old duck-cusser isn't here," says Bob.

Duck-cusser has a blind some five hundred yards farther up Quarter Gut. He earned his unusual soubriquet by his propensity for sky-busting—shooting at birds out of range—coupled with his indulgence in profanity when his wild shooting merely frightens the ducks and drives them higher.

"Watch yourself! Mallards at ten o'clock."

It is extraordinary how wildfowl will occasionally approach a blind without being seen or heard. Sometimes, indeed, it is a splashing out among the decoys that brings a startled wildfowler to his feet.

The mallards, a drake and a hen, are cautiously circling the decoys and the blind. As they respond to the few soft short *quacks* from a duck call, they start to cross the gut, dropping as they come. When they are in back of the blind, two guns rise out of the reeds, two shots ring out, and two ducks fall into the marsh. Bob has taken the leading bird and Jack the trailing one, which is to say the duck nearest to each.

The spot where each duck fell has been marked in relation to a sapling that has been stuck in the marsh for this purpose. And now George plunges in again, swims the narrow ditch, and after shaking himself with vigor on the bank, looks back toward the blind. Then, following the directional wavings of Jack's arm, he swiftly retrieves first the drake and then the hen.

For a time now, things are quiet. Up over Gardner's Marsh the sky is bereft of waterfowl and the two hunters take the opportunity to have a snack. While they are consuming their sandwiches, the faint gabble of distant geese comes to ear. Knowing looks are exchanged. Far to the south, on the refuge, geese by the thousands have been resting overnight in the fields—goose pastures, the game-management people call them—or in great rafts on the surface of the ponds. Now and again a small flight is seen to rise above the tree tops, only to drop down out of sight. The geese are nervous.

The foraging flights of Canada geese are unpredictable. They may come out early or late, or, indeed, they may not fly at all, as when with entire safety they feed in fields by the light of a full moon. Their flights may be short, an hour perhaps, or they may last nearly all day. In these matters the great birds follow a wild timetable of their own. However, the experienced wildfowler can sense their immediate occurrence by the rising pitch of their anserine converse, and by the rise and fall of the small flights.

And so, while the geese are caucusing on the refuge, the wildfowlers set about making their own preparations. Goose calls are hung around their necks so they dangle handy to the right hand. There is a shift of shells—from 6's to 4's or 2's. Then Bob leaves the blind and, feeling his way cautiously with his feet, he creeps on a submerged plank across the ditch from the island to the marsh. On the marsh he steps behind a tussock that has been built up with marsh grasses. When he seats himself on a box behind it, he is completely hidden. Now they are all set.

This island blind is good for both duck and goose shooting. This is not unique, but it is rare. The goose shooting is of the variety known to sportsmen as pass shooting—that is, taking the birds as they fly past overhead, always, it would seem, traveling faster than you think. This is difficult and a challenge to a good wing shot because the range is shortest when the bird is straight overhead. Also, since the geese fly high, if pass shooting is not done conservatively and with great care, it will soon degenerate into sky-busting. Only very occasionally and under special conditions will the geese pitch to the decoys set on the upstream end of the island and land in the gut, as they will on an upland pond that has not been over-shot—a rare thing these days.

"They're up!"

A vast cloud of black geese is in the air above the tree line on the refuge, a good mile and a half away. They are milling about, some flying clockwise, others counter-clockwise. Now and again a small flock splits off at a tangent. Then another flock follows it, and soon the flyways that the geese will follow are made clear. One is over the upland of the refuge. The other, at a right angle to this, is out across Gardner's Marsh. The destinations of these foraging flights are the cornfields of Kent County.

Now the flights are fairly well-launched, and they come streaming over the marsh in great V's, in long strings, or in ragged hay-hooks. Soon every quarter of the sky above the marsh has its quota of flying geese, and their full-throated calling makes a wild cacophonous chorus.

Crouched down out of sight in their blinds, the two wildfowlers peer through the slightly parted reeds in order to gauge the likely approach of this flight or that. They have two questions: Will they fly over the blind? Will they be low enough? In tolling these great birds, they rely on their decoys at the foot of the island and on their experienced and judicious use of a goose call. By using separate blinds, they have doubled the span of their pass shooting.

The large flights, led by old and experienced ganders, give the blinds a wide berth, traveling high, wide, and out of gunshot. It is the small flights that present the most likely prospects—like the seven geese that are now crossing the rim of the marsh. They are flying quite low, but on a course that will take them west of the island blind.

The wildfowlers start calling. The line of flight bends slightly eastward. The flock is now headed toward the island blind. Now and again they veer back toward the west, whereupon a few "o'lips" from a goose call bring them back to the desired course. At length they are fairly committed. Then the calling by the wildfowlers ceases. On their present course, the birds will pass just to the west of the island blind and well within gunshot. Tension in the blinds increases.

Prospects suddenly look even better when, on reaching the far shore of the gut, the leader turns to the east. It is the decoys that have done this. As the flight is about to pass between the two blinds, there is a shot from the island blind. Number three goose on the right line of the V folds and falls into Quarter Gut with a prodigious splash. A split second later a shot from the other blind brings the trailing goose on the other line down on the marsh. Seven geese have come in, five go out.

The morning goose flight is soon over and Bob returns to his place in the island blind. There follows another space of quiet—a time for small talk, for catnaps taken stretched out on the bench, for snacks and hot tea.

The next event of the day occurs during this interlude. It is a surprise and the two wildfowlers are caught off balance. There never was a day's gunning without some such occurrence—such as when you are out of your blind without your gun and a likely looking pair of birds takes the occasion to pitch to your decoys.

"My God! Will you look at this?"

It is raining ducks, big black ducks. They had come across the marsh unobserved, flying high, and now they are pitching to the three decoys off the west end of the island—wings set, feet outstretched, *splash, splash, splash*. Afterwards the two gunners swapped estimates: twenty to twenty-five birds. Now they swim about, this way, that way, quacking. They are nervous. Something is wrong. On the far side of the gut one explodes into flight, straight up a good ten feet. This is the signal. In a swift scattering sequence, they all leap up, and, as they do, two shots ring out. They are on Jack's end of the blind and he makes a double.

The swiftness of this action tingles the nerves of the most seasoned wildfowler. At one instant the pool is full of swimming ducks. A split second later, but two are left, both clean kills. When George fetches them ashore, it is seen that they are of the type the wildfowler calls redlegs—Canadian black ducks—and from the size of the flight they were obviously in migration. The two wildfowlers have, as they would phrase it, limited out in ducks—two mallards, two black ducks, and two teal.

Then follows a long wait. In their bag also are the two geese that were taken in the morning. They are entitled to harvest two more, and the geese that went out in the morning will be coming back over the marsh before sundown.

In the early afternoon the wind hauls over into the west and freshens. The trees on the upland can be seen thrashing.

"Those geese'll be boiling along, with this wind under their tails."

"Right!"

As the afternoon wanes and the sun declines toward the skyline, the colors strengthen and present sharp contrasts. The marsh is a gleaming span of gold and the water in the gut is a deep blue. A blue and gold day. It will be long remembered by the two waterfowlers.

When the returning flights begin, they are irregular and, as predicted, the geese fly at great speed. They present a noble sight and their calls make a noble outcry. This wild spectacle never ceases to enchant an ardent waterfowler.

"Hey! Watch that little bunch under that big flight."

Five geese come on, low enough to raise the hopes of the hidden waterfowlers. They are flying swiftly on pumping wings over the marsh on the opposite side of the gut. Short of the shore, they veer to the right. Then, following the contour of the shore, they pass in swift flight and move out of range.

"Watch yourself! They're going to swing."

In close array, they start swinging over the gut. Now they start coming up into the wind. Their great wings set. The five geese skim above the gut abreast of the decoys.

As they hover, there is a split second of awesome intensity. Then in swift sequence come two shots, and two geese tumble.

And so ends this blue and gold day out on Quarter Gut. In the parlance of the blind, they now "pick up," cross the gut in their boat, and secure it. And then each man, laden with two geese and three ducks, follows the long path off the marsh and onto the upland. The air above their passage is filled with flying geese and their resonant calling. The hunters will be back. The wildfowler never tires of his rare sport. ◉

Canada Goose

The magisterial black,
gray, and white Canada goose
(Branta canadensis)
is not only a beautiful species
but a very intelligent one, worthy
of the waterfowler's utmost
respect. There are times when
geese are difficult to fool with
either decoys or calls, but
because they present such large
targets and travel in great
numbers, many honkers are harvested by
the gun each season as the echelons
swoop between cornfields and
aquatic resting areas. While the
common Canada is among the
most familiar birds along the Atlantic
Flyway, there are several smaller,
lesser-known subspecies. For example,
the cackling goose is only
about the size of a plump mallard.
The common Canada, on the
other hand, averages ten pounds
or so. The Canada's plumage
is so heavy and tough that a
goose is hard to bring down until it
flies within close gunning
range. Inexperienced hunters may
fire at great range, thereby
alerting the flocks and causing
them to fly high and ignore the decoys.
Unfortunately, a bird may be
injured by a few stray pellets at
too great a range for a clean
kill, and may fly on for many miles
before meeting its end in
some frozen field or marsh. The
knowledgeable hunter fires
only at targets within certain range.
Among the Canada's remarkable
attributes are its stupendous
navigational instincts, cooperative
behavior within the flock, and
amazing longevity. In the wild state,
geese have been known to live
over twenty years, and a hunter recently
reported shooting one that had been
banded twenty-seven years ago.

Flyway Portraits *by Walter D. Osborne*

Mallard

Despite differences in color,
the mallard (*Anas platyrhynchos*) is
closely related to the black
duck, and crossbreeding is not
uncommon. At one time, there was a
widespread belief that the mallard
merely represented a plumage phase of the
black, though the mallard is as
gullible as the black duck is clever.
Mallards have a wide distribution.
The continent's great grain
belt, particularly where it spreads
through the Canadian Midwest,
is still the big mallard country, but
the development of the Eastern
Shore corn belt has attracted the
ducks in ever-increasing numbers. Big and
plump, the handsome greenhead and his
brownish mate are among the
finest-eating of waterfowl, and they
respond eagerly to a well-placed
decoy spread and a duck call.

Pintail

Sometimes called "sprig" because of
the male's long tail feathers,
the pintail duck (*Anas acuta*) abounds
throughout most of the Northern
Hemisphere. The handsome drake runs
a bit over two pounds, the
plainer hen somewhat less. Like
teal and widgeon, the pintail is an
early fall arrival, heralding
the migration of other waterfowl.
The pintail is among those
species that have profited enormously
from the Eastern Shore's corn
bonanza. However, a healthy population
does not mean easy shooting—
for the pintail is almost as wary
as the black duck, and is
often quite hard to call to the rig.

Black Duck

Among the largest of ducks, the black (*Anas rubripes*) weighs more than two pounds at maturity. The male and female are hard to tell apart, but the hen is usually a little smaller than the drake. Rated as one of the most wily of all waterfowl, the black duck nests in Labrador, Newfoundland, and much of southeastern Canada, as well as parts of the Great Lakes states, upper New York, and New England. The species migrates in small flocks, wintering throughout the Southeast and in southern New England, Long Island, and the lower portions of Ohio, Indiana, and Illinois. During the migratory period, heavy concentrations arrive in the Delmarva Peninsula, and in the Northeast and the mid-Atlantic states there are also nonmigratory colonies. These ducks quickly learn the tricks of the hunter. Any unnatural-looking feature of the blind or stool will keep them far from shooting range. One of their most exasperating tactics is to swim to within a tantalizing distance from the rig, then take off rapidly and almost vertically, so that the hunter must calculate his lead well above, rather than only ahead of, the target. Black ducks are often found in the company of whistling swans, feeding on the remains of vegetation which those voracious feeders tear up.

Canvasback

Larger than even the black or the mallard is the highly esteemed canvasback (*Aythya valisineria*). The male often weighs three pounds or more. In his celebrated *American Duck, Goose and Brant Shooting*, Dr. William Bruette calls the hunting of this species "the real glory of duck shooting." Canvasbacks, or "cans" as the Eastern Shore folk call them, are an odd blend of caution and curiosity. A drowsy sportsman may be startled by a flight swooping in for a quick look at the decoys, then barreling off again before a shot can be made. The fastest of all American waterfowl, the canvasback has been timed at speeds in excess of seventy miles an hour. Larry Koller, in *The Treasury of Hunting,* estimates that with a good tail wind this bird may hit ninety. Pass shooting at cans requires extreme alertness and a long lead. Equipped with such flying speed, the species does not need the cleverness of the black duck to elude gunners. In the days of market hunting, cans were butchered by the thousands, but the fact that they have dwindled so in numbers can also be laid to the drainage of Canadian nesting grounds and the destruction of the big wild-celery beds in the Susquehanna-Chesapeake region. Nevertheless, proper game regulations and management have aided greatly in rebuilding the once tremendous canvasback population.

Green-Winged Teal

With a flashy black-and-green speculum, the little green-winged teal (*Anas carolinensis*) is a dandy of the flyway. In nuptial plumage the male sports a bronze-brown head and a green eye stripe. Drakes generally weigh just under a pound, hens a little less. The meat is tasty, but hunters often refer to such small species as "breakfast ducks." Since teal are not only small but very swift, they provide difficult wingshooting.

Gadwall

The drake of the gadwall species (*Anas strepera*), weighing about two pounds, is not as gaily marked as the teal but is among the handsomest of all ducks. This is particularly true of birds in nuptial plumage—a subtle blend of grays and browns with a white speculum and coal-black rump. Gadwalls are widely distributed through the temperate zone. Like black ducks, they occasionally hybridize with mallards, and for some years the crossbreeds were erroneously classified as a distinct species. The "Brewer's duck" painted by Audubon was in fact nothing more than a gadwall-mallard hybrid.

●

The Cliffhangers

Patience
and fortitude
are rewarded with
extraordinary
insights
into the life cycle
of North America's
finest trophy
animal.
By Andy Russell
Photography
by Bill Browning

To stand at timberline at sunrise watching bighorns graze on a steep meadow hung between rocky cliffs is to enjoy one of the great sights offered by nature's living museum. For these animals are as spectacular as the country which they inhabit. Among the cloven-hoofed game of the world few species can match the marvelous mountain sheep for sagacity and beauty of form.

The massive curling horns of the rams are highly coveted trophies that lure hunters back into high country again and again until their annual pilgrimages sometimes become indeed as much a way of life as they are a pursuit of sport.

To really know the sheep, it is best to see them in spring, when the ewes are on the lambing grounds and the lambs are being born. Away up among broken rocks at the foot of high cliffs, where scattered remnants of snow mark the recent passing of winter, the lambs are dropped in as rugged an environment as North America has to offer.

Opening pages:
Six-year-old ram is good
trophy, but horns
are not yet full curl.
Patchy July coat
will soon be summer sleek.
Opposite: Bachelor
rams grazing on high-protein
bunch grass. Above:
Montana's Absaroka Plateau,
bighorn homeland.

Friendly ewes from nursery herd—one the lamb's mother, the other barren—make jostling contact. Opposite: They take mid-day siesta on high ledge while watching alertly for danger from below.

Unlike the young of mule deer, elk, and moose, they know no early awkward period when they cannot readily travel with their mothers. I once watched a lamb being born on a ledge suspended between sky and earth where there seemed scarcely room for its delivery. It was no sooner dropped than the ewe got to her feet and licked the lamb dry with such vigor that she threatened to knock it off into space. Then she led it along a ledge over an eagle thoroughfare where one slip would have been sure death for the lamb. Although wobbly and a bit uncertain, it managed to follow for a few yards to a wider place, where it suckled. Mountain sheep milk must be potent, for when the mother moved on again the lamb followed, bouncing and gamboling with astonishing vigor and agility.

At birth lambs weigh between four and five pounds. But they grow rapidly and by the time they reach maturity, a ram will weigh some two hundred and fifty pounds; much of the weight is in the horns.

As the ewes and lambs move off the lambing grounds, following the rising tide of new green growth to the summering grounds among the high

July lamb, about six weeks old, follows mother over precipitous trail. Young have adult climbing ability within week of birth. Below: Lamb learns early to check rearward.

Virile young rams
in grizzled December coat
butt each other
in test of strength as
rutting season nears.
To gratify urge,
however, they will have
to overcome herd ram.

peaks, they are watchful but relatively carefree. They travel in bunches numbering from ten to thirty or more, and thus make use of a multiplicity of senses for their protection. If two sharp eyes are good, twenty times two are that much better, and few things large or small move within range of their marvelous vision that they do not see. They have eyes many times better than man's; their vision is about equal to human sight aided by a fine pair of eight-power binoculars. Their noses are keen; but they pay little attention to what they hear unless it is a strangely repetitive sound or one foreign to the high country. The mountains are full of noise: the clatter

of falling rock, the rush of water spilling over ledges, and the roar of wind, all mixed with the sounds of birds and other animals. The sharp barking of a squirrel will not spark any interest, but the clink of iron on stone will rouse a sheep instantly to alertness.

In early summer when the lambs still are small, the usual routine is sleep, followed by a period of suckling, which usually stimulates a session of play, followed by more sleep. The lambs are never left unguarded while napping. Even when the ewes scatter out to graze they leave a nurse or two watching over the sleeping lambs. They seem to take turns at this baby-sitting chore and it is not uncommon to see a lone ewe guarding a dozen or more lambs. Sometimes, if the ewe happens to have lost her lamb or missed having one that year, not one of the group she tends will be her own.

Although bighorn social organization permits yearlings and two-year-old rams to join a band of ewes and lambs, mature rams are unlikely to mingle during the summer and fall—even while sharing the same general area. At these times the rams run in separate bunches

Left: Spooked for reasons known only to himself, ram bolts for safety across snow, carrying head in typically regal bighorn fashion. Above: Concealed hunter scans magnificent Alberta Rockies for sheep.

—bachelor's clubs of a kind—with each group under a leader, usually the biggest and oldest.

But there is some communication between them, regardless of sex. One bright morning I was sitting high on a ridge within a few yards of a big ram lying comfortably in his bed. Suddenly he stopped chewing his cud and rose to his feet to stare fixedly toward a peak across the valley where a canyon dropped down from the foot of a snowfield. At first I could see nothing that would attract his attention, but when I screwed the focus of my nine-power binoculars down sharp and fine, and combed the far slopes, I saw the heliographing flash of white rump patches in the sun. It was a bunch of ewes with lambs running and romping across a rock slide toward a meadow under the snowfield. When they stopped to feed, the ram lost interest and turned around to lie down again. He had spotted those flashing rump patches at well over a mile. No doubt when coyotes or a cougar spook some distant band, its movements are telegraphed to other bands within eyeshot and they are alerted to the danger.

Bighorns, old and young, love to play. Most of the time their games are just a rough and tumble mixture of running and butting of heads with no apparent pattern; but sometimes the games are stylized and even organized. Unlike many species of animals and birds there is no special significance attached to this play. It is just a means of blowing off steam.

I was scouting for sheep one day when I walked out on a rim overlooking a deep basin on the east face of the Continental Divide. Almost directly below, under a sheer cliff and some precipitous gullied shelves, six big rams were bedded deep in the loose shale of a talus fan. Dangling my boots over the drop-off, I leaned back to rest and watch them. They were a study in placid enjoyment—for a while. Then, with-

out warning the ram at the back of the bunch leaped to his feet and ran past the others at a high speed. Instantly, all were away in full flight down the slope with the biggest in the lead. Then the leader made a quick, end-swapping jump in mid-air, and with scarcely a break in stride headed straight up the mountain. Upon reaching the first steep shelves among some weather-worn chimneys and turrets, the old herd master proceeded to lead the bunch through a flying exhibition of the most magnificent rock acrobatics I have ever seen. It was a wild alpine quadrille—a daring pattern of balance, momentum, and sheer speed, on an almost vertical stage. It was a spectacular display of footwork overhung with flying banners of dust. After about a minute of this high-spirited play, the rams stopped to look down over their mountain domain. Then they slowly climbed back down to begin feeding, as though frivolous frolicking was farthest from their minds. Like the country that is their home, mountain sheep are creatures of sharp contrasts of character.

Another time I watched for perhaps twenty minutes as four young rams played a bighorn version of "king of the hill" on a pile of loose rock in a moraine. It was almost a duplicate of the game children play, except that the rams butted each other off their chosen "hill"—a stylized game showing organization and indicating intelligence. They also play mountain versions of "follow the leader," generally in places of a suicidal nature where a single slip would mean disaster. However, they never seem to slip.

Although I have spent a lot of time observing sheep in winter, I have never known them to play during the cold months. Probably the impulse to play on the summering ranges is a result of high spirits brought about by unlimited quantities of lush, high-energy feed. At that time they can pick and choose from a host of alpine plants that grow to the tops of the mountains. They wander in this profusion of plant life, often belly deep in brilliant flowers. It is no wonder then that bighorns grow so fat, and that the meat is considered by gourmets to be the tastiest and most tender of all game.

But in this day of shrinking natural environment—a result of using natural resources for short-term profit—the taking of bighorn for meat should be secondary to the quest for a good trophy. To take a heavy-headed old ram is not only beneficial to the herd, but also something of a break for the ram. Like all ruminants, old age and senility is presaged by the loss of the nipping teeth from the front of the lower jaw. This inevitably causes weakening from malnutrition on the limited wintering ranges. For then bighorns depend on the graze and browse of barren ridges, where the wind rarely allows snow to lie deep over the feed. Like all grazing game of the snow regions their numbers are governed by the quantity and quality of this range. There comes a day when the old sheep bogs down in the deep snow of a gully to die slowly of exposure, or by being eaten alive by coyotes or some other predator. So a well-directed hunter's bullet may be a merciful end to what is at best a short life. The average life span of the wild sheep is ten to twelve years.

Bighorns are divided into three subspecies: the Canada bighorn ranging from the headwaters of the Smoky River in northern Alberta to the Colorado Rockies, the desert bighorn of southwestern arid regions, and the California bighorn found in central British Columbia and Washington. Of these the Canada bighorn is most numerous. The only areas where hunters can pursue these without the restrictions of draws for hunting licenses are in the Canadian Rockies and three sections of Montana.

Most sheep hunters travel far to reach bighorn country and are required by law to hire guides. A good outfitter and guide is the most valuable acquisition of a visiting sheep hunter. The best way to acquire such professional service is to inquire among experienced sheep hunters. The newcomer to the game may be tempted by such things as so-called guaranteed kills and the low rates of some unscrupulous operators. These had best be avoided like poison, for no man can guarantee a shot at a decent bighorn trophy; and the low rate come-on usually indicates poor service and the possibility of annoying extras tacked onto the final bill for the trip.

Equipment is best kept as simple and functional as possible. The most important items of a sheep hunter's gear are a pair of comfortable boots, a warm bed, an accurate rifle, and a good pair of binoculars—in that order. Clothing must be light but warm, because fall temperatures can drop well below freezing. Light, tough boots with good climbing soles are a must, for nothing can ruin an enjoyable trip like sore feet. Aside from plenty of nourishing food, which is usually supplied by the outfitter, nothing ends a good day and provides for a happy tomorrow like a soft, warm bed constructed for mountain use, filled with goose down, and with a good air or foam mattress. Binoculars should be compact and light, and not less than seven power.

Deciding on the best rifle can spark arguments till the thin gray light of dawn, for in choosing a weapon basic fundamentals are often obscured. The ideal rifle should be flat shooting, accurate, and not more than seven and a half to eight pounds complete. A man accustomed to shooting a .308 Winchester will likely find a heavy-kicking Magnum something of a curse. The average hunter will shoot far better with a .270 or .30/06-class weapon, although the Magnums can be deadly if mastered. I have observed about a thousand head of game killed with almost every kind of rifle, and it is always

121

Ram keeps watchful lookout. Mountain sheep's vision is several times keener than man's.

obvious that where the animal is hit is much more important than what it is hit with. Contrary to popular belief most rams are killed within two hundred and fifty yards. So if a hunter owns a .270 or even a 6mm, with which he can hit a woodchuck at two hundred yards, he has all the rifle necessary to kill a ram.

A good reliable scope of magnification not exceeding four power and solidly mounted is a most satisfactory and helpful accessory. Variable-power scopes are a temptation to be avoided, for apart from unnecessary bulk they increase the chances of mechanical failure, and some have the nasty habit of changing zero with changes of power. A good scope allows a hunter to see his target more clearly; nobody can shoot better than he can see. While no magic is attached to such a sight, it gives a much better chance for a clean kill—the prime obligation of every hunter.

A soft leather carrying sling and a saddle scabbard with a removable hood complete the outfit of the sheep hunter.

The best remaining bighorn hunting grounds are in Alberta, where population counts show good numbers still ranging along the spine of the Rockies.

The famous East Kootenai herds in British Columbia have taken a sickening plunge these past three years from about four thousand to seven hundred head—a staggering disaster directly resulting from a mismanaged multiple-use program. Summer grazing leases for cattle and sheep were sold on vital wintering ranges of bighorn sheep. The bighorn became infected with a Pasteurella organism (a kind of shipping fever common to cattle under stress from severe confinement) and they died in bunches.

Bighorn trophy hunters must now largely confine their sport to the Alberta Rockies, where most of the record trophies have originated. The best of these have come from a one-hundred-mile stretch of mountains drained by the Oldman River. A fabulous bighorn head that hung for more than fifty years in a ranch home near Twin Butte, Alberta, was finally given official measurement and recently entered in a local trophy contest. It scored a whopping $207\frac{3}{8}$ points to capture top place for all time in the Boone and Crockett competitions. It was taken by a local rancher on Yarrow Creek about five miles from my door and broke the long-standing record head killed by Martin K. Bovey seventy-five miles north on Oyster Creek. That head, which had held top spot since 1924, was very close—$207\frac{2}{8}$ points. My own Boone and Crockett qualifying head was taken just over the summit from the head of Yarrow Creek in 1954. And in 1965, my friend Bob Woodward killed the top-ranking bighorn of the year, a beautiful head scoring $195\frac{6}{8}$ points, in almost exactly the same spot. These are only a few of the big heads collected in this region.

Naturally, the Oldman River section is famous, but with a strange disregard of values the much-vaunted multiple-use program again has caused near ruin. Timber and oil interests have been allowed to build access roads up almost every creek.

No matter where you hunt bighorns, the problems of stalking are much the same, varying only in immediate terrain and conditions encountered. The trophy ram that comes easily is the exception.

One unforgettable September day I was guiding a hunter from Chicago on the headwaters of the northwest branch of the Oldman. Mike, a newcomer to the western big-game fields, had a world of enthusiasm, which was a fortunate thing, for the weather had been foul and our luck worse. For ten days we had been hunting among some of the most rugged peaks of the Rockies, deviled by rain, wind, and snow, groping through mist, and wondering if the sun would ever shine again. The talus fans of the high basins were crisscrossed everywhere with heavy sheep trails. We found plenty of fresh sign, but were unable to see far enough ahead to find the rams that made the tracks.

One morning the wind swung around and swept the sky clear. We saddled up early. About noon we neared the top of a spur ridge jutting from the divide between two forks of the creek. After tying our horses out of sight in a hollow, we bellied up onto the rim to glass the big basin beyond. The wind slatted and banged off the top of the cliffs above us like a great sail, and we found it difficult to hold our glasses still even while lying prone among some shin-tangle scrub. Seeing nothing in the basin, we moved down across a meadow on the face of the ridge to a better vantage point.

No sooner had we put the glasses to our eyes than six rams filed up out of a deep ravine half a mile away across the basin and about seven hundred feet below our level. Three of the rams were young mediocre ones, two had nearly full-curl heads of fair proportions, and the sixth looked like it might be a good one. At first, as he climbed through some scrub brush, I could see only part of his head. For several minutes he moved about feeding, then he stepped up on a mound of loose rock and stood looking down at the rest of the bunch below him. I needed no crystal ball to tell me that this was a fine trophy ram. Both horns were massive, well spread at the tips, and symmetrical. The arch of his curls came well up and back to leave plenty of room around his ears.

"He's a real buster," I told Mike. "That's the one we've been looking for."

"Fine," Mike said, "but how do we get to him?"

It was a good question, more pointed than Mike realized, for we were in something of a spot. Behind us was a bald stretch of open ground offering no cover for a retreat. Below us was an inviting stretch of heavy timber, but we had to reach it without being seen. Even if we did, this route would lead us close under the face of the mountain, where the wind would undoubtedly curl our scent back up to the rams. The mountain face was too open and cliffy to allow a flanking approach from that side; so our only alternative was to swing wide the other way and come in above them from the crest of the opposite ridge. The way was open for the first four hundred yards, but perhaps we could fool them.

There was no hurry, because I wanted to find out where they were going to bed down before we made any move. We relaxed and ate lunch while we watched. After an hour, all six rams bunched up to lie down on a small bench along one side of the ravine not far from where they had first appeared.

It was time for us to make our play. There are only two ways to move near rams: completely camouflaged or boldly in the open. Bidding Mike to follow, I led the way along the open slope away from the sheep. Almost at once every ram had his eyes glued on us, but they stayed put. Moving casually and keeping to the same level, we proceeded until a natural dip in the ground gradually hid us from their sight. Then we turned sharply downhill, pouring ourselves at a scrambling run down a draw leading into timber.

It was rough going over dead logs and through tangles of alder brush, but we made good time across the bottom of the basin. The wind howled and roared in the trees, and a couple of times we heard a big spruce crash under the onslaught as we climbed towards the far rim.

More than an hour later we crawled out of a stringer of timberline larches to look for the rams. They had not moved and were now about six hundred yards below us on a diagonal toward the face of the mountain.

They showed sharp and clear in our glasses, their coats a rich brown in the sun. Mike whistled softly to himself, his glasses on the biggest ram. The excitement was building.

Fifty yards below us there was a bench leading down toward the sheep, offering ideal cover for the final stalk, but to reach it we had to cross open ground. To play it as safely as possible, I fell back on an old sheep-hunters' trick. Slipping back into the timber, I cut two small bushy firs with my hunting knife. Giving one to Mike and instructing him to hold it in front of him, and crawl as though his life depended on it, I again took the lead. Holding our trees upright in front of us, we bellied slowly, and smoothly across seventy-five yards of open grass to the shelter of the bench. The rams still were oblivious to our presence.

From the bench it was only a quick traverse to a shelf among some wind-twisted, low-growing pines about one hundred and fifty yards from the sheep. Mike carefully worked his way into a solid sitting position and raised his rifle to look through the scope, but I cautioned him to wait until the ram got to his feet. Then I waved my hat high over my head. Instantly every ram looked our way, and the big one stood up.

"Take him now," I said softly, and a long moment later Mike's rifle bucked and roared. The bullet struck a shade too far back. The ram humped up, lurched in a half circle, and went to his knees, but recovered as Mike fired again. He shot too quickly and the bullet went high to powder itself on a boulder with a sharp crack. The wounded ram jumped straight toward us, then turned and began to climb. But he was hard hit and soon faltered to a stop. Mike's third shot took him square in the shoulder and he was dead when he hit the ground.

It is a good idea for sheep hunters to study the angles and features of conformation which make a good trophy, and to become as competent as possible in spotting them at long range in the field. While an experienced guide's judgment is of great value in the field, there are times when a hunter will find it advantageous and even necessary to make his own decision. A shrewd judge of heads can guess the length of curl and basal circumference within fractions of an inch while the ram is grazing or asleep in his bed. Given time to look over both horns from several angles, he can even come close to the total score by the Boone and Crockett table. This kind of thing can best be done through the use of a good spotting scope of at least twenty power at long range.

To judge a head, one should get a good look at both horns. A head that may look like a world beater from one side may add up to a very poor score if the hidden horn proves to be broken off short at the tip. Both horns should flare in a good spread at the points, with the tips coming up even with the bridge of the nose. Next, get a profile look to judge the inside curl. The size of the portal formed by this inside curl is really the key to accurate guessing of the measurement of the outside curl. If the opening is big enough to barely accommodate the ram's ear, the head will likely be no more than thirty-five to thirty-eight inches on the outside measurement, even if basal circumference is a full sixteen inches. The size of a ram's ear is fairly constant and the best way to judge the head is by the distance of the horn tips in relation to the bridge of the nose, and the space around the ear.

When their horns reach a full curl and begin to interfere with their vision, bighorns almost always broom off the tips by rubbing them on rocks. When a horn comes around, massive and heavy, in a full curl with tips measuring two to three inches across, when it flares well out from the sides of the face and has an inside curl of generous proportion, and heavy bases, it will likely score

well in the record book.

Even old timers can get badly fooled on occasion. I was hunting one fall with a veteran of many sheep hunts when we spotted what looked like a very good ram asleep in a hollow across a wide basin. It was a tough spot to approach, but I found a way to avoid a tricky wind and get close enough for a shot. The fluff of mountain avons was drifting in the wind that day like tiny white parachutes, mapping the twisting currents, and when we had figured a route we made a long traverse. After toiling through a steep-sided canyon and sweating our way through a mess of brush and avalanched timber, we finally eased into position behind a big uprooted stump. The tops of the ram's horns were visible over an intervening swell of ground. He had not moved an inch. Then we discovered that the ram was stone dead! Evidently it had died in its sleep the previous night in a natural position. Also, as nearly as I could guess from a crude autopsy, sometime in its younger years it had suffered from lungworm. What from a distance had looked like a noble head was really small, for the whole ram was in miniature proportions. My hunter and I were standing there mournfully when we chanced to look at each other, and suddenly the gloom was shattered by our laughter. The joke was on us, and it has been told around many fires.

It is the atmosphere of the unexpected, the air of suspense that makes sheep hunting so attractive and enjoyable. Furthermore, the companionship among this breed of hardy mountaineers is sometimes worthy of contemplation by the little red gods that dance in the flames of the campfires. There is an intangible something that infects the blood from which no man, once bitten, ever fully recovers. It is the combination of sunshine and storm, the peace of the wilderness, and being in harmony with it. ◉

the
hard business of
surf-casting

All effort is justified,
all fatigue forgotten when your
forty-pound striper
comes cartwheeling through a comber,
silver and lavender and
smelling of thyme.

by Frank Woolner

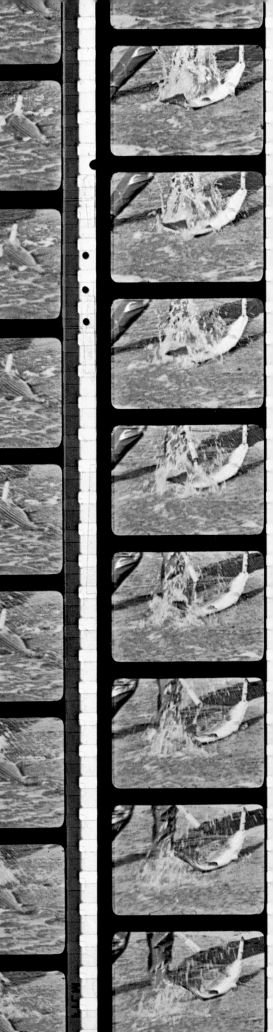

Since about 2 a.m. I had been scuffing along Thoreau's Great Beach on Cape Cod, casting surface plugs and rigged eels out into a heaving, sibilant darkness where breaking waves were ghosts and the horizon was a curious demarcation line of black on black. Then the diamonds disappeared.

Up to this point, each step had unearthed showers of blue-green luminescence in the sand and wash. Billions of microscopic diatoms (Noctiluca) were emitting sparks—the "fire in the water" that is so roundly cursed by summer surfmen, because striped bass usually ignore lures bathed in its cold flame. Now strengthening light had dissipated the brilliance of this plankton swarm.

Dawn is a subtle thing in the Northeast: It never arrives with a burst of pyrotechnics, but rather with a gradual paling, so that the horizon swims up like a photoprint in stale developer. Gradually there are highlights on the ground swells, and one may see an arctic tern curving across the faintly visible world of sand and sea.

I was weary. My waders seemed unbelievably clumsy and a dull ache pierced my shoulder blades. But the tide was right and I was committed. It would be stupid to hit the sack now. Dawn and dusk are the magic periods, especially with a great tide flooding. Muttering about a scarcity of bass, I battled drowsiness. That's another thing about surfmen: We all talk to ourselves. Make the most of it.

Retrieving, I felt the double knot slide under a line-grooved left thumb. Two turns and there'd be just enough overhang for another cast. Mechanically I swiveled, laid the big rod back and brought it forward in an accelerated sweep. Line soughed off the wide-spooled squidding reel, a long trajectory of sound, diminishing until I knew that the lure was touching down. Then I reached over with my left hand and threw the clutch into gear.

Whether it was the strengthening light that dulled the "fire," or just a combination of dawn and flood I do not know, but there was a gout of white spray where my plug had been, together with the familiar, yet always surprising shock of a striper's headlong attack. I was whole again.

Not only whole, but leaning back while my rod tip pounded. Line departed in stuttering zips. The drag was set just tight enough to be punishing, but not screwed to a breaking point. Tight drags lose more game fish than any other single factor. Grimly, I twisted my head to see whether other anglers had witnessed this triumph. Three beach buggies were silhouetted against a silvering curve of beach, but no human stirred. They were all asleep.

Gradually, the bulldogging bass yielded. He thrashed out beyond the third wave—thirty yards away—giving me one glimpse of a shining body and a broom-sized tail. The rolling combers were his ally—and mine, if I could make proper use of them. In close, after each wave exploded on the

Photography by The American Sportsman—ABC

128

FRANK WOOLNER

beach and went surging back to sea, my bass exploited the tremendous power of undertow, so I'd have to grant line. But caught in the next advancing swell, he'd be just as irresistibly borne along, and it would be my time to apply pressure.

Finally, on the crest of a towering swell, the fish was finished. I back-pedaled, maintaining a tight line. Weary, at last, he came flouncing ashore and I ran down to grab the leader, to belt him with a hardwood priest.

Forty pounds of striped bass, silver and lavender and smelling of thyme. Forty pounds of magnificent game fish, glistening in the light of a New England dawn.

It has become customary, in writing about surf-casting, to warn the reader that he had best forget the whole thing. Having said this, the writer proceeds at greater or lesser length to extol the delights of a rough-and-tough angling method that offers immense esthetic and, at times, material reward in the shape of great fish. There are two reasons for the admonition. First, of course, it commands attention: Anything advised against must be strangely, if esoterically, delicious. Second, there is more than a bit of truth in the cliché.

As a surf-caster, I have spent a great many years on a variety of beaches, from the cold wash of Maine down through Cape Cod to Hatteras and beyond. I have belted lures at roosterfish on the west coast of Costa Rica and I have worked up the Pacific seaboard to San Francisco. Species change with the latitudes, and each of the great ones requires some variation in lure presentation and tactics, but there is no such sea-change in the surf-caster or the things that make him tick. He is a specialist, quite as thorough a craftsman as the citizen who has learned to drop a lightly cocked bivisible some few yards above a brown trout.

In America, the high surf—and I plead guilty to inventing this term some two decades back to distinguish between ordinary shore fishing conditions and the furious breakers of an outer beach—means striped bass and channel bass. S. Kip Farrington will hate me for excluding South America's great roosterfish (I would agree with him were more of us able to angle for *pez gallo*).

Other formidable gamesters are hooked in the suds: bluefish and weakies, corvina, pompano, and a host of sharks. They're all fine when the time is right, but anglers still associate the great striper of the Northeast and of San Francisco, together with the broad-shouldered channel bass of Virginia's Barrier Islands and North Carolina's Outer Banks, with surf-casting at its furious best.

The striper remains my choice, possibly because I am steeped in New England brine. What makes this fish unique? Other fish-shaped fish can run faster, pull harder, and jump higher. But none is quite so unpredictable—and there is the challenge. When you catch a trophy bass in the 40- to 60-pound bracket, you have achieved something.

Stripers rarely leap after the manner of an Atlantic salmon or tarpon, but they do so occasionally. More typical is the powerful, wallowing surface cartwheel, during which the fish makes much use of its huge, square tail to slap the water. The striped bass is a pugnacious, active gladiator, catholic in its tastes. Therefore, anglers who employ natural bait suffer no handicap. Indeed, there are occasions when the bottom-bouncer outfishes the purist who uses nothing but metal or a treble-hooked plug.

I hope certain chambers of commerce will forgive me if I puncture a few daydreams.

Major striper-range extends from the Outer Banks of North Carolina northward into the Maritime Provinces, and, on the Pacific Coast, from San Francisco into the clean rips of Coos Bay, Oregon. In other places, there are landlocked bass, most notably in South Carolina's Santee-Cooper impoundments, and there are stripers in the inland fresh waters of the Gulf of Mexico. If you are seeking trophies, however, range is drastically reduced.

Curiously—because commercial fishermen continue to prove they are there—Chesapeake Bay, the world's foremost striper nursery, rarely produces record-crowding bass for rod-and-line anglers. Similarly, monsters are present on the Outer Banks from early December through February, where they are harvested by haul seiners, yet seldom by sportsmen.

The best fishing begins in New Jersey and extends northward through Long Island and the coasts of Rhode Island and Massachusetts. Connecticut somehow is by-passed by most of the heavyweights during their annual migrations, and Maine is best known for an abundance of schoolies.

On the Pacific seaboard (where the species was introduced during the late nineteenth century), there are two locations of importance to high-surf enthusiasts. One is the Ocean Beach area immediately adjacent to San Francisco's Golden Gate, and the other is Coos Bay. Perhaps the latter is a sleeper, if only because Oregon anglers are prone to place the native king and silver salmon above the imported striper as game.

Zero in, and you will find that all records indicate Massachusetts and Rhode Island to be the principal states for surfers who hunt striped bass. There, more trophy bass are brought to account each year than in all other areas combined. I have enjoyed great sport with *Roccus* in the Chesapeake, in San Francisco, and at Montauk, but for

Rod braced between his legs, Woolner beaches striper taken on a plug as Curt Gowdy looks on.

sheer numbers of heavyweights give me that rugged Yankee coast, bounded by Rhode Island's Charleston Inlet to the south, and Cape Cod to the north.

Moreover, during a New England season, which begins in May and continues through October, this mercurial slugger is taken at all hours of the day and night, a characteristic that guarantees red-eyed, unshaven regulars who live for the next tide and who never admit defeat. Ridiculous people! I am one of them.

In self-defense, if for no other reason, there is a thing about surf-casting that is unique. It is difficult to put into words, because there is no single facet to grasp and to declare typical. I am tempted to say that surf-casting, compared to inland angling, is the difference between elemental fury and tranquility. Wind, fog, crashing combers, and surging currents are the rule on a sea beach. An angler is a combatant, not a seeker of Izaak Walton's gentle relaxation.

Every surfman lives for a "blitz" of bass, and often these frenzied feeding periods coincide with weather guaranteed to keep normal, thoughtful people at home. No wind ever blows too hard for a striper, and no surf dismays the fish. Once, years ago, I caught a bass during that short, glowering period of calm which is called the eye of a hurricane. Again, on Nauset Beach, midway on Cape Cod, I hooked a striper as lightning split a thunderous night sky. In the weird glare of the forking bolt I saw the bass boil up to take a plug and cartwheel wildly. Normally, I'm a first-class coward, but on that night I was fishing with Arnold Laine of Templeton, Massachusetts, a great commercial rod and liner. He wouldn't quit and so, being a stubborn man, neither would I. Throughout that vicious electrical storm, bass walloped our plugs.

Every surfman flirts with disaster—and counts it part of the adventure. Annually, men are washed off wave-battered rock jetties and tumbled in the smothering combers. It is a wet, cold, and thoroughly wonderful business! Still, there are nights when the ocean breathes evenly, when the swells come dreamily ashore, when dim starlight is reflected from a wet silk surface.

Perhaps much of the allure lies in the fact that surfmen probe a last frontier. The roaring ocean remains unconquered, and her fish are no pale descendants of hatchery spawn. Here, the unbelievable is quite possible. I have been startled by a great whale with halitosis (they always have halitosis) bursting out of the inshore swells like something from the prehistoric past. No sea monster is beyond belief in that pale hour of dawn when the ocean pulses and sighs.

Nor is it all nighttime and a sense of things that might be seen, but are not. Beachcombers sometimes observe a sight that is reserved for few men. When the brilliant white light of midmorning lances through advancing combers, one may occasionally see a striped bass suspended in the heart of an emerald wave. No transfixed, split-second image so thoroughly conveys the striper's power as this airy, swift, yet unhurried passage through a comber racing forward, cresting, and aiming its pile-driving power at an unyielding beach.

Nowadays spinning tackle is the preference of the majority. I like coffee grinders, and yet I continue to go back to the old high surf squidding outfit when the fish are big. I think it takes more skill to employ orthodox tackle—although "orthodox" may soon mean another thing if spinning continues to conquer the multitudes.

Whatever the gear, a surfman must be a craftsman, able to cast a lure to extreme range, which means approximately a hundred yards. He must do this instinctively, for there is no time or opportunity to lay the line with mathematical precision during a nighttime retrieve. A man's left thumb becomes educated; it sweeps back and forth like a metronome, geared to the rate of retrieve. Any lump on the orthodox spool will mean a backlash on the next cast.

Spin-casters are not plagued by this difficulty, but they have to live with other handicaps. For one thing, the fixed-spool addict is hard put to throw heavy lures to the distances often required in high surf. Once tied into a fish, there is less control and, because of the light monofilament line used with this rig, a greater degree of peril.

Selection of proper lures is important. There are, for example, about nine basic plug designs, together with many variations, engineered to swim, pop, or skip on the surface, to swim or dart at mid-depths, and to dredge the bottom. Metal squids, forerunners of all modern high-surf tempters, are much used. Natural rigged eels, with or without casting weights attached to their heads, and patent, soft plastic eels are hot items on bass.

Now we deal with tides and currents, with moon phases and "fire in the water." It is necessary to recognize bait and to divine its action as a clue to the proximity of game fish. We must be bird-watchers, too, for the gulls and terns of any seaboard are a surfman's light cavalry. A single striper's slashing attack on bait fish in choppy waters may not be registered by human eyes, but a herring gull or tern, sitting on the beach with its fellows—all facing into the wind like weather vanes—will immediately lift off and speed to the scene. A wheeling, diving gaggle of birds usually means game fish beneath, pushing bait to the surface.

Generally, game fish such as the striped bass prefer to feed in "live water." A general rule of thumb, therefore, holds that fishing will be best "two hours before and two hours after the top of the tide." This is generalization at its best, because rips, inlets, and estuaries change the situation. Moreover, the bass is unpredictable enough to vary his feeding pattern occasionally.

But "live water" is a good phrase, because it means moving water. When water moves, bait is swept along with it—and big fish eat little fish, that's one of the laws of creation. So you're there at the right time, supposedly in the right place, armed with the correct tackle. Add a new dimension: In salt water you'd best be an opportunist, ready to take immediate advantage of anything strange or unusual. The sudden swoop of birds, the twinkling surface flurry of bait, a slick, or even a curious smell.

Any expert surfman can smell striped bass, bluefish, or red drum. Beginners always doubt this, but it is so. The striper exudes a fresh, cloying scent that has been likened to cut melon or thyme. I opt for the latter, believing that cut melon more accurately describes the scent of bluefish. Channel bass throw off a more acrid scent, something almost chemical—and how any of them do this is unresolved. Probably the scent is an excrescence; I don't think anyone knows, but the various aromas are far from imagination. Once isolated they are weapons in the expertise of the surf-caster.

Now I chance incurring the wrath of sportsmen who rely on natural bait alone. I can sympathize with them, for they have much to argue about. The great fishes of our sea rim will take a wide variety of fresh baits, ranging from sea worms through squid, crabs, mackerel, herring, and sand launces to ordinary clam flesh. There are many natural tempters, and I leave them to the specialists, who will probably rack up a world's-record catch before I tangle with another bona fide trophy. But to me, and evidently to a growing number of marine anglers, there is nothing so satisfactory as a great game fish on an artificial lure. There is something peculiarly gratifying in fooling a sought-after game fish with a thing of metal or plastic or wood.

Initially, the marine purist was a squidder—a man who used nothing other than a cleverly shaped hunk of block tin, with or without feather-hooked dressing. The squidder remains a classicist, and he is well-represented in today's high surf, but a new aristocrat has arisen: the plugger.

Plugs, contrary to the august International Game Fish Association, confer no special advantage, other than their tendency to draw strikes. Indeed, treble hooks often prove a handicap, because each barb works against another to aid keyholing, straightening, and ultimate rejection. Often a bass will strike a lure head-on, embedding a forward treble in its mouth, while the plug's tail hook pierces a gill cover. A fish of 20 pounds or more is powerful enough to shake its head and completely straighten one or both of these barbs, even if they are 5/0 heavy-duty types. If hooks hold during this maneuver, the opposing forces involved are likely to create keyholing. Thereafter, if the angler permits any amount of slack, especially during that period when a bass is cartwheeling on the surface, his quarry may eject the lure.

The ability of an angler to cast accurately and then to work his plug or squid with consummate skill is in direct proportion to his success. Any surfman worth his salt is capable of slowing a cast at an opportune moment to drop a lure just beyond an advancing ground swell, and not in front of that moving body of turbulent water. By so doing he insures that the artificial will be swimming in a relatively clear area, and not tumbling in the froth of the breaker.

Top hands not only achieve tack-hole accuracy, they learn to feather spinning-reel spools, or throw the clutch on conventional winches, at that precise moment when forward momentum is nil, the lure poised to touch down. Retrieve begins immediately and speed is gauged to water conditions.

This is an art difficult to teach, since it is achieved only after much trial and error. Accuracy and reflexes that respond to immediate needs cannot be guaranteed by any correspondence school. There is the feel of it, like the feel of a properly cast fly line when a Light Cahill drops exactly right. It is ice skating and skiing and wing shooting—a moment when all things seem to fall right after an extended period of bungling.

Nor is it possible to describe the faculty with which a seasoned surf-caster can absorb the rustle of bait on a pitch-black night, over the boom of breakers and the rush and slide of beach sand. The sights and the sounds are there, distinct over and between other sounds and recollections, but it takes a craftsman to give them their proper places.

How does one reach the beginner? How can he understand the surfman's "black spot," actually an inshore weed bed or shell bar transformed to a darker shade than the surrounding water by the alchemy of polarized lenses? Striped bass frequent black spots, for the weeds and shells harbor bait.

To a beginner, all sea is a succession of crashing combers and wide blue yonder. How can one point out the subtle differences in white water and rip and current that indicate a slough where the great game fish drift in on a flooding tide to devour crabs and other sea creatures? The signs are there, but they are nuances, not neon-lit directions.

I'd like to help, but perhaps it is best this way. Those who would excel will ask questions and seek fine instructors. They will go down to the ocean and walk the sands and ponder the tides. They will become masters of their tackle—a thing necessary if they are to scale the heights of any rod-and-reel sport —and they will then enter the realm of the regulars—the ten percent of anglers who catch ninety percent of the fish.

No bugle ever sounds to vector surfmen into a specific area at a given moment in time, but regulars gather when all of the nebulous clues indicate action. They come striding over the dunes, grotesque in waders and foul-weather parkas, or they arrive in elaborately equipped beach buggies. Often this concentration is triggered by an ideal tidal phase or wind direction; always it follows good fishing on a preceding tide. If bass are here on today's flood, they're likely to be back tomorrow at the same time.

The real pros materialize an hour or so before fish are likely to move in, and they look at the sea. "Good water" is alive and turbulent, but relatively free of suspended sand. A lack of clarity is no handicap, although a lot of sand and debris kicked up by a storm keeps stripers well off shore. "Dirty water" is not a reference to sewage; it refers to storm-torn weeds that discourage the presentation of bait or lure.

The average surfman is fiercely competitive, yet he admires fellow craftsmen. Before the tide is "right," little groups of bewhiskered regulars lounge around the beach buggies, trading shop talk. Always a scattered few explore the surf, hoping to beat bass at their own unpredictable game and find a school on tap prior to the appointed time.

Perhaps thirty minutes before a calculated zero hour, each surfman grabs his long squidding rod, hitches a plug bag higher on one hip, and trudges down into the wash. Each casts methodically, meanwhile searching the sea, the sky, and the competition. It is serious business.

First evidence of bass may be a bent rod etched sharply against the sky somewhere along the picket line. More likely it will be a sudden, sprinkling flurry of small bait which indicates predators below, or even bait washed up by the waves. Of course, any glimpse of a bulging swirl or a quick bomb-burst of white water, which marks a feeding fish, alerts all hands. Wheeling birds insure an immediate stampede of anglers, each striving to be first with a plug on target.

Where sand bars and rock piles lie well off the beach, it often takes a surprisingly long cast to reach feeding fish. A pro swivels, puts back, arms, and legs into one smoothly coordinated motion, and the plug sails eighty to a hundred yards. Duffers backlash, snap their lines, curse, and splash ashore to repair the damage. When this happens, and the lost plug arcs seaward, somebody always yells: "Good cast! Too bad the line wasn't tied to it!"

Thanks to a little-known Law of General Cussedness, a productive bar or rock pile usually lies just beyond a long cast. The solution is to wade far out, until each successive wave becomes a crisis in the making. Sand-beach waders must move constantly, lest the current's gouging action take them down. Where rocks pave the bottom, each will be slippery. Dedicated surfers take frequent cold baths, come up spitting blue-water words—and go right back to work.

Complete success usually depends on tactical skill. If bass are rushing bait on the surface, then a popping plug may best simulate natural forage. Squid, chameleon-like, turn red-amber when they are excited, hence a lure of the same color is most likely to succeed when stripers are slapping them into the air. Frequently an inshore wind defeats the long cast with a plug, and then no lure will prove so deadly as the time-tested tin squid. During the retrieve, each artificial is worked at a speed contrived to match the natural bait in its harried flight from predators. Beginners, lost in the frantic excitement of a blitz, always reel too fast. They get fish, but rarely with the machine-like efficiency of the regular.

No seasoned campaigner shouts with glee as the barbs go home in a thrashing striper. He grunts, leans back, and feels quiet elation rather than panic as line peels off against a preset drag. Rod butt tucked between his legs, the long fiberglass tip bent in a throbbing arc, such a man may stagger to maintain balance as ground swells hit

him, but he backs slowly and methodically to the beach. Sometimes a long cast results in an immediate strike. If the bass is big, it may go submarining seaward until all line is gone; then the tip assumes an alarming bend and, finally, there is the sharp report of parting gear. Always there is the thought that this was a true record-breaker.

Enthusiasts speak of "fishing a tide," here defined as about four hours of optimum water conditions. That's a long time in high surf with the wind blowing and combers whacking you in the breadbasket, yet time passes all too quickly in the heat of action. You never feel utter weariness until it is all over and the ocean seems a biological desert and the birds are back on the dunes haggling over stranded bait.

Then the groups gather again to admire fine bass and to tell of the monsters that just kept going, taking line down to a bare spool —and beyond. No striped-bass fisherman in our watery world doubts that he will some-day hang a record lineside.

There is much in the high surf that cannot be explained to the uninitiated, but must be experienced. There is cold and high wind and elemental fury. There is failure when sweat and wet are indistinguishable; there are hours of hard labor and broken lines. But there is success as well, triumph in catching truly wild fish. There is satisfaction in challenging the immortal sea and the tides and the roaring combers.

We are going to see much more of this, because America's affluence and modern transportation place the seas within hours of a traveler, regardless of his home base.

Some will go to the plush charter boats, and some to the jetties and the piers. I think it certain that incurable romantics must seek the high surf—where a man faces our last frontier with nothing but a slim wand of fiberglass, a reel, a line, and a lure designed to catch fish-shaped fishes. ◉

The Strange Ways of Grouse

by George Bird Evans

In analyzing the behavior of ruffed grouse—
where they're likely to feed and roost,
how they flush and fly—an expert offers pointers on
getting the best performance from dog and gun.

Anyone who has gunned at all seriously for ruffed grouse, or "pats" if you prefer, has learned that these birds can behave unpredictably—one of the reasons why so many upland gunners acquire a lifelong passion for grouse shooting: Much of what ruffed grouse do under stress is instinct, but a lot of it must be something else. Some young grouse will flush into a tree and perch there with raised crest, piping as they would in the presence of a fox; others that have never seen a pointing dog or heard the sing of pellets will behave as adult grouse do, whether or not you fire a shot. How do they know to go up with a roar of wings, to take the far side out, to travel a long distance, and to pitch into thick cover instead of landing in an open clearing?

You may say it is instinct to get far away from any animal—dog or man—once it is obvious that hiding is useless. But why doesn't the yearling that perches in a tree feel that fear? And why doesn't man on horseback or in an automobile appear equally threatening? A grouse will stand in the middle of a road to be hit by a car.

It is easier to understand responses acquired from experience. Methods of escape that have worked are used again—and again, if they are good enough. But what about that yearling that couldn't have seen a gun and yet flushed on opening day like a veteran? I suspect that some of this is a sort of "inherited experience" from ancestors that survived because they learned to do it that way and lived to pass on the same responses. For there must be instincts that have evolved since the prototype. Canadian grouse, which have not been gunned as much as the more sophisticated grouse in the eastern United States, behave differently before a dog. If their responses were entirely basic instinct, this would not be so. Grouse in hunted areas have become increasingly wary. Not every generation was bred from parents that escaped shot (and this may explain the young birds that act less wisely), but enough experience has been infused to put its mark on the blood.

An example of inherited experience may

be the grouse's fondness for abandoned tramroads. Traces of old tramroads lace the mountains in Pennsylvania, Maryland, and West Virginia, following the contours of the ridges. From the 1890's through the 1920's, these lumber railroads hauled logs to sawmills that operated throughout the Allegheny Mountains. After they were abandoned and the rails removed, weeds grew up in the roadbeds, then blackberries, and finally trees. Most are so obliterated that only close examination reveals old cross-ties rotting in the earth. For forty years I have known these tramroads to be good places to find grouse. Being on contour, they make easy walking and once were open paths from which to shoot. More than that, grouse stayed near them because they found grapes and berries along the roadbed and because grouse like an escape up and out of cover. When flushed, if the birds didn't top out they often crossed or even flew along the tramroad corridor.

As the woods reclaimed the tramroads, grouse have continued to use them. They can no longer find the roads attractive as openings, for overhead cover has closed in and few food plants remain. It is my opinion that today's grouse use the ghost tramroads because each succeeding generation has seen its parents and other grouse use them, though recent generations have derived little benefit. Some tramroad grades were later utilized as log roads, keeping them open

JACK GATES

138

and extending their usefulness to grouse and the hunter. If you haven't gunned for grouse along a tramroad winding through autumn woods, you have missed a memorable experience. With a conscientious dog quartering left and right across the grade, it is a productive and delightful way to shoot.

One of the charms of grouse shooting is that, no matter how long a man pursues it, he seems to encounter something new. On a cold sunny day in November of 1957, my wife Kay and I were exploring a tributary of Stony River on Allegheny Mountain in West Virginia. The high terrain seemed too open for grouse, but it was as near to being wilderness as anything in the East and that was excitement enough.

We were using our father-and-son brace of setters, Ruff and Shadows. At a little run bordered with rhododendron, hemlock, and spruce, a grouse flushed ahead of Shadows, and he went on point. Two more flushed without shots and we followed them to dense spruce farther up the stream where, obeying my impulse to hunt the woods, we spent the afternoon attempting to ferret birds out of nearly impenetrable evergreens. In the huge cover we would find Ruff on point and be treated only to the sound of grouse going out, with no chance to shoot. When the sun reached the tree tops we started back.

Rather than return by the long way we had come, I headed for a knob I judged to be in line with our station wagon. This led us across a big flat grown to waist-high blackberry canes. Both dogs were working it nicely when I saw a grouse flush to the right of Shadows. Finding grouse in the open, two hundred yards from woods, was new to me and equally surprising to young Shadows who took one look at the bird heading for a beech woods and started after it. As he broke, two more grouse left the same spot, then a fourth. The air seemed full of birds, all out of gun range, with Shadows leaping at them as if he'd never heard of stopping at flush. As number six took off, I swung through and missed with my left barrel, only to see number seven flush even farther out. It was too far for the right barrel but I was frantic. I might as well have saved the shell. Number eight took off, with me a shaking wreck holding an empty gun.

We reflushed a few of them in the dry, noisy beech woods—wild flushes too far ahead to shoot. With cold and darkness overtaking us, we pushed for the knob. On the way we saw grouse roosts in open grass. We had moved twenty-two grouse and the only thing I managed to do right was to get us out of that wilderness before pitch-dark. I had not known that grouse will roost in an open area on a cold night, though I later read that flatlands seem to be most attractive to grouse when weather is colder than normal. And every night is cold in

Author and his dogs work along traces of abandoned tramroad skirting woods. Such areas often provide excellent grouse coverts.

139

that high country at Allegheny Mountain.

Grouse behavior varies with terrain. Woodlot grouse of abandoned farms and foothills present shooting unlike that on steep hills in the river country of Pennsylvania and West Virginia, and grouse in the big coverts of West Virginia's Blackwater and Dolly Sods high country differ in feeding and flight habits from the birds in the hawthorn and alder glades of Maryland's Tableland. In the strange highlands atop Allegheny Mountain, the most challenging coverts are in and around the swamps, more like Canadian muskeg than West Virginia terrain. There are spruce flats with beaver ponds in expanses of sphagnum and haircap moss where red globes of cranberries grow in ice-cold water.

This is good cold-weather cover after the grouse are bunched, and I have memories of days when it seemed only a matter of working my dogs farther along the spruce edges to locate more grouse feeding in the sphagnum flats. I can still see one of Ruff's points with a brace of grouse pinned—both birds flying low and straight for an arm of spruce cover. Next to a grape-fed grouse, I would rate as most delectable a November bird that has fed on cranberries until its pink flesh has acquired the distinct cranberry tang.

Although the snowshoe hare, a typical north-woods animal, inhabits these high bogs, the grouse there are not the *togata* subspecies of the North but the *Bonasa umbellus monticola* of all of West Virginia, so nearly like *Bonasa umbellus umbellus* as to be indistinguishable to most of us.

It is difficult for a grouse shooter accustomed to grapevine ridges and hawthorn bottoms to immediately appreciate this terrain. Grouse go for thick cover when flushed, but I often find them in the open, lying in bracken or frost-killed goldenrod, or in blackberry canes with piles of droppings to suggest they spend the night there. Unless there is cover, they usually fly low.

I try not to look for the bird on the ground in front of my dogs' points, for to glue your eyes to a sitting bird will slow your focus at the flush. Much better, keep your gaze at "universal," above and in front of the dog, where sudden motion will draw your eyes to the flushing bird. In spite of intention, I occasionally see a woodcock or grouse under a point. The woodcock is almost always flattened, with head drawn back into the body, and from that position it jump-flushes nearly straight up. Some grouse stand erect before a point, neck elongated and crest raised, but many lie flattened like woodcock, a bright eye following your every move. A grouse once held this position on a drumming log and let me pass within six yards without flushing.

Driving along an old mountain road, I saw a grouse standing in the middle about seventy yards ahead. Interested only in a point if possible, I reached back and carefully opened the rear door of the station wagon and let Bliss slip out. She knew what to expect but not where, and when she cast in front, the grouse saw her and instead of flushing squatted like a brooding hen. Trying to put a dog onto sighted birds is rarely successful. As Bliss swung into the side cover, a second grouse flushed from the bank above the first bird, which also took off. It was a fair picture of what grouse sometimes do as dogs approach.

Except in obvious situations the grouse's takeoff is unpredictable and may be anything from nearly vertical to a low skimming flight. The classic evasive tactic is the flush that dodges behind a tree trunk. Many grouse hunters believe the bird intentionally keeps the tree between itself and the gun until it is beyond range for a shot. I can't go along with this notion. Darting behind the nearest obstacle is understandable, but

Currier & Ives print, dated 1865, depicts pointer and setter holding stanchly as grouse flushes.

anyone who has tried walking a line from a given spot without looking back or taking sightings will realize it is chance, not intention, that causes a bird to continue in line behind the tree instead of showing itself.

Some grouse take the wide-open way out, others crash through twigs and leafy branches. I tell myself to shoot as though the trees weren't there and I sometimes drop grouse in early season by completing my swing and firing after the bird has disappeared into dense foliage. While some grouse come straight at your head, I don't believe they do so knowing it will unnerve the gunner, though God knows it does.

The closer I am to the flush, the more devastating it is on my nerves. Late on a cold February day I came to Bliss pointing into a grapevine tangle, with Dixie backing. I waded in behind Bliss in deep snow,

each step letting me down into concealed brush and vines. At such times passages from books on shooting flash through my brain—"toes of the boots should be about nine inches apart, heels about three . . . balance and poise of the body must be even." In the terrain I gun I'm lucky if I'm on either foot when I shoot. There was no flush, but Bliss held while I backed out and circled to the opposite side. I got to within eight feet of her and kicked the grapevine but still nothing happened. Looking as if she couldn't believe it, Bliss moved three steps closer and froze again. Suddenly what I thought was a rabbit bored out of the snowy tangle at my feet, spread its wings like a fast-motion movie of a flower blooming, climbed vertically, and topped a pair of saplings that jutted from the mass of grapevines. I waited until the grouse reappeared

141

before I shot as it leveled. I missed, but it took talent to do it.

Each grouse flush is influenced by the character of the cover. I have hunted coverts that seemed stiff with grouse without shooting one bird. In other coverts with few grouse, I have had good shooting. I love to hunt where there are plenty of grouse, if only for the excitement of dog work and hearing the birds go out. Heavy rhododendron-hemlock cover is this type, as is dense spruce. Tall beech woods never produce any good shooting for me; whip-size regrowth choked with blackberry canes offers no footing; and climbing a rock ledge is no way to get a shot. Yet there are often grouse in such places, and when they flush it is in a manner distinct to each type of cover, which makes it hard to resist hunting there. A covert with few grouse often offers better breaks simply by the nature of the place.

Much of this is luck and the way the birds are coming up on any particular day, but being aware of these subtle differences in grouse country can contribute that extra bit that makes Lady Luck smile, and sometimes grin most pleasantly.

One of the "rules" is that grouse will be on top of a mountain in certain kinds of weather, and on the slopes or in the valley under different conditions. Grouse often use upper levels of a low ridge during the day, then drop to the valley a hundred feet below to spend the night, or to shelter from wind or low temperatures, or heavy snow. But I am not persuaded that grouse that live on high plateaus around four thousand feet, such as the top of Allegheny Front or Cabin Mountain in the Blackwater country, ever get to the valleys miles away. In the big mountains, when grouse are found on the lower slopes or in large valleys, they are there because they spend their lives there, not because they have just dropped down to escape fog or wind.

Another rule some gunners cling to is that the best times for grouse shooting are early morning and late afternoon. I think it was Samuel Johnson who said, "It is but lost labour that ye haste to rise up early," and for my part that goes for grouse hunting. I love to hunt grouse in the late hours of the day. If weather has been warm and dry, scent becomes more perceptible during the temperature drop of the last hour before sunset. At this time, tired dog and tired man gather strength, and grouse seem to lie best, possibly because, having settled for the night, they hope to be passed by. You may not shoot at your top form during this late hour, especially if you haven't had a shot all day, but if you make a hit there are few times when it means so much.

However, I shoot as many grouse between noon and three p.m. as at any time of day. The authors of *The Ruffed Grouse*, published by the New York State Conservation Department in 1947, list the hours in which more than eighteen hundred grouse flushes occurred during the autumns of 1930 through 1936. Far more grouse were flushed in each of the midday periods than in early morning or late afternoon. Early afternoon, considered by many grouse hunters to be the poorest time of day, produced four and a half times as many flushes as the highly touted early morning. Even my favorite late-afternoon period produced fewer birds than any of the middle-of-the-day periods.

Grouse have a way of behaving contrary to many popular beliefs and professional opinions. Some top grouse men have suggested that you can judge the sex of grouse by the manner of flush, claiming that males usually climb steeply when flushing, while females tend to fly off low. In forty years of shooting grouse in West Virginia, Pennsylvania, and Maryland, I have not noticed a pattern of flushing characteristic of either cock or hen. To check, I went over my gun diary, selecting the last one hundred and ten grouse shot. Nine flushed from trees; one gave no clue as to how it took off. That left one hundred whose flushes I could be sure of. There were forty hens and sixty cocks. Exactly twenty hens took off low, twenty rose in flushing; twenty-eight cocks took off low, thirty-two rose in flushing. Disregarding sex, forty-eight took off low, fifty-two rose, with no relation of adult or young to low or rising flushes. The only sex characteristic I could notice regarding flushing was that hens, being smaller than cock grouse, got off the ground faster. Considering grouse speed, that is a fine distinction.

No experienced grouse shooter will question that grouse fly faster at certain times and that sometimes they take off silently instead of with a roar. The wind (behind or against the bird), the character of the cover, and accessibility of escape all have bearing on getaway and speed of a grouse's flight.

It is nearly impossible to accurately measure a game bird's flight speed. The New York Conservation Department carefully clocked a grouse at 47.2 mph, which included takeoff time and a flight of two hundred and fifty-one feet slightly downhill to a definite spot where the bird entered a woods. This is about seventy feet per second, according to the formula $1\frac{1}{2} \times$ mph = feet per second. Most estimates are not this accurate, and a bird shot at and hit by a fast swing seems to be flying slower than that same bird would if snapped at and missed.

One of the most talked-about grouse-flight characteristics is the "crazy flight," or "mad moon," when the birds fly as if intoxicated. At the risk of appearing totally heretical, I doubt that this occurs as a defined phenomenon in grouse of the Alleghenies. I first read of the mad moon in Ernest Thompson Seton's *Wild Animals I Have Known*, which I received on my tenth birthday. I had not

begun to shoot and I found his story of Redruff very moving. He placed the month of the mad moon as November and described the unpredictable flights of grouse at night, with daylight finding them in odd places far from their normal habitat. Seton called this behavior a trait of young birds exhibited during their first and sometimes second season, never afterward.

Some authorities believe that infestation by stomach worms causes the crazy flight; others attribute it to a residual migratory instinct, and suggest that it is nature's way of dispersing surplus young. Leaf fall in autumn has been considered as cause for abnormal nervousness, but trees are bare by the time of Seton's November mad moon, especially in Ontario where he described it.

I am skeptical about the dispersal theory. I find groups of first-year grouse together throughout the shooting season into late February. In the Alleghenies, dispersal takes place in March and April as part of the mating season. The extreme forms of the mad-moon phenomenon seem to be reported in the northerly grouse ranges and I wonder if, like more clearly defined grouse population cycles, it may be more characteristic of the *togata* subspecies.

The grouse flight that most concerns the gunner is the flight before the gun. I have often wished to be at the far end of a grouse's flight to see what the bird did. Not to ferret it out when it had sportingly evaded me, but because much of the time I am so damned bewildered as to where it went. Sometimes tracks in snow will give the answer; at others, your dog will give you circumstantial evidence and your imagination fills in the blanks. But many grouse disappear in contradiction to logic.

A large number of initial flushes is often luck, but a high number of reflushes is a sign of good dog work aided by careful marking. I've become fairly adept at marking grouse flights in relation to a distant snag or conspicuous contour. This is elementary to the sport, yet I have known men who simply couldn't mark a grouse. If a bird topped out over the trees they were certain it had left the country; if it took off low they were sure it had gone only a short distance; and I've seen some of them follow "a straight line of flight" in a beautiful curve.

With grouse that flush in front of a point without giving the gun a glimpse, it is sometimes possible to estimate direction of flight by the sound, or by the attitude of the dog —a quick turn of the dog's head or a short break-at-wing, preferably only a few steps.

A grouse that climbs, then levels over high timber does not always go the great distance it may appear to. Conversely, starting with a low takeoff, a bird may zoom up after it is out of sight and travel far. Flights that can't be observed to their completion—and few can—are subject for conjecture. You may determine the direction and, plotting the course, rely on your dog to relocate the bird. But in a normal grouse flight, a slight change in direction by the bird is magnified greatly at the far end. It is important to watch the bird as long as you can see it.

In flatlands grouse may go any direction. When you are gunning steep hillsides you will notice a general pattern with birds remaining pretty much on contour, except those flushed near the top, which often top over the crest, and those flushed low on the ridge which sometimes pitch for the bottom.

In cover, I find that most grouse fly at least two hundred to two hundred and fifty yards. During the past season I flushed a brace on an edge of woods bordering a paved road. Both birds took the middle of the road down a straight stretch and banked into the woods, where I marked and reflushed them. I checked the distance on my car odometer as .25 of a mile—four hundred

and forty yards—and yet it didn't appear an excessively long grouse flight. Flight length varies with birds and cover—young grouse occasionally landing sooner than adults, with thick cover encouraging shorter flights. Except for very young birds, I find it rare for a grouse to land within one hundred and fifty yards of where it was flushed. If it does, expect a wounded bird.

There have been a few times when I've been privileged to see what occurred at the far end. Once, shooting with a friend in spruce cover along a sphagnum bog, I heard "Mark!" and looked up to see a grouse pitch and land on the floor of the spruce forest forty yards from me. The bird righted itself, stood a moment and then reflushed at an angle to its original line of flight. The sound of the reflush couldn't reach my friend, who had no way of knowing that the bird was not somewhere ahead in the direction of the first takeoff. This is probably what has taken place when your dog makes a stanch but empty point somewhere along the line of flight when you are following a grouse. You may call it ground scent, but it is actually lingering hot body scent.

Another opportunity to observe a flight from the far end occurred in the Blackwater-Canaan area, shooting over Dixie. She had cast toward me and a grouse flushed wild. For a moment I thought it was going away low, then I saw that it was boring straight at me. Before it could have seen me it made a sixty-degree turn, climbed, and was topping the trees when I caught it with a long right-barrel shot. Seen from the site of the flush, the flight could have been misjudged as a straightaway carrying the bird directly ahead. Many birds that appear to fly straight ahead aren't there when you and your dog arrive simply because they never went there. Remember that direction of flight is more critical than distance in relocating grouse after a flush.

An old hunter where I grew up had a thing about following the first grouse he flushed because it would take him to other grouse. There is some wisdom in this. By following, you know there is at least one bird ahead of you, and it may be one of a scattered brood flushing back to the group. Also, a grouse will usually lie tighter for a dog on subsequent finds, especially if it has been shot at—unlike a woodcock, which is inclined to be more jumpy after a shot. Again unlike woodcock, grouse don't plop down at the end of a flight and just sit. They may not run far, but tracks in snow reveal that they go at least to the nearest hiding place.

Next in fame to the grouse that keeps a tree between itself and the gunner is the grouse that lets the gunner walk past and then flushes behind him. The man who finds that a number of grouse are doing this is probably barreling through the woods as if he were in a hurry to get it over with. The other extreme is the man who pokes along, pausing every few minutes to wait for a flush. Sudden stops sometimes flush grouse, but where? The bird you flush may go out ahead where you would have been within range for a shot if you had continued walking. If a grouse lets you pass, it will probably go out within seconds after you have passed it, whether you stop or not. I don't suggest never stopping, but the walk-and-pause method is for the man who hunts without a dog. I like to keep a moderate, steady pace that does not tire, a pace that my dog can depend upon and adjust to.

The last day of a recent season was cold, with deep snow on the ground, and Kay and I found ourselves in an unproductive covert. Rather than end in a negative mood, we returned to the station wagon and drove to another valley for the last half-hour of daylight and, as a final splurge, used all

three setters. We came to grouse tracks almost immediately but though we hunted until nearly dusk, we had no contact with birds.

Turning back, we followed a log road that held to the side of the ridge through slashings. As we approached a power line with big cables sagging from one side of the valley to the other, I saw Bliss stiffen in the path, a brisk wind hitting her in the face. Step at a time she moved, reaching, until she was pointing at the edge of the right-of-way, her head high with both ears swept back by the wind. This would seem to locate the grouse either in the open swath or in dense cover on the far edge. Dixie joined Shadows who, almost blind with age, stayed in front of me, nearly tripping me as I advanced beyond Bliss into the right-of-way. In the half-light neither dog had seen Bliss pointing. There is some feeling that grouse flush into the wind if they have a choice, which would still give me a shot if the bird lay in the open. Instead, the grouse went out above and behind me, the wind carrying the sound away, and I turned to see it sail back over Bliss. Seconds later, another grouse took off from the same spot, following the first but to one side of Bliss, and I in my eagerness fired the right barrel knowing as I pulled that the bird was too far away. It was stupid shooting but it had been a fine piece of dog work, from the first hint of scent in the wind to the established point.

As for the grouse, they had behaved about as should be expected—unpredictably. They had selected that open situation on a bitter night in preference to brush piles all around them or to heavy rhododendron in the valley; they had held tight, not unusual at such an hour but exceptional in a high wind; they had flushed back over the pointing dog. And true to form, they had disconcerted me. ◉

HUNTING THE SOUTHWESTERN MONARCH

by John Wootters

To down a mule deer in the Southwest, knowledge of terrain and the animal's habits is just as essential as choice of rifle or binoculars.

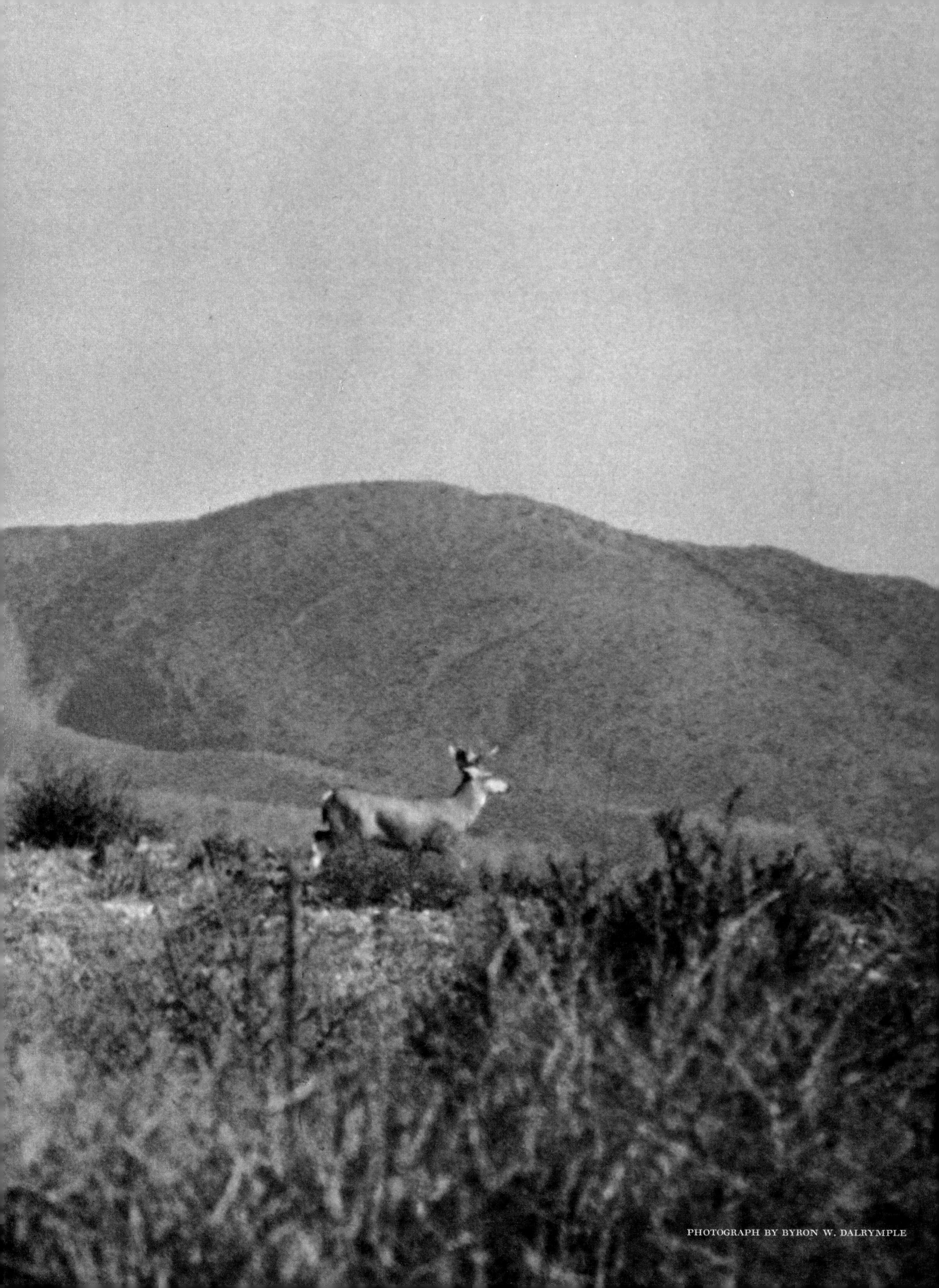

PHOTOGRAPH BY BYRON W. DALRYMPLE

A frozen sun-disc inched its way upward to clear the rim of a mesa across the canyon, its rays spangling every leaf and twig and blade of grass with frost-fire. In the basin below my perch, I checked several trails through my binoculars, noting that not many deer had used them during the night. As I glassed the meadows a mule deer doe and fawn appeared, quick-stepping along one of the trails, but no buck followed them. I lowered the glasses and scanned the basin, shivering, wishing the sun would hurry, but at the same time knowing that the day would soon be too warm for comfort.

My companion, Winston Burnham, and I were seated atop a towering chimney rock, part of an eroded ridge which was the ancient spine of the mesa. Behind us loomed the mesa's shoulder. The flat top of the mountain, twenty thousand acres of table-flat meadows and groves of aspens and ponderosa pine, was the summer range of a herd of elk and mule deer. From our position and within range of our rifles, we could overlook at least three major migration trails, trending downward off the mountain's point into the canyons and valleys where the deer would pass the winter months. Far below us, in the valley six miles distant, closely mown alfalfa fields shone in the early sun like standing water.

It was the morning of the second day of the hunting season, here in southwestern Colorado's vast Uncompahgre Plateau, and that fact was significant. The only con-venient access for hunters was along the high ridge at the far end of the mesa. As usual, hunting pressure had begun there along a forest road on opening morning and rolled in waves the length of the mountain's level top. From long experience in the area, my companions and I could predict the reaction of the resident deer herd to this pressure. For a day or two the animals would circle and dodge, reluctant to leave their summering grounds even though riflemen were combing this high country. However, the herd was on the verge of beginning its annual downhill drift, especially since snows had blanketed the country a few days before. The infiltration by the hunters would trigger the movement. In high Rocky Mountain regions, where timberline rises to eleven thousand feet and all access is from below, the oldest, biggest mulie bucks are the last of the deer to drop downhill as snow deepens. But in this mesa country, where elevations range from five to eight thousand feet, maximum, and hunters can work from the top down, the big bucks are the first to go. It takes just about twenty-four hours of hunting to convince the heavy-headed old bucks that the time has come to leave the easy living in the high meadows. When they get the message they begin a parade down those trails, overlooked by our chimney-rock perch, which has to be seen to be believed.

Every animal, during those first few days of the general season, will be headed the same direction—downward—and almost every one of them will be a mature buck. By the end of the sixth or seventh day, the mesa top will still hold a sizable, and nervous, heard of does, fawns, and young males, but very few of the craggy old patriarchs will be found there.

Our tactics are simple: We spend those first few days on the chimney rock and pick and choose between the racks of antlers passing in review below us, meanwhile wishing the horde of hunters stomping through the mesa-top meadows all the luck in the world.

On this particular morning the sun had hardly cleared the opposite mountain when the parade started. Winston jabbed me in the ribs and pointed downward, where I saw a pair of mule bucks on the nearest trail. One was a four-pointer (western count) with spindly horns, but the other carried a set of antlers that made me grunt, roll over onto my belly, and slip my arm into the rifle's sling. It was an easy shot, with the deer standing broadside in the open, no more than one hundred and fifty yards away. I took my time and placed the bullet precisely behind the shoulder, well up in the lungs. The buck died on his feet.

Before we could gather up our gear and scramble down from the rock, a third buck ambled into view on the same trail, and his antlers were even better, with exceptional height and symmetry. Winston reached for his own 7mm Magnum and

Preceding pages: Texas hunter has stalked close for offhand shot at buck which is now aware and fleeing. Above: Film for The American Sportsman-ABC shows spooked mule deer streaking over snow-covered hill in New Mexico.

rolled the buck over. Almost before the sun was up, we had a pair of fine bucks to dress, thanks to the hunters above. Three days later, the third member of our party, Murry Burnham, went back to this same chimney formation and selected from among a dozen bucks he scoped that morning a magnificent mulie with massive, nontypical antlers spreading thirty-eight and one-quarter inches at the widest point.

This migratory habit of the mule deer is perhaps the most distinctive of the several differences a whitetail hunter will have to adjust to when he makes his first mule deer hunt. Almost nothing short of a residential subdevelopment or a forest fire can drive a whitetail permanently out of his small home range. The mulies of the Southwest, however, change their living quarters twice each year, and their migrations are both vertical and horizontal. One herd, which winters in California, travels more than one hundred miles to spend the summer in Oregon. Most populations do not wander so far, their "migrations" being better described as a mere vertical drift occasioned by changing weather and forage conditions. Even so, the movements and their timing are of crucial importance to the hunter throughout most of the southwestern range. In some of the area under consideration here—trans-Pecos Texas, New Mexico, Arizona, the Oklahoma Panhandle, and southern Colorado—there is little change in elevation and therefore no vertical migra-

tion. In West Texas mule deer country, for example, the animals are found in abundance in rolling prairie terrain cut by ravines, or in the foothills of the small mountains (which seldom rise more than a couple of thousand feet above the surrounding tableland). Western Oklahoma, some of the prime mulie country in New Mexico, and much of Arizona, too, is more desert than alpine. In more mountainous terrain, the primary problem may be pinpointing the elevation of the herds at the time of hunt. A hunter should bear in mind that the big trophy bucks are last to leave high country where hunting pressure is from below, and the first to leave where hunters can come at them in numbers from above. If local information is not available, or reliable, it pays to spend a few days before opening morning scouting various elevations for sightings, fresh beds and sign, and evidences of feeding.

The southwestern states offer a surprising variety of deer country, from the towering Sangre de Cristo Mountains of New Mexico to the rocky deserts of Arizona, and the mule deer has adapted to almost every environment. The species was originally reported, by the Lewis and Clark expedition, to be a plains animal, but improvident conservation practices in the early days and the invasion of their territory by livestock have pushed the mule deer back into remote areas where mankind permits him to abide.

Throughout his range, the mule deer is

a much more open-country animal than his whitetailed cousin, whose range overlaps that of the mule deer in much of the Southwest. The habits of the two species are radically different. The whitetail is a skulker, a creature of the environmental "edges," a thicket-dweller taking advantage of every scrap of cover. A burglar-bold old whitetail will lie low, even when a hunter passes within a few yards, as long as he thinks he hasn't been noticed, but when he flees, he does it with purpose, putting lots of cover between himself and danger and never stopping until safely concealed. Wounded, he almost invariably goes downhill, especially if leg-shot.

The mulie, on the other hand, is a more innocent soul, even in the same general terrain, posing grandly in the open, fleeing uphill with his comical, pogo-stick gait, even when wounded, and almost invariably pausing to gaze back at the hunter just before he reaches cover or a ridge crest. It has been a fatal error of thousands of deer. And he lacks the nerve of the whitetail; surprise him in his bed and he'll go crashing away in a panic.

In the southwestern regions, mule deer are hunted under two distinctly different sets of circumstances. The first is during the general big-game seasons of the various states, opening from mid-October through November. The weather may be quite warm, there is little or no snow, and the herds may still be peacefully established on their summering grounds. The other set of conditions is encountered during the post-season hunts commonly held in southern Colorado and some parts of New Mexico. These may be declared at any time in November, December, or even January, to allow the harvest of surplus animals which survived the general season, but most of the hunts are in December, when heavy snow has shut the high country off to the deer, and the rut is in full swing.

During the general seasons the mature bucks are ranging alone or in small bachelor bands of two to four individuals. Although does and fawns may be using the same areas, a trophy buck will rarely be found in their company at this time of year. Hunting techniques comprise all the standard ones for deer hunting—point-sitting, still-hunting, and watching feeding areas at dawn and dusk. The man out after a real trophy head had better haunt the roughest and most inaccessible pockets of country he can find, timberline areas, rugged rimrocks, and slides. Big-headed mule bucks tend to lie down during the warm part of the day near the ends of points where they have shade and a clear view of their back trails, and where rising thermals will carry the scent of danger to their nostrils from below on either side of the point. Like other mountain species, mulies seem not to be as conscious of the possibility of danger from above, but timber on these preferred points frequently makes a silent approach from above impossible. An excellent tactic involves two hunters working together, combing out each side of a point simultaneously. Either may push a buck over the ridge and right into the cross hairs of the other's rifle scope.

In lower country, the typical bedding spots will be just below the rimrock bluffs. Juniper and piñon shrubs offer shade and shelter in such spots, and the lazing deer have good warning of danger from either above or below. Hunting them from above is impossible, but the hunter who isn't afraid of running shots may be surprised at the game he can flush at midday by working slowly along the slopes or slides a few yards below these bedding areas.

In the warmer reaches of the Southwest, mule deer appear to suffer somewhat from heat during the general hunting season, having already grown their winter coats by this time, and I've found them actually lying in a bank of old snow. If no snow is available, they'll do their nooning in deep shade on the northern slopes, so it is a mistake to do all your hunting on the sunny, protected, south-facing points which fairly shout *deer beds*.

Hunting the postseasons is a different proposition altogether. The snow is usually deep in normal years, not only in the timberline country but also in the valleys, and the cold is an enemy to be reckoned with by deer and hunters alike. These are the "trophy hunts," held when even the biggest bucks are ranging in the valleys, and the rut is like fire in their veins. Deer concentrations are easy to locate in the snow, and the animals themselves are conspicuous against the white background from great distances. In much of the postseason region, the staple winter fodder of mule deer is sagebrush, and they may be observed a long way from any cover, far out on the open flats. That same openness of terrain, however, can complicate the task of stalking within sure rifle range. Other favored feeding areas in December will be those offering bearberry, scrub oak, juniper, or serviceberry bushes.

These snowy postseason hunts have been held regularly in the San Juan region of southern Colorado and on the Jicarilla Apache Indian Reservation in northern New Mexico, and occasionally in other areas of both states. The southwestern hunter who covets a mule-deer trophy for the Boone and Crockett Club listings probably has better odds during this "trophy hunt" on the Jicarilla Reservation than anywhere else in North America. During the last few years more record heads have been taken here than in any other similar-sized region—at least sixteen, as of my latest information. One hunting party from Texas killed three

Colorado does, typically alert, watch intruder.

record heads on a single trip to this reservation in 1966. The Apaches charge a stiff tribal fee for the hunt, and limit the number of permits issued, but the results seem to be worth the price of admission for a serious trophy hunter. The tribe also holds a regular-season hunt, and some exceptional heads always seem to turn up on this less-expensive hunt, too.

West Texas, particularly the region between the towns of Marfa and Presidio, has at least as many mule deer per square mile as any other portion of the range, but this is the Mexican, or "desert," subspecies, substantially smaller in body and horn than the Rocky Mountain race found farther north. The very biggest heads of this variety are rarely better than the average, mature Rocky Mountain trophy, so if an outstanding mule deer head is your primary goal, be certain to inquire of the state game and fish department as to which regions hold the larger subspecies.

Where elk are not also on the agenda, the mulie hunter enjoys wide latitude in selecting his shooting equipment. My own favorite combination for all western hunting is a battered, beloved old Remington bolt-action rifle, chambered for the 7mm Magnum cartridge and mounting a 2X-7X variable scope. The cartridge may be a bit much for most mule deer hunting, but it has ridden so many miles on my shoulder or in a saddle scabbard in the mountains and on the plains that I'd be betraying a friend if I left it behind. Furthermore, everything I shoot at with the old Remington falls down, and my confidence in the rifle is unshakable.

That confidence and familiarity with a given rifle is, in my opinion, far more important than any technical specifications, and this belief has been supported by companions who are just as deadly with their .270's, .280 Remingtons, .284's, .30/06's, .308's, and 7x57 Mausers as I am with my "Big Seven." The 6mm family of cartridges, with proper bullets and in the right hands, is perfectly adequate for mule deer, as is the ancient .257 Roberts. Even the .30/30 class of cartridges, including the .32 Special, the various .303's, and the .35 Remington, has undeniably slain more than its fair share of mule deer, but the average visiting hunter, with limited time and a relatively large investment in the hunt, is better assured of success and satisfaction with more modern ballistics at his disposal, plus a good scope sight of at least four power.

In short, almost any good whitetail rifle will serve well enough for mulies, which are no tougher and not as much bigger than whitetails as popularly supposed. The chief difference is in the ranges at which the two species are taken; the whitetail average is well under one hundred paces, while mulies average closer to one hundred and fifty yards in most areas, with a possibility of shots up to three hundred.

Plenty of mule deer are downed each season with the several .300 Magnum cartridges, but both game and hunter will more than likely be overgunned by such cannons, and they are usually heavy for scrambling around all day at the higher elevations.

Far more important than selection of a cartridge is the choice of bullets, and more important yet is the placement of those bullets on the target. For all the more modern .30-caliber rifles, the 150-grain bullet is the correct choice, and it's not bad in the various 7mm's, either. The rounds of .25 caliber and smaller demand the heaviest available slugs, whether handloaded or factory-loaded. Moderately quick expanding bullets are desirable for mule deer, as contrasted with the emphasis placed upon penetration for shooting bigger game such as elk or moose.

I regard a good pair of binoculars as equally essential to my mulie hunting kit as a good rifle. Magnification of 7X to 8X is about right, and can be had in compact glasses, but sharp definition, or resolving power, is more important.

To an experienced whitetail hunter, the antlers of the first adult mulie buck he sees will appear tremendous, through the binoculars or otherwise. Where an outstanding whitetail rack may spread to twenty inches (inside), a mule deer head is not in the bragging class until inside spread reaches close to thirty inches. I've measured the ear spread of a giant mulie buck at twenty-two inches (probably slightly less in life, with his ears held at the alert) so it's obvious that any rack which barely spreads outside the ears is inferior. However, when the first main fork of the beams extends outside those ears, the head is getting interesting. Seen from front or rear, a good rack has a distinctive, boxy, square appearance, seeming to be about as high as wide, with massive beams and long points. In fact, a trophy head will not only be wider than the ear tips, but wider than any other part of the body. Symmetry, in a potential record head, counts heavily, so the trophy hunter must make certain that the typical mule deer formation is complete—each beam branching, with each branch forking once more, for a total of five prongs on each side, counting the stubby brow tines. If there are additional points, it's desirable that they be paired (one on each side).

A record-class nontypical mule deer's antlers are nearly indescribable, but the instant you see them there'll be no doubt in your mind that they're something special. In general, if the head has the big, square look, with lots of spread and heavy beams, it's necessary only to make certain that no obvious deformity exists before shooting.

I've found—and most experienced trophy hunters agree—that any rack of antlers always looks smaller than it really is when viewed from a position steeply above the animal. (This is true of all antlered game.)

Altogether, my favorite tactics are to camp high in the game country (keeping quiet around camp), walking, riding, or being hauled as high as possible before daylight, and spending the day hunting down the mountain at my own pace. That pace is ultraslow, allowing plenty of time to study the terrain below me, planning routes, glassing likely lying-up spots during the midday hours, and generally soaking up all the sights and sounds and smells of the forest at my leisure. Every kind of mule deer country has its distinctive character and its own delights. The towering mountain country offers the incredible cleanliness and majesty of high parks and ridges, with cross-canyon vistas of aspen stands saffron against the green-black spruces. There is a stillness and a privacy here, a sensation of possessing all the eye can see, that justifies the effort, deer or no deer. The perfume of this land is the pungency of moist, dead aspen leaves alternating with that of the conifers, and it stirs my hunter's heart every autumn.

The desert reaches of the mulies' range have a completely different appeal, at least for me. This is harsh country, a man's kind of country, where every form of life commands respect. The ocotillo, staghorn, and prickly-pear cactus are formidable, and the yucca's daggers will never be risked a second time by the newcomer. All the birds, mammals, and reptiles are tough and hardy and defiant. Everything in the desert seems to run to extremes—daily temperature ranges may be as great as fifty degrees, the weather is either extremely dry or extremely wet, and plant life adaptations are so extreme that the stranger will term them weird. But the deer are here, too, softening the arid land with their grace and beauty.

The mule deer is, to my eye, the loveliest of America's deer. In the segments of his range north of the southwestern regions discussed here, he is larger, but there he takes second place among big game to elk, moose, and other animals. In the Southwest, he is our biggest game. And since he must often be taken at very long range in open country, he is among our most demanding.

His whitetailed cousin is a politician. He accommodates; he adopts a subtle détente with his enemy, Man. The whitetail is the slick quick-change artist, living by his nerve and wits, learning new habits and modifying old ones into a behavior pattern which has become perhaps the most successful in big-game history.

But the mulie is, by contrast, our defiant aborigine, an honest, noble, straightforward, perhaps rather simple, beast of surpassing grace. Both species are admirable, but, in the Southwest the mule deer is a well-crowned king. ◉

155

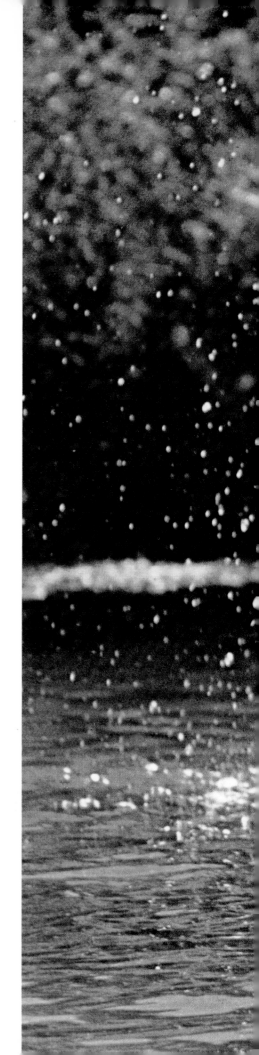

His
flaring spirit
has men
wading rivers
around the world
to engage him
in battle.

Searching
for
the
Wild Rainbow

by

David Shetzline

Photography by Bill Browning

When I sold my first novel I quit my forestry job in the Oregon woods and moved my family to Seal Rock on the coast. We bought a small ranch through which a stream wanders to the nearby sea, like the shallow trough of a sunstruck mole, mindlessly oxbowing until it deepens into a tidal slick and hurls itself into the breakers. We came to our ranch in doubt; we were leaving familiar country where I'd been able to get work and where we had killed deer and harvested our garden and smoked fish. We were leaving the high-lake rainbow country because we could not stand to be long away from an ocean; there was something in us that made us coastal people, something in the blood or the brain. It was witnessing the catch of a rainbow-banded fish at our new stream that enabled me to accept "home is where you make it," and I had indeed finally made mine.

The neighbor's boy stood by a tangle of alders and swung a salmon egg from an old fly rod, swung this hook-impaled orange pearl out over the pasture edge and let it wander deep in the slow water while I paused in walking my unfamiliar fields. He strained, his body suggesting he had seen a fish move and he simply *knew* he would connect. For an instant my mind slipped back and I remembered myself — awkward, all angles —

going through that initiation of the neophyte, when you first feel your body responding to some hint of the fish. Then the boy's rod twitched, throbbed as he struck his trout. His body composed while he and his captive plied their ancient contest, the fish leaping, leaping until the dance was done and he lay senseless in the grass.

The air, the moil of the water, the bank smell—all a replay of twenty years and three thousand miles gone by, when I had caught my first rainbow from a favorite bend of water in the East Aspetuck River of Connecticut.

I had my own secret pool, a bend of Aspetuck water that may by now be scourged by hurricane floods, yet in my head remains the finest lay of brook that I have ever fished. I was fishing a somewhat nondescript bucktail streamer when my working line tangled. Angler enough to know you have to possess decent backing to work a pool which holds good brown trout, I decided to neglect my cast and mend the snarl. At the exact instant my bird's nest was picked and reeled up, and my hitherto free-diving bucktail was cinched to tight line, from deep under a backwater something fastened its life to me

and muscled downstream. Once it leaped. Then again, again, again, again, again. *A smallmouth bass?* I thought. *A pink-colored smallmouth streamlined bass?* Fifteen minutes later I squatted bulge-eyed on the bank, examining a two-pound piece of spent fish striped with vermilion.

How exotic the rainbow seemed to me then—an import, a hatchery treat from the sovereign Nutmeg State, feeding wild, but of the same western stock that had caught fire in the waters of Argentina, Chile, Kenya, New Zealand, Australia, and Tasmania. And at that moment on that Connec-

Far left: Frustrated by fruitless casts, Waterman re-examines hatch in hopes of making a better match. Casting sequence: false cast over rise; turning the fly over; natural drop. To fool them on this crystal mountain water, fly must float free—without drag—on gossamer 5X tippet.

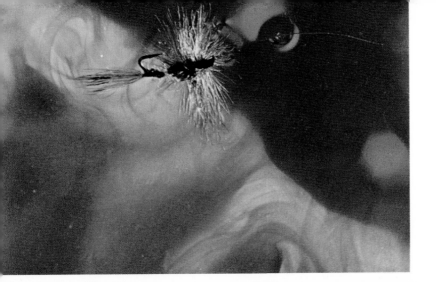

These pictures, made by Photographer Browning with waterproofed 35mm camera, show beguiling flies as they may appear to a cautious rainbow trout. Clockwise from opposite page: Ginger Quill, Gray Wulff, and two Cahills.

ticut stream I promised myself I would see him someday in his native waters, and beyond—where he grows to maximum.

As I walked up to introduce myself to my new neighbor on my backyard Oregon stream, was I not keeping that promise, meeting myself again? The boy's fish was a steelhead showing the rainbow color—as they often do after entering fresh waters. It does not matter. From that day I accepted I was home. Now, when I prepare for the first of the season's fishing, it is as if I am going out to meet my oldest friend.

From where did the lovely rainbow trout come?

It is of the salmons—scientifically, *Salmo gairdneri*, closer to the Atlantic salmon, *Salmo salar*, than to the brook trout—and its natural range, before artificial dispersion started, extended from the Aleutians to the mountains of northern Mexico. So these trout were with the early western Indians, amazing them with their colors, and—with the chinook salmon and others—providing them with abundant nourishment.

Dried, smoked, powdered, or sun-leached, the Salmonidae were the staff of life for the most highly advanced North American empire before the white man's iron and whiskey and paper-promises relegated the poetry, dance, architecture, and exquisitely stylized carvings of the Pacific Coast Indians to a barely viable tourist trade. And now with the most mindless of energy sources—the atomic reactor—raising the temperature of our rivers, it may be that in a dozen generations the salmons, and their cousin the giant rainbow trout, will be reduced to inhabiting a few regulated fenced and nurtured streams, little more than aquatic garden preserves,

Opposite: Moment of hesitation, as wet fly whisks past nose of great rainbow trout.
Above: Caution thrown to the currents, fish attacks a feather minnow.
Left: Frantic attempt to escape carries him surging to surface of river.

where, for some eleven thousand years, they have spawned free.

The rainbow trout must survive. Pound for pound it is the most beautiful, tenacious, and acrobatic creature in the sportsman's bag. For sportsmen of means, rainbows of ten to twenty pounds and daily catches of a dozen three- and four-pounders are available in water throughout North America, especially west of the Rockies and north to the Arctic Circle; and in Argentina, Chile, Tasmania, Africa, Australia, and—most reliably—New Zealand rainbows abound. Except in British Columbia and Canada, these fish occupy waters that were virtually sterile to sportsmen a hundred years ago. They exist with other imports—both hybrid and relatively pure-strain—through the cooperation of fishing enthusiasts whose instinct to stalk, lure, capture, and kill exotic creatures is never abated. Man will, no doubt, someday enjoy a life span as long as that of the Galapagos turtle, and then perhaps he will tire of seeking and killing. He will amuse himself instead training astonished rainbow trout to jump hoops and dance water ballet.

Rainbow are virtually everywhere for the American sportsman. The question remains: In your search for wild rainbow, just how many fish per hour of action will satisfy? And do you seek the steadily good fish—six and eight and ten pounds? As for tackle, you must settle that with your own conscience. The rainbow, as with his close relative, the Atlantic salmon, will feed on the tiniest of flies, on virtually all the high-fat aquatic beasties, and—in his great size—on his own

kind. The fly man can try for the famous twenty-two-twenty formula—a midge tied to a #20 hook, secured by a two-pound tippet, festering in the outraged jaw of an amuck twenty-pound rainbow. Or he can deep-troll streamer flies suggesting shrimp or minnow. The hardware man can cast the daintiest Colorado spinerettes or drag Ford fenders, for all I care. I am a fly fisherman, though I do not tie my own. I like the subtleties—knowing what I am about, and what this fish is I am after, what are his ways.

Since there is a rainbow-like form, the Kamchatka salmon, native to the Russian coast, it was once held that the American trout originated in Asia, migrated to southeast Alaska, thence to the Fraser and Columbia systems, thence to the Yellowstone and Missouri. From the Snake to the great inland sea basins of Utah and Nevada, and, of course, from Oregon southward into Mexico, with all sea-running forms passing from stream to stream. The western Salmo trouts, the steelhead rainbow and cutthroat, were essentially Arctic migratory fish pushed southward by glaciers, sea-run fish caught up in vast watersheds of fresh water. On the West Coast, where the rainbow and cutthroat have access to the sea, they often elect to spend their lives in salt water, the cutthroat trudging upstream to spawn. This cutthroat is called a blueback, often simply a sea trout. In the narrow creek that ruts my pasture to the sea, I've seen them taken at twenty inches, with flesh the color of the small salmon we call here shakers. (One is supposed to shake small salmon free when trolling for the chinook or silver, hence the name.) Teenage fishermen sometimes bravado the wardens and sneak a shaker home in their shirts to impress a neighbor with their pluck. At that point the "shaker" becomes a "poacher." Poached in a bit of decent white wine, the shaker is virtually indistinguishable from the sea-run cutthroat. Which, in turn, is only superseded in flavor by the kokanee, a sort of landlocked salmon appreciated alike by the gourmet, and a monstrous creature called the Kamloops. The Kamloops is a rainbow trout, indigenous to the Kamloops area of British Columbia. It is truly a rainbow, but under prime conditions of meat feed it can exceed fifty pounds. That's correct: fifty pounds.

For the fisherman, there are really but two native *western* trouts: the cutthroat, with its sea-run form; and the rainbow and its sea-run stepbrother, the steelhead.

Small rainbow and steelhead are virtually indistinguishable. However, they attain a different orientation, the steelhead fry dutifully seeking the sea, while the rainbow fry linger in freshwater riffles or drop into lakes where—under the adage "the bigger the water, the bigger the fish"—they meat up to their most enormous. Beyond the fry stage, ichthyologists can differentiate steelhead from rainbow, but the rule of the field seems to be this: If your fish, no matter how deep and splendid his rainbow stripe, has an empty stomach, he is a steelhead, probably on his way to spawn. If his stomach has any sort of food he is invariably a rainbow. If there is no outlet to the sea, unquestionably you've caught your wild rainbow. The brown? The brook? The Dolly Varden? The brown, or Loch Leven, was introduced from Scotland and Europe. The brook is a native eastern American critter. The Dolly Varden is a western char. The golden? The speckled? The whatever? Ancient hybrids, ancient relatives of the original western trout, ma-

rooned, isolated, abandoned to their own spectrum of dazzle and color and tenacity by the glaciers and upheavals that pocketed watersheds and lakes tens of thousands of years ago.

As these glaciers drove all living matter south, then receded, the rainbow, cutthroat, and steelhead remained—the rainbow adapting so well it now will take in any water system with proper temperature and aquatic cycle. Rainbows will survive in water down to thirty-two degrees, but their functions almost cease and if fed the fish may die, as the food will decay in the stomach before it is digested.

The native rainbow's time of glory was no doubt a hundred years ago in western America. When the great fisherman Edward Hewitt was a boy he visited the proposed Yellowstone Park and found it full of fish, all seemingly between three and four pounds. Hewitt caught five hundred pounds of rainbows to feed an escort of thirty of General Sheridan's soldiers. They were all caught between breakfast and midafternoon on a single day by the young fisherman.

Under Federal auspices, rainbows were shipped in the early 1870's from the McCloud River, a tributary of the Sacramento, to wherever sportsmen believed they could afford the experiment. Where the adults can spawn and the fry survive, they endure. But longevity is not species-specific. Rainbow seldom live over six years; even the giant Kamloops is a dying specimen at eight. And thus in some backwater they were planted, grew immense, and then, before they could be fished-out, seemed inexplicably to disappear.

Once I hiked up a wild creek in southern Oregon to see if I could kill an elk. Instead, I met an old prospector who in his youth had had his "back rubbed with gin and finished off with Paris talc by one of the best madames in Frisco. That was after quite

170

a night of sport...." Yet he had been a day sportsman as well, and told of a lake in the high Sierras miles back: the tiniest bead of water glimmering through a notch in the trail. He had reined his horse, quartered into the pines, and made camp. There she lay: the most beautiful water he had ever seen. The year was 1915, and the old tin Government sign read: "Stocked in 1909. Do not fish until 1912."

"But they had forgotten her. Would you believe? Lost or forgotten her there! And she was filled with rainbows. Damn, damn, I caught them and turned them back, four, five pounds apiece, until my arms ached. I swore I'd never tell another soul. And I didn't. I always figured to try her again. I always meant to get back. But...you know...."

I remember him staring out one of the tiny windows of his cedar shack, down upon the waters of the tumbling coastal creek above whose bed he had come to eat up his Social Security checks and die, amusing himself by plucking at flakes of gold washed down from the mountain, dreaming of a nugget, though Chinese laborers had sweated over every existing pocket a lifetime before. His eyes were fastened to that high Sierra lake, his paradise of rainbows. "If only I could get back...." I did not tell him the truth. In such a tiny secret pocket of water, planted rainbows simply expire of old age.

It is a shame that fish placed in fine high lakes cannot spawn—for they must have running water in which to run, and the right gravel and currents for protection and aeration of the eggs. So they run from lakes to rivers—from Superior into the Brule, from New York's Lake Seneca into Catherine Creek—and so they run from the sea into the great rivers of the West. But from small lakes they find no exit.

Given fine spawning water, the rainbow may actually over-spawn itself. This I learned ten years ago on a slip of water below a Colorado beaver pond. My partner and I had hiked six miles down the crumbling hogback of a ravine to get to a trickle. We lowered ourselves from ledge to ledge, whooping celebration of our release from the dull peacetime Army in which we had languished—with rare bouts of dove shooting—interspersed with parachuting from airplanes, which in turn gave us extra pay to save for things like the Colorado fish feast. Now, below the ravine, we tackled up and fished waters most private, perhaps flecked with a fly once a year. Dozens of troutlets rose, grouped at each cast. Quickly we learned to move fast, seeking deep water where the tinies did not rise. There the heavier wild fish lay: eight and nine inches. We hardly attempted to match our flies with the native hatch. I possessed nothing but eastern patterns anyway. Yet we took dozens, dozens of rainbows. Each, every single fish fought until seemingly lifeless.

This is the unique signature of the rainbow. From some ancient seat of instinct he is programmed to leap and throw himself about as if he were trying to astonish his way free of the steel. If you use the lightest of gear and he has any weight at all—even a half pound—you have royal entertainment. We tired of it, as one eventually does with small fish and small trickly water; but it brought us sharp appetites. My partner produced a very small iron egg pan and a glob of margarine that had suffered our descent very badly; and he then introduced me to a most illegal delight. Stalking a lens of water filled with tiny 'bows, he skittered his smallest fly and plucked two- and three-inch spasms of color out, one by one, as a man might pull single perfect hairs from the tail of a restless horse. I lay them upon a clean wet handkerchief, and when we had twenty or so they went into the hot pan and margarine. We ate them whole, entrails and the lot. Like tiny smelts. I think of myself as an objective man, but I don't believe I've put much between my teeth since then rivaling their delicacy. If only, instead of margarine, we had thought to bring butter.

If you fish consistently, you tire of the little ones. For the rainbow must have some size, some seasoning, before his faculties mature and he is truly prime game. In his prime he is much more sensitive to ultra-violet light (he may be more sensitive to colors in general than man); he is keen in determining size and shape; his night vision is superior to man's; he sees better in less clear conditions; he maintains better side vision. His reaction to vibration seems to be as acute as the fisherman's hearing; his smell as keen, no doubt keener; and nerves leading from the mouth, tongue, and lips to the brain explain the marked preference feeding rainbows have at times for flying ants, at other times for mayflies. But he tends to have a one-rut mind. Experiments with shape and size suggest that radical changes of flies are most effective: changing the size of a fly rather than varying its color pattern.

The sportsman seeks mature game and the question must return: Where, in your search for your wild rainbow, are you most likely to come up with consistently big fish? And where are the truly huge rainbows, ten- to twenty-pounders?

Hanging from a parachute over Kentucky, I first sensed the *round* of the world, my eye following the rivers over the horizon. Catfish rivers. After being discharged from service I had the chance to go West, working with the Forest Service in the Cascade Mountains. There, in Davis Lake, I found my first western rainbows. Yet in days and days of fishing, in many advertised and unadvertised places, I could not find rainbows in the number or size I craved.

Rumor favored New Zealand. One might dream about New Zealand. One heard of a special fishing contest there which brought in rainbows averaging three-and-one-half pounds. Lake Tarawera produced a ten-pounder every day. But the ten-pounders are hard to catch. If you fish hard all day you might get two or three fish in the eight- to ten-pound bracket. On Lake Taupo in New Zealand, the very large lake where rainbow gather to run the rivers and herd up the tiny white native minnow, the average take was four-and-one-half pounds, with the local warden weighing in eight-pounders daily. Five-, six-, and seven-pounders are quite common and although seven hundred tons of trout were harvested last year, the season on lakes Taupo and Rotorua is open all year to keep up the 'harvest and ensure sizable fish. Indeed, Taupo is considered by many the one single body of water most distinguished for consistently heavy fish. The year one might expect a thirty-pounder somewhere in two solid weeks of fishing, though, has passed. Fishing is also excellent on the south island of New Zealand, with reasonable catches in Tasmania and New South Wales. In all the places down under where the English introduced the rainbow into systems of water heavy with aquatic shrimp, insects, minnow, and nymph, the fish has flourished: solid, heavy, with small, perfectly proportioned heads and total energy.

One evening, in the throes of my planning, I simply telephoned Ted Trueblood, one of the most respected American sportsmen, and asked where in the world he would go to count upon catching a six- to eight-pound rainbow. He answered, "I'd go to New Zealand. Lake Taupo and Tangarriro River flowing into the south end of Taupo."

And stateside?

"I don't know where you could catch a six- to eight-pound rainbow and count on it," Trueblood answered. "I've never been able to count on it yet in British Columbia. I've caught some nice fish there, but I wouldn't bet I'd get one if I just went after him."

Another respected angler, Joe Brooks, told me: "Yes, New Zealand would be the best. There are nice rainbows in Argentina and Chile . . . big ones in Tasmania, but not as many. I'd have to say New Zealand."

Where in the U.S.?

"There are some lakes that hold tremendously big rainbows. But lakes come and go. Kamloops run the biggest, of course. In lakes, probably the biggest are in Pend Oreille, Idaho, where all the world records are held. Georgetown Lake, Montana. But there are not too many rivers where you come up with big rainbows in the states— or anywhere for that matter. In many cases they get out of bounds for the fly fisherman because they go to meat. With any kind of fishing they're still hard to take in big numbers. It is not so much a question of favorite waters, but producing waters. I've caught lots of rainbows in Argentina. Up to twenty pounds; they have them there. But you don't catch many of them. They have rivers like the Collón Curá for example. You catch nothing less than three- to five-pounders, but few over. There are so many fish they've become stunted."

During late August and September, big rainbows come after the sockeye spawn in the Battle River of the Kenai Peninsula. And Funnel Creek and Brooks River. Probably the best place in the country easily accessible to catching big trout on flies is Henry's Lake, Idaho. Out of Babine Lake in Canada the Babine River receives tiny sockeye fry, some still laden with their yolk sacs. Usually in late May big trout follow downriver, feeding. Unfortunately, the waters can be moiled at this time, so superior fishing cannot be absolutely assured there each year.

In my own opinion, the dean of trout fishermen is Dr. Roderick Haig-Brown. I put my inquiry to him and was told: "The obvious answer is New Zealand or possibly Argentina, or extreme southern Chile where the fish run very heavy, but the conditions are horrible. . . . In British Columbia you have some spectacular rainbow fishing. Certain lakes produce some very large rainbows; Stump Lake, up beyond Merritt. But you have to be there at the right time to get onto them. And then you stand a pretty good chance of hooking fish between twelve and twenty pounds on a fly. And that's pretty significant. Then we have a run of fish in the Thompson River near Kamloops. On occasion there can be rather spectacular conditions for the Kamloops at the outlet of Adams River into Shuswap Lake and the outlet of Lettle River from main Shuswap into Little Shuswap. And when the Adams River sockeye are migrating as fry or yearlings you can get some quite extraordinary fishing; very exciting, strong rainbows up to ten and twelve pounds. But again: *on* some years, *off* some years. At the right moment, fishing in British Columbia would rival New Zealand, but the latter would be more consistent, with a longer season. If you are interested in lake fishing, and many people are, then you would probably have to say the finest lake fishing for rainbow trout in the world is probably B.C. I don't know anywhere else in the world where you could find as many lakes producing such a variety of excellent fishing for Kamloops."

Great men, important men, book jet seats to carry them to the corners of the world for rainbow trout. Their rods ride in special velvet-lined cases.

But there are rainbows here, good ones, rainbows left behind, and if you are a hard-hunting meat fisherman you can find them. I have rainbows in my own pasture by the Pacific, and a boy to show me how. ◉

THE ULTIMATE FLY ROD

Masters of the art of
splitting and joining
bamboo are dwindling,
but from their
hands come rods worthy
of great fish.

by Leonard M. Wright, Jr.
Photography by
J. Barry O'Rourke

Men are emotional about fly rods. Trout rods in particular, yet perhaps even about the hefty rods used in salt water for bonefish and tarpon, or about freshwater rods used for bass bugging and streamer fishing. Men may love a salmon rod. But light, split-cane fly rods are objects of reverence. A Payne, Halstead, Gillum, Garrison, Leonard, Orvis, Winston, Young, Thomas, or an Edwards trout rod may well be the most cherished piece of equipment used in any sport.

The only serious rival is the wing shooter's fine double shotgun. In fact, fly rod and shotgun have much in common. Both are used in the beauty of the wild outdoors. And both become intimate extensions of the body in motion. In some respects, though, the fly rod is the more intimate companion. It seems to be alive. It bends and moves in response to the angler's touch. The rod is a more constant friend, too. Fishing seasons are longer than shooting seasons, and, while a bird shooter may fire several times in a day afield, the trouter will number his casts in the thousands.

Add to this that a day on his favorite stream is a semireligious experience for the dedicated angler. The trout stream is set apart from other scenes of sport—by hemlock and rhododendron, willow and warbler, the play of sunlight on a riffle. Many fine authors have tried to capture this magic, but it beggars description. A great naturalist once described a stream as "the artery of the forest." It is that and more. It is also the life blood of the trouter.

In this setting and in this spirit, a rod becomes far more than just a tool for casting. And, fortunately, this

Preceding pages: Custom-made
bamboo fly rods by Gillum (top)
and Jim Payne. Opposite: A
recent Leonard, with Hardy reel.
Above: Antique twelve-footer,
in eight sections with extra tip,
was shaped from solid wood.
Left and below: Flashy metalwork
of 1880's frightened
fish, is now taboo. Left below:
Old guide variations.

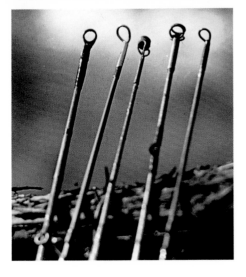

Opposite (from left):
Orvis's Wes Jordan fly rod;
early Leonard; early
rod by Jordan. Bird-cage
reel dates to c. 1890.
Above: Wrapped joints were
common on camp rods
set up once a season. Right:
Unlaminated rods of shaved
greenheart predate dry-fly era.

bond between rod and man is an especially happy one. The experienced angler seldom blames his rod. In fact, he is all too liable to consider it perfection.

This happiness with things as they are can be observed in almost any fine tackle store. There are seldom requests for unconventional rod actions or special embellishments. If you examine a sampling of rods by the finest makers, you will see that they are almost uniformly modest in appearance. The brown cane glows warmly through the clear varnish. The reel seat is a harmonious cedar or walnut. Windings will usually be a neutral tan. This is the quiet beauty of the partridge, not the gaudy beauty of the cock pheasant.

And yet, despite the generic description above, each maker subtly signs his own work. Custom-made reel fittings differ from one another. The shape of the cork grip often indicates the maker. And then there's the cane itself. Most Leonards are quite light-colored. So are Garrisons and Gillums. Paynes are medium brown. Halsteads and Orvises are quite dark brown.

Any of these fine rods is fairly expensive. One may cost from $150 to perhaps slightly more than $250. But it is definitely not a rich man's plaything, or a status symbol. A great many of these rods are in the hands of people of very modest means. I once saw a farmer fishing with a Gillum in the stream that ran behind his barn. When I admired the rod he looked a bit sheepish and admitted, "I've always wanted one of these, and then I made a bit of extra money trapping last winter. But my wife sure doesn't know how much I paid for it."

You can be sure that many lunches have been skimped or skipped in order to pay for a dream rod.

Is a $250 bamboo rod ten times as good as a $25 glass rod? There's no pat answer. It all depends on your sense of values.

Everett Garrison, one of the very finest custom makers, can back up his art with some science. "A glass rod doesn't throw the smooth curve of line that a fine bamboo does. Stop-motion photography proves this." All well and good, but why do most tournament distance casters now use glass? "It's a very powerful material, all right," Garrison admits. "But they haven't got the tapers worked out yet. Perhaps some day."

There's more to it than that. There's a "sweet feel" to a great bamboo rod that just can't be duplicated. When you're casting thousands of times a day, this advantage may be worth a lot in pure enjoyment—even if it won't catch more fish. A bamboo rod should last the average fisherman at least twenty years. That comes to $12.50 per year, or merely the price of two tankfuls of gas. When you look at it that way, a great rod isn't an extravagance.

There's a joker in that twenty-year life expectancy, though. It's only a median figure. A rod may last a man a lifetime if he fishes only several times a year. On the other hand, the screen door has ended the life of many a rod before it delivered its first cast. Each year hundreds of fine rods are crushed underfoot, splintered against tree trunks, or chopped off by car doors. Surprisingly, rod breakage while actually playing a trout is one of the rarest forms of disaster.

Perhaps it isn't fair to measure a rod's life in terms of years. Barring accidents, it should be measured in numbers of casts. For each time a bamboo rod flexes, it dies a little. It may take years to notice a change in power and action, for an angler unwittingly suits his casting style to the rod in hand. But fatigue is inexorable. The finest, steeliest dry-fly rod I ever owned—or ever handled for that matter—was an eight-foot Halstead. I still own it and cherish it, but I seldom fish with it. After some seven hundred and fifty days of dogged dry-fly fishing, it's a slow, lazy parody of its former self.

All great rods don't die; some escape both catastrophe and senility. But they survive in collections, like pinned insects, as a matter of record. In one notable collection is a priceless "gold" rod. Its history belongs to a brasher era, when the president of a kerosene company (which grew into Standard Oil) refused to be outdone by royalty. When this captain of industry heard that Queen Victoria had a rod with all-gold fittings, he decided to match her. He commissioned America's top rodmaker to make him a rod with all-gold ferrules and reel seat—then had all the metal intricately engraved by the finest gun engraver of the day!

In the same collection is a more modest, yet more historic rod. It was the favorite of Theodore Gordon, who, before his death in 1915, pioneered and established dry-fly fishing in America. The many excellent rods of the great Edward R. Hewitt seemed to have escaped the collectors, even though Hewitt died only about a dozen years ago. His grandchildren don't know where they all went. Have they fallen unceremoniously into the hands of the great-grandchildren? I hate to think that these rods might be suffering the same fate as my grandfather's ten-foot Thomas. I well remember using it with a quarter-ounce sinker, fishing for flounders off Cape Ann, Massachusetts, when I was a larcenous and untutored eight-year-old.

Sadly, great rods are being ruined or retired faster than they are being built. Demand for the very finest easily exceeds supply in our affluent society.

One hundred years ago, production was also negligible. The ardent angler made his

Heavy 1890 fly rod was used by Joseph Jefferson, angling actor famous for Rip Van Winkle role.

own rods and perhaps a few extras for his friends; these rods of ash, lancewood, or greenheart, while finely finished and ferruled, were relatively simple in construction. Rod guides were often simple unbraced rings which flopped as the line struggled through. Samuel Phillippe changed all this.

The art of lamination had been used in older bows; in the early nineteenth century, English rod tips of three-part design were used, and some glued work must have appeared then. Phillippe was an Easton, Pennsylvania, gunsmith who fished. He made violins as well. With the skill of a minor Stradivarius, he revolutionized the trout rod.

What was probably the first entire split-cane rod appeared in America in 1848—Phillippe's "rent and glued-up cane" rod, as it was called then. He wisely chose the six-part,

hexagonal cross section, which offers a flat, glued plane for flexion. Nine-, eight-, five-, and four-segment rods would be tried and discarded.

Phillippe's son, Solon, and later Charles Murphy, learned from the master. In 1870, the great self-taught builder Hiram L. Leonard began varnishing wonderful rods in Bangor, Maine. Thomas, Edwards, and the elder Edward Payne, whose son James became the finest rodbuilder who has ever touched a plane, learned at Leonard's bench.

George Parker Holden, a hobbyist and writer on rods many years ago, made his own, and trained Everett Garrison, an architect, who still builds by fits and starts for the custom trade. But Nat Uslan, who learned from Payne, has retired. Edwards has died, and so has Thomas, though his company

Antique salmon rod by Canada's Scribner & Son.

is still in business, making fine rods.

Shortly before this article was begun, Jim Payne told a friend, "I'm leaving the shop, I don't know when I'll be back." He died one month later. The announcement of his death in the New York papers precipitated a run on Abercrombie & Fitch's stock of used Payne rods—his output had been low for years. Paynes have doubled in price; the big salmon rods, which he stopped making fifteen years ago, are worth $750, prime condition, against $150. Younger hands struggle to keep the Payne shop going. Pinkey Gillum, Payne's fine apprentice, who built rods independently for years, died eight years ago. The masters are not being replaced.

The Charles Orvis Company in Manchester, Vermont, must be credited with offering the contemporary angler a fine rod on the retail rack. Their twenty-five hundred pieces a year, along with the production of Young of Detroit, Winston of San Francisco, and Leonard of Rockland County, New York, barely touch present demand, despite the inroads of glass. Very little that is wonderful is coming out of England or France, and the Japanese seem to have failed as rodmakers.

What makes one rod great, another mediocre? Materials and workmanship. The trout rod is pared to an irreducible minimum, a trend that began when the dry-fly method reached fad proportions under Theodore Gordon's tutelage in the early 1900's. False casting, short float, and recasting made the old ten-foot rods instruments of torture after an hour or so of fishing. Builders competed for lightness by sixteenths of an ounce. While the salmon rod remained a symphony, the dry-fly rod became a quartet. The slightest flaw in taper or action is quickly transmitted to the hand. The real devotee pursues his jewel-sided quarry with bamboo; glass is rare in the top trout clubs.

Bamboo, the muscle and sinew of the rod, is a large grass of which there are many species, sizes, and qualities. The first rods— perhaps Phillippe's original rods—were built of Calcutta bamboo. Today this is porch furniture bamboo, not rod material.

Modern rods are built of what is called Tonkin bamboo, said to be found only in a small area in southern China. One legend has it that only those stalks that grow on the hilltops are first rate, because they have been strengthened by resisting the wind. Another story is that this bamboo has ceased to exist in a wild state and is a cultivated crop. Most likely, there are several species of bamboo that have the desired strength and straightness for rod building.

A store of well-aged and dried canes of this type is the rodmaker's bank account. They are eight feet long, three inches in diameter, and may have cost only $2 apiece. They are the first key to quality, as is the stock of

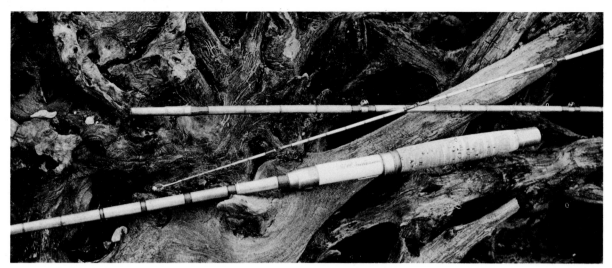

Rare Thomas, Edwards, and Payne fly rod of 1890's; all three craftsmen studied under Leonard.

hackle necks or a particular strain of live roosters to a fly tier.

But even a plentiful supply of the best cane is no assurance of perfect materials, for individual canes must be specifically selected for special tasks. Here a knowledge of the microscopic construction of bamboo and how it works is essential. A cross section of a piece of bamboo reveals small, powerful fibers that run the length of the section of cane and are embedded in a relatively neutral, but binding, matrix. A closer examination of this cross section reveals that these fibers are very close together on the outside of the cane, or nearest the exterior enamel, and that they become less and less dense as you approach the pithier interior.

A rodmaker examines this cross section very carefully as he selects a cane for a particular purpose. If he is going to build a seven-and-a-half-foot dry-fly rod, he looks for a cane with a dense cluster of fibers on the outside edge. He may have to examine and discard several canes to find this type. On the other hand, he may find one with an exceptionally dense power structure running well into the interior. This is a special prize, but not for the seven-and-a-half-foot trout

rod. All of those prized and rare inner power fibers would be planed away in making a rod of narrow diameter. This cane he marks and puts away as a special cane for use in a larger, more powerful salmon rod.

Only when a suitable cane has been selected from an already highly-selected batch of bamboo can the work proper commence. This consists of turning a single piece of cane into a fly rod of several sections, each of which is made up of six separate but absolutely equal slices of bamboo. While this fact of hexagonal structure is widely known, it is also often the sum total of an angler's knowledge about bamboo rods—even among men who own several of the finest. Yet, this is about the same as a sports car driver knowing only that all cars have four wheels!

Actually, the hand making of a fine rod is part art, part craftsmanship, and it is a lengthy and painstaking process. Here are some of the major steps involved in the order that some, but not all, rodmakers follow.

First, the selected cane is split in half and the partitions inside each node are cut out with a gouge. If the rod is to be the popular seven-and-a-half-footer, in two pieces and with an extra tip, one half is split into six equal sections and put aside for the butt section. The other half is split into twelve pieces for the two tips. The pieces forming each section are cut and arranged with the nodes staggered so that no two fall opposite each other. Pieces are numbered so they can be reassembled in the same sequence.

Each piece is then placed in a V former, and the two split sides planed to an angle. The nodes, which protrude slightly on the enamel side, are then filed approximately flush, and now the eighteen strips are ready for straightening. If the bamboo had been sawed into strips—as is the case with many high-quality rods made by larger concerns—this step would not be necessary. But Tonkin cane grows straight once in a blue moon; normally, split cane sections veer off a few degrees at each node, and it is at these awkward natural joints that the rodmaker sets to work.

Fortunately, bamboo has very plastic qualities when heated to a certain, rather high temperature. By holding the node over a small lamp and turning it carefully to prevent burning or charring, bamboo may be straightened by applying moderate pressure, and the strip will hold its shape after it has cooled.

The straightened strips are then heat-treated to give them the extra steely quality that even well-seasoned cane does not possess. It would be easier to do this baking after they had been planed to size, but the process causes some shrinkage that might make the final rod thinner than planned. It is best to heat-treat before planing even though the extra hardness will make the planing a bit more difficult.

Hours of this delicate work make all six pieces of each section alike to within one-thousandth of an inch. The strip is placed into a V form which has caliper adjustments every several inches; all six pieces comprising that section are cut flush to the form. Only two sides of the strip may be worked

on. A cut off one side. Turn the strip. A cut off the other. Near the end of this process, the enamel, which has no power, is removed with one clean stroke. No further planing on the rind side is permissible on a fine rod.

From the artisan's point of view, the rod is now done; its final action and feel have been fully imprinted into the bamboo. Of course, there are many hours of work left: glueing and pressure-winding the strips, trueing them up, seating of the ferrules, fitting the grip and reel seat, winding and fixing the guides, and three coats of varnish. But though it must be meticulously done, all this is journeyman's work.

A top rodmaker says it takes him a minimum of twenty-five hours to make a rod. Working hours—not counting the hours and days he must wait for glue or varnish to set. I think he's underestimating his labor considerably.

When you consider that the top custom-made trout rods sold for as little as $100 only ten years ago, the economics of fine rod-making seems incredible. Without figuring in the rent, the materials, or the tools, the finest craftsmen in the field were probably making less than $4 an hour!

But these are proud and devoted men. You stand in line for a rod. Often you have to wheedle and cajole. I know one board chairman of a huge company who waited a year and a half for his nine-foot salmon rod. Finally he called the rodmaker and approached the matter with tact. He was told, "I haven't had time to start it yet. I'll call you when it's ready."

Another builder, troubled by telephone interruptions, calmly ripped the old-fashioned receiver off the wall and went on about his business.

It was a fine, monastic life, at four dollars an hour.

The trade cannot possibly survive; the rods, and the tradition, do. ◉

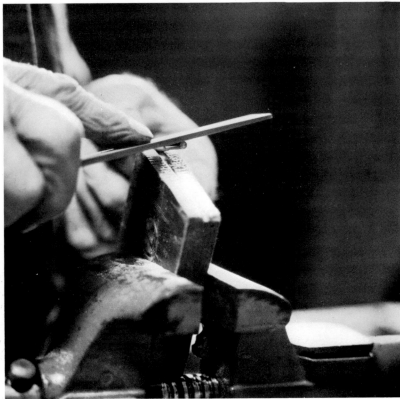

*Crafting the modern
rod: Precision cutter replaces
handwork in splitting;
planing and filing have not
changed in century.
Hands deftly planing (above)
are those of "Hap" Mills,
a master builder in Leonard
shop and one of the few
young men in profession.*

In Search of Trout

by Roderick Haig-Brown

A
great angler
on the
sport that can never
grow old

Fish such as black bass, Atlantic salmon, dorado, bonefish, striped bass, muskies, tarpon, pickerel, or what have you, may be local fishermen's favorites. But for universal popularity and worldwide distribution there is no other fish to compare with the trouts. Trout are practically synonymous with angling, and there are few anglers who do not try for them sooner or later. Many will fish for nothing else during their entire angling lives, and most of these enthusiasts will go as far as funds and time will let them in search of trout fishing that is better or perhaps merely different in some small way from any they have known. If a trout fisherman must stay for a long time in a land where there are no trout, he will almost inevitably look into ways of introducing them; and as often as not he will find some way. Many trout fishermen turn to other fish from time to time, but most are inclined to think of these infidelities as rather questionable adventures—fishing, perhaps, but not really serious fishing.

There are many obvious reasons for the trouts' popularity. Trout are very elegant creatures, clean and graceful in form, usu-ally handsome or even beautiful in coloration. They are vigorous and active in performance, prompt and hearty feeders, and a delicacy on the table. They frequent, by preference, pleasant and beautiful places: charming meadow streams, hill torrents, river estuaries, the shoals and reedy shallows of mountain and lowland lakes. They are to be found at the edges of the sea and two miles above the sea among mountain peaks, in blue waters and brown waters and in waters so clear that the only colors are those of washed gravel and trailing weeds.

In addition to all this the trouts are, for the most part, dwellers in shallow water, usually feeding at or near the surface on a wide variety of fascinating aquatic insects, many of which are themselves very beautiful. They tend to be dainty and selective feeders and they learn quickly to beware of the shadow of man and all the delicate devices he creates for their deception. This naturally leads man on to further extravagances of cunning and ingenuity and so keeps the whole thing going.

The quest of trout started long ago with the brown trout of Europe. Well before the

fifteenth century he was recognized as the flyfisher's fish and, with the salmon, something of an aristocrat. Juliana Berners, after declaring the salmon "the moost stately fyssh that ony man maye angle to in fresshe water," complains that though "a gentyll fysshe…he is comborous for to take." She wastes no time after that: "The troughte for by cause he is a right deyntous fyssh and also a ryght feruente-byter we shall speke nexte of hym." Izaak Walton notes that "The Salmon is accounted the king of fresh-water-Fish" but calls the trout, without any hesitation, his favorite—"which I love to angle for above any fish." And so the glory grows through the angling works of the seventeenth and eighteenth centuries to the great flowering of the nineteenth century when writer after writer celebrated the trout's glory and precedence, and the sophisticated lore and techniques and equipment of the modern trout fisher took full form and shape.

While the brown trout was attaining his formidable position in the respect and affections of Old World anglers, American settlers were finding and celebrating a trout-like fish in the new world. That it turned out to be a char rather than a trout matters not at all. "No higher praise can be given to a salmonoid than to call it a char." Few fish have more dedicated admirers than has the eastern brook trout, and certainly there is none whose beauty has called forth more resounding praise. A description of the great speckled trout of Lake Edward and Lake Nipigon, wrought by E. T. O. Chambers around the turn of the century is typical: "Here…the American brook trout is found in his most gorgeous apparel. His whole being is aflame with burning passion and nuptial desire, which reveal themselves in the fiery flushes of deepest crimson upon his shapely sides and lower fins. The creamy white margins of the pectoral, anal and ventral fins distinctly mark the course of the fish in the dark water, and form a striking contrast to his olive-colored and vermiculated back and dorsal fin. Here, he has caught the varying tints of the submerged rocks, and of the forest-clad mountains which form the basin of the lake, and in the brilliant brocade of his spotted sides he reflects the gold of the setting sun, and the

Preceding pages: Roderick Haig-Brown angles for rainbow of British Columbia. Above: Labrador waits patiently as Haig-Brown adjusts rod.

*"Last summer I fished for a few days
in northern British Columbia, in wild waters . . .
whose possibilities had been little tested."*

purple sheen of the distant hills."

So much splendor in a single fish—yet that is the way anglers have felt and written about him time after time, celebrating also his strength and cunning and violent activity on the end of a line. And the brook trout *is* handsome as few fish are, a lover of clear, cold water and unspoiled streams. If he is less abundant than he once was, it is because he is less tolerant of civilization than other trout and perhaps more responsive to the flies and lures and baits of anglers.

As settlement advanced into the West and finally to the Pacific coast, two more trouts were discovered—the rainbow and the cutthroat. There are many other fish that are or have been called trout—the lake trout and the Dolly Varden, for instance, both of them chars. But it is on these four—brown, eastern brook, rainbow and cutthroat, with their several subspecies—that the trout fisherman's world is built.

All four have sea-running forms of great beauty and highest performance—the European sea trout, the sea-running eastern brook trout so abundant in Labrador, the winter and summer steelheads of the Pacific Coast, and the sea-run cutthroat of the Pacific Northwest. Each of these is a special experience, and most trout fishers go in search of them sooner or later. But trout fishing, in all its main traditions and development, is primarily a freshwater sport; it was so to Walton and Cotton, Halford and Skues, Theodore Gordon, George LaBranche, and Edward Hewitt.

The trouts are exacting creatures. They demand abundance of clear, well-oxygenated water; streams with clean gravel for their spawning, rich in insect life for their feeding; summer temperatures generally below 70°F; shade and shelter from the enemies that beset them, under rocks, under banks or in deep pools. They are at their best in water that is high in mineral content—the chalkstreams of Britain and France, the spring-fed limestone brooks of the eastern United States, the dry-country lakes of British Columbia and Idaho. Yet they thrive also, and often spectacularly, in swamp-water ponds and tea-colored burns, in the soft-water lakes and rushing creeks of high rainfall areas. They are exacting, yet also highly adaptable.

Of the four, the brown trout is the most cosmopolitan. Long established in Europe, from the British Isles to Yugoslavia and in every country between, he is now a well-assimilated resident in North America from coast to coast. In the southern hemisphere he is happily settled in Chile, Argentina, New Zealand, Australia, South Africa and probably in other countries with suitable waters. He is the wariest and wisest of the trouts, the most selective in his feeding and the most difficult to deceive by strictly honorable means.

The rainbow is almost as widely distributed, though he has given difficulty at times by disappearing, I suspect because a sea-running stock was introduced rather than a resident freshwater stock. He flourishes close to the equator, on the slopes of Mount Kenya, and twelve thousand feet up in the Andes at Lake Titicaca in Peru and seven thousand feet up at Lake Maule in Chile. He is incomparably the most active and violent of the trouts, as Theodore Gordon

recognized long ago in welcoming him to eastern streams. "A better game fish," he wrote, "does not exist...the rainbow leaps again and again and always runs downstream. Brown and brook trout almost invariably run up, at least their first run is up; but the rainbow, after throwing itself into the air, tears desperately down and you must follow if the fish is any size. Men not accustomed to this trout are apt to lose all the large fish they hook for some time. It fights to the last and when landed has scarcely a kick left in it."

The brook trout has not traveled so far, perhaps because of his preference for colder waters. But he has settled comfortably west of the Rockies and I have found him, large and handsome, in the rivers and lakes of Argentina.

The cutthroat remains the rarest and wildest of the trouts. The hatchery men, I am happy to say, have found him hard to handle; for that reason he has been little transplanted. He flourishes in eastern British Columbia, Idaho, Montana, and Wyoming as the Yellowstone cutthroat, black-spotted, with red-gold sides and a scarlet slash under his jaw. But I admire him most in his sea-running form, when he can be bright as a rainbow and wild as a rainbow, but with a sulky power all his own at the last.

Why do we search for these four fish so hard, so persistently, so obsessively? There are many obvious reasons. Some of us search constantly for trophy fish, those monster trout that make the record books and keep the taxidermists busy. Some search ever for that miraculous river where every cast brings a fine fish to the fly. Some of us are

in love with the gear—delicate yet powerful rod, smoothly balanced lines, leaders calibrated to turn over perfectly even into the wind, flies tied so elegantly that neither fish nor fisherman can resist them. Some of us are firmly and permanently in love with all the surroundings of trout streams or lakes—bird and animal life, trees and bushes, reeds and water grasses, gravel and rock and sand, the water itself, and the way it moves and sounds.

All of us take with us to the waterside some blending of all these loves and fascinations. But there is nearly always something else, too, more subtle and more complicated. We are hoping to create or re-create some ideal situation. This may vary from time to time, changing in its intensity or emphasis. But I am convinced it holds its general shape throughout a trout fisherman's life.

I was raised on a south-of-England chalk-

stream and by the time I was fourteen or fifteen my first ideal situation was firmly established in my mind. I sought it assiduously. A big fish (which meant anything over a pound) rising steadily, upstream of me and well away, probably close under a grassy bank or overhanging bushes. If I could cast a fly above him and have it float over smoothly and closely enough to bring a confident rise, the ideal was pretty well realized. If the fish was then firmly hooked and brought to bank, so much the better. But the ideal was in the scene and in the action up to the setting of the hook. What happened afterwards in those weed-choked streams was often anticlimactic and even a little untidy.

I had another ideal in time, dimly formed from the reading of many books about fishing: that of the downstream wet fly, sweeping across fast, broken water in a big stream,

the heavy strike and instantaneous first run of a big fish. This was realized almost as soon as I came to the Pacific Northwest, best of all in the rapids and runs of the Nimpkish River on Vancouver Island. Here I found three- and four-pound sea-run cutthroats and rainbows feeding in the white water. They were not numerous, but a hard day of wading and casting would yield me five or six fine fish, and for the first time I knew trout that would run line well down into the backing from the strike and jump half a dozen times before they were beached.

I was usually alone on these expeditions and I knew, even while I was camping under the great spruce trees or in one of the bridge-crew shelters up on the logging track, that I was realizing another ideal that would always be important to me. These were undiscovered waters from a flyfisherman's point of view, their possibilities no more than vague rumors in nearby logging camps. I had to learn the water and the way about it, find the fish and their preferences for myself. An eighteen-year-old enthusiast could scarcely have asked for more than that great gleaming river all to himself.

Big streams, heavy wading, fast water, and the wet fly became the standards of my fishing from then on. On the Nimpkish I had usually fished with two flies on my leader, one bright, one dark. I soon cut back to a single fly, but otherwise found little reason to change, even to catch fall-running coho salmon and winter steelhead. Much as I loved all these splendid things, though, I still carried my box of chalkstream dry flies wherever I went. Every so often I found myself recognizing something like the old ideal, the perfect dry-fly set-up. Whenever I did so I quickly profited by it, sometimes spectacularly. Once I saw sea-run cutthroats rising quietly along the shallow edge of a stream. Wading up outside them and casting in toward the overhanging alders I took six or eight perfect fish on a No. 16 olive dun in less than an hour. One July morning, at the edge of a fast run where a small stream came in at the head of a lake, I saw a big fish roll. He took a small English dry fly, as did three others, all big fish that had moved up from the deep lake to follow the sockeye salmon.

From chancing on such opportunities and putting them to use, it was a short step to looking for them and even trying to create them. I learned about hairwing dry flies and their floating qualities in fast and broken water. I searched riffles and runs and glides from downstream, with a fly dancing over the surface, instead of from upstream with a wet fly swimming under the surface. It was the old, original ideal, but grown much larger. Instead of the quiet interception of a fifteen- or sixteen-inch brown trout I was looking for the lazy, breathtaking roll of a ten-pound steelhead.

I am oversimplifying, of course. I have not abandoned wet-fly fishing, nor do I forget for a single moment the sharp pleasures of the sudden heavy pull and the first wild run away from the strike. When the conditions are right for this I take advantage of them with little hesitation. But the other thought is always in my mind, the moment when time stops utterly, that moment between the slow break of a powerful fish to the fly and the lifting of the rod to set the hook.

Chile and Argentina, the latter especially, have some of the finest wet-fly streams in the world, where big brown trout, rainbows, brook trout, and landlocked salmon live and feed under ideal conditions. I have fished many of these streams, by no means neglecting the wet fly. One of my favorite Chilean streams is the blue-water Petrohue, flowing out of Todos Los Santos Lake. It is a big stream, wild and tumbling over rock ledges and among great boulders. One can wade it with some confidence, because the footing is generally good. There are places where every lengthening of the cast, every step farther into the fast water, seems to bring another good fish, rainbow or brown. Yet I remember best of all a little spring-fed tributary forcing out from under the Osorno volcano, where trout were rising in weedy water among grassy islands. The water was shallow and very clear and the fish, in spite of their steady feeding, were wild and shy. I fished floating flies upstream with care and caution and had fair success there until one evening when nothing went right. I realized belatedly that the fish were nymphing, bulging the water with their backs and tails but never breaking to surface-feed. In what was left of the evening I took three good fish on the upstream nymph and promised myself to do much better the next day. Fifteen years have passed. I never did get back there, but I still remember that little side stream as a trout fisherman's ideal.

The Argentine pampas streams are superb, clean and brilliant, leaping and gliding and driving their way among the brown hills as I imagine the streams of the Rocky Mountain States did long ago. The Chimehuin is not least among them. I have waded into its rapids and taken two- and three-pound browns and rainbows almost at will on sunk flies, delighted by the ease of it and the wildness of the fish. But I remember best of all a long, narrow island that split the river, forcing a deep dark flow smoothly under a cut-bank. It was dry-fly water and nothing else, but I was certain no artificial fly had ever floated over it before. It was mid-day, with a high hot sun, and I saw no fish rise. Halfway up the glide, almost against the sharp break of the bank, a five-pound brown trout dimpled and took down a floating purple upright. Thirty or forty yards farther up a three-pound rainbow came to the same fly much less tidily, but he was just as securely hooked.

The magnificent Martinez Pool lies just below the junction of the Liucura and Trancura Rivers in Chile. It is enormous. It holds many fish and some very big ones. The two rivers burst in at the head with a rush that only gradually subsides through the quarter-mile length of the pool. The water is deep on both sides, so wading is difficult and limited, and I have never been there when it was not windy. It is logical to fish a wet fly there and I have done so with good effect. But the lower half of the pool, its relatively smooth surface marked here and there by great sunken boulders, tempts the dry-fly enthusiast in spite of its difficulties. Fish rise here and there, and a dozen different places promise smooth exciting floats—if they can be reached.

I have never managed to do things just the way I think they should be done in the Martinez Pool, though I have taken some nice fish there on floating flies. My sharpest memory of the pool is focused on a huge rock that just breaks the surface of the water near the tail of the pool, thirty or forty yards out from the north bank; a McKenzie yellow caddis sliding along it, floating high; a long, gleaming bar of silver, twisting slightly to catch the light, seen momentarily against the dark rock; the fly gone, my rod raised into solid resistance, another gleam of silver and the fly coming back to me. The rainbows are very bright in the Martinez Pool and this one was a full ten pounds.

So we search for trout in many ways and many places, each of us, I suspect, with some secret inward vision, subconscious as often as not, of what trout fishing really is. We will settle for less, often much less, and we may even find other, unexpected experiences more brilliant than the one we seek. I have many friends who never stop traveling in search of trout. They speak to me of Alaska and Africa, of Normandy, Czechoslovakia, Yugoslavia, of Scandinavia and Tierra del Fuego, of trout in Ceylon and Kashmir and Colorado, in New Zealand and New York State. They are all enthusiasts and, though I know some of their individual special enthusiasms, I would not try to guess the ideal that each one surely carries in his mind.

Frederick Halford believed he was not trout fishing unless he was casting to a rising fish the most perfect imitation he could create of the natural fly that the fish was feeding on. Few of us choose to limit pleasure so narrowly. Yet there is something of this spirit in all trout fishermen. We aim for the natural, unsuspecting response which tells us that everything—choice of water, approach, cast, leader and fly—has been perfectly planned and executed. But if we are sometimes short of perfection and the results are good anyway, we accept them happily enough.

Last summer I fished for a few days in northern British Columbia, in wild waters far from roads, whose possibilities had been little tested. The weather was bad even in early August, with snowstorms in the mountains, mudslides and night frosts along the river. Yet I felt again all the dawn-fresh excitements of discovery that I had known forty years ago.

Here, in the calm outlet of a stormy lake, rainbow trout and Arctic grayling were rising. The fish were bright and clean, fourteen to sixteen inches long for the most part, by no means suicidal, but easy enough to rise and hook. In the upper pool, as often as not, a five- or six-pound Dolly Varden came up to chase the hooked fish wildly through the shallows.

Nineteenth-century British cartoon spoofs ineptitude and awkwardness of gentlemen anglers. Caption advised, "Be quiet & go a-Angling." It was part of the McLean Collection of Caricatures.

Later, down along a big river, storm-swollen and thick with silt, there was a sliver of clean blue water from an entering creek. Grayling rose there, faithfully and accurately, to small flies that danced on the broken water. Grayling are not trout and they do not fight like trout. But they are as beautiful as any fish that swims and I often think trout could learn a good deal from them about surface feeding and honest response to a well-presented artificial.

At the head of the big river is a small lake, more than four thousand feet above sea level, the mountains around it seeming like low hills in spite of the summer snow on their slopes. A good stream enters at the head of the lake, straight from the glaciers and snowfields, across a flat cut up by tracks of woodland caribou, moose, wolves, and grizzlies. The stream was high and milky with storm water, but good-sized rainbows were jumping again and again where it entered the lake. I had only a little while to fish, so I used some of it to put up two rods, one with a sinking line. Then I offered the jumping fish a dry fly, as was only fair and reasonable. They jumped on, paying not the slightest attention to it, which did not surprise me. I offered them a credible wet fly, a sedge of some kind, still on the floating line. They were not interested. I turned to the other rod, which had a No. 6 Silver Doctor to go with the sinking line. Even so, I had to get it well down. But once I had the depth there were fish at every cast, strong, deep-bodied, splendidly clean rainbows of sixteen and eighteen inches that jumped like the wild things they were.

Later in the year I fished for a few short days in Wyoming and Montana. It was too early, I was told. Stream temperatures were too high and the big fish had not moved up from the reservoirs. I caught some smallish cutthroat-rainbow hybrids in a small but beautiful stream in Wyoming and a few more impressive fish from the big rivers of Montana. But fish were scattered and hard to find. Then, one late afternoon, I found myself on the bank of a spring-fed meadow stream, a tributary of the Madison, under a high hot sun. Only the water was cool, and very clear, rippling across flats and around great banks of tight green weed, gurgling along curving cut-banks, flat and smooth in the eddies. A few mayflies were coming down and a much larger hatch of at least three different types of sedge was just starting. Trout were rising, quietly and efficiently, and though none looked large I knew there were big fish in the stream.

I went to work cautiously, keeping well down, throwing a No. 16 fly on a 5X leader. Three fish came short to it before I hooked a pretty little ten-inch brown. I was satisfied then that they were no fools and began trying to match the two smaller sedges that were hatching.

Nothing was easy, but when I did everything right I rose and hooked fish. Time passed swiftly and soon the sun was touching the mountain-tops. I had released eight or ten fish, all browns, none over fourteen inches, most of them around ten inches. But the sedge hatch was on the water now and fish were rising everywhere. I missed two

and hooked two in a roily piece of water below a small island. It was dusk by then and a good fish rose in backwater above the island. I made three perfect casts in succession to the spot, laying my leader over a weed bank. Nothing happened.

In a glide tight under the curve of the far bank I saw a tiny rise and put my fly a foot above it, brushing the grasses. The tiny rise came again and my fly disappeared. I struck and moved back from the bank fast. The fish ran upstream, taking line from the reel with a firmness and speed that commanded respect. Then he turned and came back, very fast, spreading heavy ripples over the smooth, dark surface. I recovered fast, but there was no fish there, only the fly.

As I dried off the fly there was another tiny rise, thirty or forty feet farther up against the grasses at the edge of the same glide. I covered it, the fish rose, I struck — and a four-inch brown trout came flying through the air toward me.

There was time to rise and lose one more good fish, then it was dark and time to go. It was only later I realized that there, in the range lands of Montana, under the high mountains, I had fished an evening rise exactly like those of the gentle streams of my youth.

Of such things as these, and many others, are a trout fisherman's days and ways. It is a sport that can never grow old. We follow the traditions, but do not hesitate to bend and twist them to our needs. We dream dreams and make plans and nearly always fail in the execution of them. We surprise ourselves often, perhaps because we know so little about it all, perhaps because we are such simple souls. But wherever we go in the world we find other men speaking the same language, planning the same plans, dreaming the same dreams. And one of the big four — brownie or brookie, cutthroat or rainbow — is the cause of it all. ◉

Elk

There are more today than ever before,
but stalking them takes stamina,
and the hunter must have a well-tuned ear
for the language of the bugle.

by Bob Hagel
Photography by Bill Browning

*In sheltered
valleys, elk browse on
winter pasture.
Quaking aspen, favorite
food, seldom matures
on elk range. With
spring come spotted
calves, and for
males the shedding
of antlers.*

Bull caught napping. Cow and calf may not be his. No family ties follow mating; bulls usually stay aloof and wary, but close to herd.

It had been a long, hard day. I had started from camp just as the first pale light seeped into the high, sub-alpine basin. The day had turned unusually warm for early October at this elevation in central Idaho. As the sun rose over the peaks to the east, the elk had deserted their nighttime feeding grounds on the open slopes for the shade of heavy timber on the north faces and cool basins.

There is but one way to find elk on such a day: Hunt them where they sleep—the way a cougar does—and hope for the best. In this area, as in most of the elk ranges of the West, this means crawling for miles through, around, over, and under miles of dead and toppled lodgepole pine. Large sections of the blow-down are interlaced with jack-alders that bring a curse from even the most mild-tempered elk hunter. I had fought this tangle of brush and logs through the steep canyons and into the basins, where I drifted silently down benched ridges onto the bedgrounds. I'd found a lot of old tracks but no live elk. The only game I'd seen was a family of spruce grouse that trustingly walked along the logs to within a few feet of me, casting bright, questioning glances and talking in low, twittering tones. I always have time to stop and spend a few minutes with these friendly little inhabitants of the elk ranges. Setting up the camera with a telephoto lens, I took a few shots, then moved slowly on in quest of elk.

Now the sun was sliding down its deep blue path toward the western ridges. I was tired, tired almost to the point where I didn't care if there

A bugled challenge
met: Bull in foreground
deferred, losing
harem rights. Twenty
or thirty cows
are commonly the stake
in these hammering
but seldom fatal duels.

*Right: A bugle
from the herd bull.
Females and
rival bulls respond
(below). Primed to fight,
bull (right bottom)
vents anger on sapling.
Broken branches,
hoof marks alert hunter
that elk is near.*

were any elk between me and the camp that was five up-and-down miles away. I knew that off to the left of the trail I was taking back to camp there was a basin—a high basin rimmed with cliffs, with plenty of dense timber for daytime shade, sedge-covered slopes for feed, and the little streams and bog-holes elk love so well. Slowly I worked through the limber pine and alpine fir that were casting long shadows along the slope. When I got to the rim overlooking the basin I settled down on the mat of pine needles with my back against a tree.

Sitting midway along the horseshoe rim of cliffs that formed the head of the basin, I had the whole scene in view. The cliffs dropped down for per-haps three hundred feet to the basin floor, which sloped away in a series of

benches. The upper benches were covered with a mixture of elk sedge and bunch grass. From the toe of the slope tiny spring-fed streams sparkled between brilliant green moss-covered boulders. The lower benches of the basin were heavily timbered with spruce and alpine fir, and here and there a golden splash of aspen added color. The light updraft of evening air brought with it the wonderful odor of autumn.

There might not be any elk in this basin, but it was worth all of the sweat and effort it had taken getting here just to be able to sit and relax in the warm afternoon sun and devour a scene that few people ever see.

There was no sound from below, not even the call of a jay or the swish of a breeze-tossed branch. It seemed a shame to break the tranquility, but I

was here to hunt elk; there should be elk in the basin, and a few notes on the bamboo whistle might stir something up. Almost reluctantly, I raised the bugle and sent a challenge drifting down into the timber to any bull that might be shaded-up there. As the last shrill note of the bugle died away, there came an answering blast. The challenge started in deep-throated tones, seeming to start far down in the lungs, rising, changing from note to note, to end in a high-pitched, near scream. No youngster, this bull. Only the big herd bulls produce that kind of bugle.

The bull had bugled from far down the basin just inside the heavy timber. If he came out into the open at this point he'd be more than five hundred yards from where I sat, farther than one should shoot if there is any chance of getting closer. From the sound of things, he wasn't about to take any backtalk from the upstart on the rim. He'd come out all right, no doubt about that, maybe too soon. If I didn't get within decent shooting range fast, he might decide that this was not a legitimate challenge and drift back into the heavy stuff.

I eased back off the rim into the timber and headed for a rock point that jutted out above the bull. My weariness had dropped away. My feet suddenly were light, my senses turned to every sound, smell, and movement. As I slipped along as fast as possible behind the cover of the rim, the big bull continued his uproar in the basin below. Once I peeped from behind a bushy pine and saw him come out of the timber, head low, and long six-point antlers swinging menacingly from side to side. A few feet out in the open he stopped, lifted his nose until the ivory-tipped back points of his antlers swept his ribs, and another bugle echoed against the cliffs. I gave a timid answer and headed once more for the point, wondering if the bull would stay until I made it.

A few minutes later as I crawled out onto the point above the bull, he was still going strong. He had found that a small limber pine gave him something on which to vent his rage. As I got into position for the shot, some three hundred yards away, he alternately fought the bushy little pine and sent forth his challenge. For several minutes I sat and watched the great bull bellowing and pawing the ground as he horned the tree and sent limbs and bark flying. At last he tired of the mock-battle, looked up at the rim, saw nothing, and, turning slowly, started back into the timber. I knew I'd have to take him before he made the timber. One shrill note on the bugle stopped the bull broadside in the open. The cross hair settled up near the top of his back at the rear edge of the shoulder, and the .333 O.K.H. Belted sent a

250-grain bullet on its way. The bull collapsed without a kick.

→≫≪←

It is unlikely that the first buckskin-clad white men who hunted the rough, mountain country where most elk are hunted today found many elk to shoot. In fact, there were far fewer elk than inhabit those same regions now. According to the diaries left by the Lewis and Clark expedition, and the few records left by trappers and fur traders, the wapiti was mostly an animal of the plains and foothills. Lewis and Clark mention seeing very few elk (and killing none) after entering the rough country near the headwaters of the Missouri, along what is now the Idaho-Montana line, on their trek to the West Coast. They had encountered huge herds farther to the east in the plains-foothill country, and would see others on the lower Columbia River, near where Astoria now stands. But the great Rocky Mountains contained few elk.

Later, as civilization spread westward, the plow turned the prairie sod, grain grew where grass once waved, and fences pushed the elk from its chosen range back into the mountains. Cattle and domestic sheep moved ever deeper into the elk pastures. Market hunters killed elk for meat for the mining camps, as well as for their teeth. There was a time, not long ago, when *Cervus canadensis* seemed about to go the way of the bison.

But the wapiti is an adaptable animal, and has responded well to conservation efforts. With a little good management of its remaining herds, and transplants from the reservoir of Yellowtone Park, it has thrived and spread. Today elk are probably distributed in greater numbers throughout the mountain wilderness areas than at any time since the white man arrived on the continent.

Within the past few years planted elk herds have offered limited hunting east of the Mississippi. They again roam the moun-

Leaving river bottom after nocturnal feeding in timber, elk wend upward on worn switchback trail.

grazed, the elk can be, and often is, its own worst enemy. If allowed to increase under too stringent protection, it will literally eat itself out of house and home. Anyone who yearns for complete protection of an elk herd so that large numbers of the big animals can be seen from the paved highway, should sometime have to see the elk on an overstocked winter range as they starve to death an inch at a time—see the calves with stomachs bursting from eating browse too coarse to be digested; cows that are heavy with calf bound to the creek bottoms, too weak to move to better range; and even the largest bulls staggering from bush to bush, where countless elk have fed before leaving nothing but bare stems, to finally drop, a pile of bones covered with hide, never to rise and bugle again. It is not a pretty picture. Neither is it rare, and it will surely happen to any elk herd that is not properly harvested.

The wapiti is gregarious, and this habit of "togetherness" brings large concentrations to favored winter ranges as soon as snow starts to pile up in the high country. They are also animals of strong habit. Once migration routes are established to and from winter ranges, they continue to use them year after year. Thus, a range once depleted is hard to bring back into production, and no elk herd can be larger than the winter range will support.

As spring breaks and the snow line creeps back toward the heights, the elk follow closely. They love the tender new grass and forbs that spring up behind the retreating snow. For the most part the bulls and cows have been separated since the end of the rut the previous fall, and now the bulls usually precede the cows on the upward drift.

Some bulls, particularly the older ones, will have lost their antlers by early March, but many young bulls will wear theirs as late as early May. That is why many shed elk antlers are found at rather high altitudes—

tains of the Southwest, from the rim of the Grand Canyon in northwest Arizona to the Gila Wilderness of southwest New Mexico. The big animals are apparently increasing as far north as the Prophet and Muskwa river country of British Columbia. And you can hunt elk, along with brown bears, on Alaska's Afognak Island, where it is claimed that the wapiti attains greater weight than on any other range in the world.

Yes, the wapiti is indeed adaptable, and it will increase with great rapidity. In fact, with the limited amount of winter range available since nearly all of the desirable valley land has been fenced, tilled, and

and why it is often wrongly assumed that elk wintered there. Most have been dropped by bulls on their return to summer ranges.

As summer advances and the days become warmer, the cows head for the calving grounds, where they usually return year after year. Here each cow will have a single calf. Twins are very rare. These calving grounds are usually at quite high elevations in or near the summer range. After calving is over, usually by mid-June, the elk will spread out into smaller bunches and drift toward the highest basins. The bulls will already have moved on into summer pastures—pastures with plenty of water, heavy timber for shade, and mountain meadows that furnish the feed necessary to give them the fat and vitality they must have before the rut begins in early September.

During the hot summer months, the bulls and cows see little of each other. The cows are occupied raising their spotted calves, frightening summer's hordes of flies and mosquitos, and filling their winter-starved bellies with the lush food of the high country.

The bulls laze around in small bunches, two or three, maybe half a dozen together. They are growing their antlers, a process that consumes tremendous amounts of energy and which is completed in as little as three months—between mid-May (for late starters) and mid-August. During this relatively brief time the antlers grow to a huge size and the bulls are enervated. They feed a lot, sleep a lot, and take care of those tender, velvet-covered horns. This is the time of companionship and lazy contentment, a time to grow fat and fill out the winter-shrunk muscles that must be strong enough to carry them through the marathon.

In the summer months the elk, like its smaller cousins of the deer family, turns red with the growing of its short summer coat after the long winter hair has been shed. As fall approaches, this short summer hair will in turn be shed and replaced with the yellow-brown body coat and near-black neck and mane. It is during this transformation that the calves lose their spots.

By the middle of August the bulls begin

Tender in velvet, bulls recline. Their antlers grow quickly, fed by the blood-rich membrane.

to get restless. Their antlers are now fully developed; the blood stops circulating in them and they harden. The velvet—the hairy skin that has protected them during growth —loosens and hangs in long streamers. The bulls finish the shedding process by rubbing the antlers on trees and brush, removing the velvet and polishing the hardened antlers in preparation for the fighting to come.

The actual time when elk will go into the rut may vary somewhat from year to year and section to section. Exactly why this variation occurs I do not know; perhaps weather conditions have something to do with it. I have heard the bulls start to bugle as early as the last week in August, but generally they start around the first of September.

Of course, the fact that some of the bulls are bugling does not mean that they are actually in the rut, or that they are even gathering their harems of cows, or that they will come to the bugle of another bull. For several days before the rut gets under way in earnest, the bulls that have been together all summer will separate and start wandering singly. They bugle in the early morning and late evening and are always restless, though they still spend much time bedded during the middle of the day. They work around the edges of the herds of cows, but seem to ignore them, and they do not yet fight each other.

This may go on as late as the middle of September. A few years ago I made a trip into Yellowstone Park to photograph elk at the start of the rut, and I chose the second week of September as the right time to be there. When I arrived in the Indian Creek section, where a large part of the northern herd summers, I found that while they were bugling in the early morning and late evening there was not a single mature bull with any of the many herds of cows. In the back country, where most of the elk were, I was hard pressed to bugle a bull or two up to camera range in the short time between the first evening answers and the time the sun dipped behind the peaks bordering Bighorn Pass. By September 16, those bulls were still not paying court to the cows or making war with their summertime companions. They bugled, but mostly to exercise their lungs.

Usually elk stop bugling by about the end of the first week in October, though I have heard them going strong beyond the middle of the month. Occasionally a bull will bugle very late in the fall or early winter, but it usually comes from being suddenly startled and is not a true bugle.

It is doubtful if there is a more polygamous animal than the elk, and when they do go into full rut, the big herd bulls gather and herd as many cows as they are physically capable of caring for. As soon as a bull gathers a few cows, there is bound to be some other big bull around who will dispute his right to them. The only way the herd bull can keep his harem is to whip the rival, and run him off to look for greener pastures.

Whipping every big bull that attempts to usurp his place is only part of the herd bull's troubles. There are always several small bulls hanging around the edge of any large herd, and as soon as the herd bull is engaged in battle with some other big bull, or has bluffed him (as is often the case), and is running him away, the small bulls dash in and try to make off with any cow that they can round up. When the herd bull finally gets rid of his competitor, often with heaving flanks and bloody shoulder, he is faced with the new problem of putting several young upstarts in their place.

If there is a more wonderful sound than the bugle of a mature bull elk, I have yet to hear it. I am still stirred by those long, quavering notes as they drift up from the timber of some alpine basin into the sunset—and I have heard them thousands of times.

There seems to be much confusion regarding methods of bugling elk, what results to expect, and even how the typical bugle of a mature bull sounds. This is understandable, since the age and temper of the bull at the time of bugling, the time of day, the weather, and the stage of the rut, all variables, may well affect the call of the elk.

The typical bugle of a mature bull is one of three to five notes. This is the challenge call sent out for all to hear, not the sound of battle. The first note will be almost a grunt, a low note which rises and breaks to a higher note, which rises to a still higher, very shrill note. Usually this high note is the climax of the call and is drawn out for several seconds. At times, when some old bull is just calling for the pure delight of making himself heard, he will go back down the first two notes after reaching the high pitch, making five notes in all. There may be some variation of this, but it is the basic call.

To the seasoned elk hunter, it is easy to tell if the bugle you hear comes from an old bull or a young one. The old bulls bugle in much deeper tones and the whole is usually of longer duration than the high-pitched tones of a young bull. Some of the oldtimers will bray more like an overgrown jackass than an elk. A yearling or spike bull will bark more like a cow, or perhaps squeal; the two-year-olds don't do much better, but do manage a few squeals and wails. These young bulls trying to bugle remind me of a young rooster.

The hunter who has bugled many elk can tell not only if the bull is old or young by the sound, he can also tell a herd bull from a singleton bull of similar age and size that is in search of cows.

The clues are clear. If a bull is looking for a herd of cows, or for a fight, he is almost sure to start toward the bugle's sound, answering as he comes. If he is a bull that already has a harem, he is busy enough chasing smaller bulls away, and won't leave his cows unguarded to go pick a fight with some other bull. He will answer, yes, but he'll do it

where he can keep an eye on the harem. You have to go to him. If he continues to answer your efforts, stays in one place, but does not come, it is safe to assume he is a herd bull.

But if he answers a few times, then drifts away, it may be for a number of reasons. It is quite possible that he has already been duped by some other hunter and is suspicious. Or he may have just been whipped soundly by some other bull; while he'll grumble and talk fight, he just hasn't the stomach for any more at the moment. If he just bugles once or twice, then quits, he's simply not interested in fight or frolic, and there is no use trying to keep him going.

Even during the heat of the rut you can't be certain that the bulls will be bugling on any given day. They may bugle steadily for a week, then cut off for no apparent reason. Weather likely has something to do with this, but I've never figured out a pattern; they may bugle during a storm and stop as soon as it clears, or they may stay quiet while the storm is on, then start up when it's over.

They usually do most bugling from daylight until sunup, and from an hour before sundown until dark, but they will also bugle all day and all night. One thing for sure, if you want an answer, the best time to get one is when you hear them first. However, I've started them going when I hadn't heard a bugle in hours.

As for calling technique, time and conditions are the key. If you want to start bulls, or answer a lone call you have just heard, give with the three long notes, concentrating on the last one. Or you can go back down the scale through the first two. Then, when you have a bull going, mimic him. What this means in elk talk, I don't know, but it must be pretty outrageous, because a bull that is mimicked will usually charge right up to you, looking for a fight.

Many times I have bugled only to be answered by another hunter. Ordinarily, an experienced hand can tell the real thing, but at times distance and the skill of the other hunter make it difficult to be sure. A long conversation in "elk talk" may be carried on before either party is aware of the mistake.

During the rut, the bulls may make fools of themselves by blasting off and letting everyone know where they are, but after the stimulus has receded, their natural intelligence takes over and elk hunting gets tough.

While some bulls will be found with the cows after the rut has passed, most of them pull off by themselves or in twos and threes, and now, whether you hunt bulls or cows, you see the other side of elk hunting. They have now returned to the high country from the well-watered creek bottoms where they moved during the early part of the rut. As the weather grows colder, they spend more time in the ridges and less time in the canyons, unless forced there by hunting pressure.

The high, sub-alpine basins and autumn-brown mountain meadows are their feeding grounds, and the curing elk sedge is their main diet. They will feed these openings during the night, coming out anywhere from around sundown until dark, and they will leave the open just as the first ray of the morning sun hit it.

If they have been hunted earlier, they will be extremely alert and hard to catch unaware. When they leave the feeding grounds they head off into the heavy timber of some north-facing mountainside. They find a bench, usually on some spur ridge, where they bed for the day. They position themselves so that they can watch for and hear any approach on their back-trail, and where one long jump can get them out of sight.

Personally, I prefer to find a feeding ground, pick a spot within range, then wait for the elk to show just before dark or just after daylight. With a good long-range rifle, the hunter will often be able to sit and watch from the opposite side of the canyon and, when the elk appear, take plenty of time to pick the one he wants and make a good, clean kill. This kind of hunting is especially important to the trophy hunter, as it gives him a chance to be sure that the antlers are of the quality he must have before he shoots. Stalking elk in the heavy stuff makes it hard to size up antlers, and rarely permits placing the bullet in the right spot for a quick, humane kill. In the open you can make a fairly good estimate of an animal's equipment.

Judging record-class trophy elk antlers requires a practiced eye, due to the great size of the antlers as well as the large size of the animal. Then, too, there are different types of heads, some having a decided backward curve from the fourth point back, and some tending to be straighter on the beam. The straighter antlers appear to be longer than those deeply curved, often they are not.

Begin by learning the standards an elk head must meet to give the minimum Boone and Crockett Club score of 360 points that puts it in the book. First, most of the high-scoring heads have seven points on the side, and even if they have only six, they must normally have a length of main beam of

Placid cow is object of feisty mate's attentions.

better than 50 inches. Second, and perhaps next most important, all points must be very long and uniform in length on both sides. Third, antlers must be heavy in the beam. Spread should be at least 40 inches; the wider it is, the higher the head's score.

Remembering that a mature bull will stand 66 inches at the shoulders, you can get some idea of the length of his antlers by comparing them with his shoulder height, especially if you can see him feeding with his nose on the ground. The length of his head from horn base to end of nose will run 16 inches or more, so you'll have to subtract this from shoulder height in determining beam length. You can also use the length of his head to judge the length of the points.

The first and second points should look as long as his head from the base of the horn to the end of the nose, which will make them run close to 20 inches if they have normal curve. If the third points are two-thirds as long as the first or brow points, they are good. The fourth points, or royal or sword points as they are often called, should be very long, at least 20 inches, and heavy at the bottom.

When we consider the back points—the fifth and sixth points on a six-point bull—it becomes obvious why few six-point bulls make the book. Those that do must have a lot of main beam between the base of the fourth point and the fork of the fifth and sixth points, and these two back points will have to be very long. You can guess their length by the distance between the tips and the angle of the fork.

The heavier the main beam and the points are, the better the head will look on the den wall and the better it will score. The length of the points on opposite sides will have to be quite even, and not just for the sake of symmetry; if they are not even, the penalty will subtract many points from the total score.

Spread on an elk is very difficult to judge accurately, but again, the height at the shoulder will help some, and the fact that a big bull will measure about three feet from hairline of shoulder to hairline of brisket. A spread of 48 inches is good, but remember that the official spread is taken on the inside of the main beam at the widest point, not at the widest outside point.

One thing for sure: You will not be able to accurately judge elk heads that are rapidly departing over down logs and through brush, so take care not to spook your bull.

When the stalk is finished, or the bull has been bugled into sight, when the chips are at last all played, the success of the hunt depends on the rifle you pack and your ability to use it. And no matter how well you can shoot, your rifle had better be capable of doing the job well if you don't want that helpless, sick feeling that comes with the wounding of a noble animal.

What are the best calibers and cartridges for hunting elk? The opinions are as varied as those on the best breed of dog for grouse.

A mature bull elk is a big animal by any standard. He will stand from 62 to 66 inches at the shoulder, and weigh around a thousand pounds; he has heavy muscles and big bones. There have been thousands of elk killed with small, light bullets from cartridges of inadequate power, but that doesn't make them ideal for elk hunting.

Since much of the shooting in the mountain West is in partly open country—and often across some canyon at an unknown range—the ideal elk rifle should use a cartridge of flat trajectory to assure vital long-range hits. On the other hand, you may have to stalk him in heavy cover where the ideal shot will not present itself, and the bullet may have to plow through a lot of tough elk to reach the vital organs. This requires a long heavy bullet that will give deep penetration.

The ideal elk cartridge, therefore, should be capable of handling a bullet of good sectional density (roughly, bore-weight rela-

Six-point rack carries brow and bez ("bay") tines, trez ("tray"), royal, and two sur-royals.

tion) at high velocity. This would eliminate anything smaller than the .270 Winchester with the 150-grain bullet for all hunting conditions. Personally, I like something larger. Of the smaller calibers, the 7mm Magnums stand at the top with bullets of 160 to 175 grains in weight. The .30/06 with bullets of from 180 to 220 grains will do a good job, and the various .300 Magnums are much better. In fact, the big 7's and the big .30's are tops for all-around elk hunting. The .338 Winchester and the .340 Weatherby Magnum cartridges are excellent elk stoppers, but not every hunter can handle the kind of recoil they put out. Remember, if you can't hit 'em, you sure as hell can't kill 'em. It is better to use a smaller cartridge with less recoil and put that bullet in the right place, than it is to put the bullet from a big one somewhere around the edges.

Of all of the various kinds of elk hunting —and I like to hunt elk under all conditions— the most appealing is the hunt during the rut in late September and early October. It is not only the marvelous melody that is the bugle of a bull elk, but the very fact of being there to hear it. It is to hear the raucous call of the Clark nutcracker as he swoops from tree to tree prying open the cones of the limber pine to reach the nuts inside. It is to see the sparkle of a million diamonds as the sun first touches the frosted grass in early morning, and to feel the slanting rays of the sun warm on your back at midday.

To smell the scents of autumn, the odor of curing grass, decaying wood, and dying leaves, and the smell of the sun on pine needles. To be there when the leaves of the quakies turn to gold, and the mountain maple takes a touch of crimson. Color is there for a day, a week, and all nature rejoices in that brief time before the snows of winter.

To know the companionship of a good hunting partner in the lonely elk camp at the end of the day. And to sit by a roaring campfire with the sparks whirling, climbing, drifting off into the darkness that envelops the great, silent land of the wapiti. ◉

FISHING DEEP FOR BASS

The trick is how to go where the fish congregate. ■ by Grits Gresham photography by Elgin Ciampi

The black bass is the most popular game fish in America. Millions of anglers fish for it each year, many of them being dedicated to this species to the exclusion of all others. For these sportsmen, no aspect of bass behavior or of bass-fishing tackle and technique is insignificant.

They talk about bass fishing at every opportunity; they read everything available about bass and bass fishing; they dream and plot and scheme of ways to outwit bass. They buy more artificial bass-fishing lures than are bought by all anglers with any other species in mind.

Despite all this, most of these fishermen fail to learn a fact about bass behavior which is tremendously important to their fishing success: Most bass are deep most of the time!

How deep is deep? This is a relative term, of course, but in the context of bass fishing the word "deep" is easily made meaningful. Most bass fishermen never fish a lure deeper than six or eight feet. Water beyond that depth range is, for our purposes, deep.

There are many accounts of anglers who have inadvertently allowed a lure to sink to the bottom in deep water, usually while untangling a backlash, and who have caught bass on the retrieve. By a peculiar quirk of human nature, most of them ignore the clue and resume their shallow fishing.

It frequently happens that these accidental catches are trophy fish, and this is understandable. Big bass adhere to deep-living behavior more rigidly than the bass population as a whole. It seems to be true that the larger the fish, the more reluctant he is to move into shallow water.

One reason for this is that bass, lacking eyelids, dislike high light intensities. Nor can they contract the pupils of their eyes to shut out light. Their alternative is to stay deep where light rays from the sun do not penetrate so intensely.

Another reason why bass go deep is to avoid becoming uncomfortably warm when the sun is bright and the water clear. As a cold-blooded animal, the fish tends to assume the temperature of his surroundings; but while the water temperature may be perfect for bass, the direct rays of the sun will force the fish to seek relief from the heat. The situation is similar to the one we all have experienced while riding in an automobile, where a leg or an arm catching the rays of the sun becomes uncomfortably hot although the air temperature is cool.

Sunlight has its greatest effect in driving bass deep in the summertime. This is natural, of course, for at this time of year water and air temperatures are higher, the rays of the sun strike the water more directly, and there are fewer cloudy, overcast days than in the winter, spring, and fall.

Bass can cope with light intensities and heat in ways other than by going deep. They can move into the shallows at night, and they can seek relief in the shade of logs, trees, banks, rocks, lily pads, and boat docks —as any bass fisherman knows.

There is another point about bass behavior which complements the deep-living habit and is of equal or even greater importance to the bass fisherman. It is the fact

Preceding pages: Gaping largemouth hits plug. Vibrating nylon line shot at slow speed seems heavier than it is.

that bass, when they are deep, gather in tightly knit concentrations. Hitting one is a ten-strike, but finding it can be a nightmare. Where there are concentrations, there inevitably are substantial areas of the lake where few, if any, bass exist. The angler who fishes a lake in homogeneous fashion, therefore, expecting to find bass distributed like trees in an orchard, is wasting most of his time.

Now let's add one other fact which is essential knowledge for the successful angler. Those concentrations of bass are on the *bottom* of the lake. Bottom is the key word. The fish aren't suspended in the water three or four feet off the bottom; they're on it! And to catch them you must fish your lures on the bottom—not two or three or four feet off the bottom.

In situations where bass are in the shallows, say, eight feet of water or less, they will frequently move all the way to the surface to take a plug. When they are in their deep-water concentrations this is not the case. Then you must bump the bottom.

The problem of the deep-water bass fisherman is twofold: to find the deep-water bass sanctuaries, and to effectively fish the bass when they're hugging the bottom of one of these lairs.

The sanctuary location frequently has typical characteristics that help a fisherman to find it. A composite would show a spot from twelve to twenty-five feet deep, which has a clean bottom; it is on a rather flat bench, and has quick and easy access to deeper water. It is often on an underwater ridge leading toward shore. Also favorable are any abrupt changes in the bottom contour of the lake. Ledges, reefs, bars, and submerged hilltops—these are the kinds of structures which attract bass in numbers.

Even an artificial structure can become a sanctuary. When digging a flood control canal some years ago, a contractor found a huge fallen tree. Rather than remove it, he had bulldozers cover it with dirt. He created a small underwater island, the top of which was about ten feet deep when the canal was filled with water. It became a hot spot for bass.

How hot? I watched a friend of mine catch fifteen bass on thirteen successive casts from the place, twice bringing in doubles. On another day, another friend and I caught more than sixty bass from this kitchen-size lair in less than three hours—without moving our boat.

Construction of hundreds of reservoirs across this nation has created perfect opportunities for deep-water bass prospecting. Many of the bends of the flooded river offer all of the ingredients of a typical sanctuary location. The sandbar which builds up on the inner side of many river bends provides that clean resting spot; it is on a ridge of sorts, else there would be no river bend. Bass which select such a sandbar as a lair have immediate access to deeper escape water by simply slipping over into the old river channel.

A point of land which juts out into a lake almost invariably has an underwater extension. At some point along this underwater

Indiscriminate diet of
voracious bass includes ducklings,
snakes, other fish—and frogs.

ridge bass can find the proper sanctuary conditions, and these are the easiest concentrations for the beginning bass prospector to find. Locate the ridge visually, then fish the bottom along it.

Trolling a deep-running lure is a good way to explore the bottom characteristics of a lake, and to fish the ridges for a bass concentration. Crisscross the ridge back and forth at various depths, making sure that your lure is bumping along the bottom each time. Take bearings by lining up each trolling pass with two objects on shore, so you can return to the same line if the trip is productive.

Where trolling is not legal, anchor your boat at various points along and to one side of the ridge and fish it by casting. Casting is usually necessary where the water is deeper than twenty feet, since it is very difficult to work a trolled lure along the bottom in greater depths.

Two tremendous aids to the bass prospector are the hydrographic map and the electronic depth finder. The map, by showing the underwater contours of the lake, indicates general areas where sanctuary possibilities exist. A sensitive depth finder pinpoints those possibilities more precisely.

With the best of these electronic sonar devices, such as the Fish Lo-K-Tor (Lowrance Electronics, 7809 E. Admiral Place, Tulsa, Oklahoma), you can actually "see" the fish.

Let me emphasize that the area a bottom-hugging bass school occupies may be as small as twenty-five square feet, and will average perhaps a hundred square feet. That five-by-

*Hooked bass are notable
for rugged resistance and wildly
explosive topside action.*

five or ten-by-ten spot is very difficult to locate, particularly if it is far from shore as is often the case. Keep in mind that if your lure fails to pass through that small area, you miss all the fish.

A small styrofoam marker is valuable in bass prospecting. Drop one overboard when you hook a bass while trolling, and use them to mark likely spots (or schools of fish) which show up on your depth finder.

The best lures for fishing the bottom are bucktails and jigs, spoons, weighted spinners, weighted pork eels, and weighted plastic worms. Some of my favorites are: bucktails and jigs—Upperman, Cordell, Doll Fly, Bass Buster, Glen L. Evans; spoons—Weber's Mr. Champ; weighted spinners—Johnny Reb, Rider, Spider, Hilderbrandt's "Jigolo," Heddon Machete, Shannon Twin Spinner; weighted pork eels—Petigo on a Cordell Weedless Bucktail, Lutz on a jig, bucktail, or weedless hook; floating deep-diving lures —Bomber, Whopper-Stopper's Hellbender; plastic worms—any of several brands.

There are times when each of these is best, but day in and day out the plastic worm is the most effective of the lot. More bass, and more big bass, have been caught in the past decade than ever before, and it is no coincidence that this is the period when the plastic worm came into use.

It is not practical to fish a multihook lure on the bottom of most lakes, simply because it too frequently snags on submerged trees, rocks, and other debris. Thus, in rigging a plastic worm for deep fishing, use a single hook.

Most of my deep fishing is done with a worm impaled on a leadhead jig. This jig is a hook with a lead weight molded around it near the eye, sometimes with a weedguard and sometimes without. There are many on the market. Two good ones are the Cordell Weedless Banana Head Jig and a Johnny Reb leadhead.

One trick we use to make a bare hook weedless is to bury the point of the hook back into the body of the plastic worm.

Use the lightest weight necessary to sink your worm to the bottom in a practical length of time. Most of the time this will be a one-eighth ounce, one-quarter ounce, or a three-eighths ounce—the deeper the water the heavier the weight.

Another method of rigging which is very effective in some situations is to place the weight on the line, using an unweighted hook for the worm. If the water is quite shallow, a split shot or buckshot pinched on the line about six inches from the hook does a good job. Some anglers use a sinker which will slide up and down the line, claiming that this has the advantage of allowing a bass to move off with the worm without feeling the weight.

That brings us to a key reason for the success of the plastic worm and to a technique of fishing them which is essential to that success. This is that the plastic worm is soft, flexible, and lifelike, so much so that bass will swallow it. Compare that to their reaction when they touch lures made of wood, plastic, or metal. Unless they're hooked immediately, they eject the lure

with amazing speed.

Bass seldom strike a plastic worm. They pick it up, mouth it a bit, usually move off a distance with it, and sometimes swallow it. The method of fishing a plastic worm, then, must obviously be different from the technique with other lures.

Fishing the worm is a game of feel, and to be skillful at it the fisherman must be able to visualize what is happening to his lure down in the depths of the lake. To learn how a worm lure feels when certain things are happening, he should practice fishing it in clear, shallow water where he can see as well as feel.

The bottom-bumping worm is fished by crawling, hopping, and twitching it along the lake bottom. Do this in that shallow water over various types of bottom formations, over sunken logs and trees and rocks, and there will soon be a link between what the worm is doing and what you feel through your hands on the rod.

For best results when fishing a worm down deep, your boat must be stationary. That calls for an anchor, and preferably one at each end of the boat if the wind is blowing. If the boat is moving you cannot distinguish between a bass taking the worm and the worm being dragged against something.

After making a worm cast, keep your rod at a forty-five degree angle while you let the worm sink to the bottom. While it's sinking, keep one hand on the rod handle and the other on the reel handle, since you can "feel" better by doing so. Your grip on rod and reel should be firm, but not tense.

Your line will go slack when the worm reaches the bottom. Hold your rod position for five or ten seconds. Lower your rod a foot or two while you reel in the slack line without moving the lure. Lift the worm with a slight sweep of the rod, then let it settle back to the bottom again.

Repeat the procedure until the worm is directly beneath your boat. Jiggle it a couple of times and, if nothing happens, reel in and make another cast.

There are obviously endless variations of retrieves—short sweeps and long sweeps, short pauses and long pauses. None of them works best all the time, which means that you should experiment until you find the right formula for the day.

While the worm is sinking, after you make a cast, watch your line. If you see it move suddenly to one side or the other, take up slack and set the hook, for a bass has taken it on the way down.

The feel when a bass takes a worm is just about what you would imagine. It's like a bass nibbling on a plastic worm, and can vary from a slight movement to a sharp pull. When you feel this it is your cue to give him line, to give him time to get the hook into his mouth.

How much line and time to give? I begin by giving the fish the length that I can reach with rod and arms extended. If I miss a few fish doing this, I give a bit more line by opening the bail of a spinning reel, or by pushing the button on my free-spool casting reel.

There are days—I don't know why—when you can hook most of the bass by striking the instant you feel them. That's the exception, however; usually it's a guessing game of "now, or wait?"

When you set the hook on a bass down deep, do it with gusto. Snatch back on your rod hard enough to make the boat shudder, for you have several factors working against getting the hook firmly into the fish's jaw.

One of them is the inevitable bow in a line fished down deep. Your sweeping strike must remove that bow before it has much effect on the lure. If you have the point of the hook buried back into the worm to make it weedless, your strike must be sufficient to drive the point of the hook on through the worm and into the bass. If the bass has the worm all balled up in his mouth, and your strike is gentle, you will merely pull the bass through the water.

Another reason for a hefty strike is that big bass have big, tough jaws—and when you begin bumping the bottom with plastic worms you are in big bass country.

A strong line is best for this type of fishing. I use twelve- or fifteen-pound test monofilament on my spinning reel, and fifteen- or twenty-pound test mono on my Ambassadeur 5000 plug-casting reel. If this seems unnecessarily strong, let me assure you that it is not. It's required to stand the strain of the strike and of pulling big bass off the debris-laden bottom of a lake.

When you hook a bass in a deep-water concentration, horse him up out of his companions without ceremony. This accomplishes several things. It moves him away from the school and decreases the chance of spooking the rest of the fish. It tends to get the fish up out of most of the underwater obstructions on which he could foul the line, and this is very, very important if the bass happens to be trophy size. A really big bass, unless moved while still disoriented from the strike, is almost impossible to keep from breaking the line on a limb or stump. If the lake bottom is free of obstructions, there's no problem. In any event, if you let big fish thrash around in the sanctuary it usually scatters the school.

Color can be very important, despite the fact that you are fishing at a level where visibility is often low. Purple, blue, black, red, and green plastic worms are the most effective colors, with purple best.

You won't always find bass at home even in a known sanctuary. They migrate, usually up the ridge toward shore, at some time during the day and sometimes twice. They may go all the way to shore and scatter up and down the lake edge, and during the half

hour or so they are there, any lucky angler who happens to be working the shoreline gets action. He may think that the bass started hitting and then stopped, but in fact he has simply been on hand for their arrival and departure.

Buck Perry discovered bass sanctuaries and migrations in his home state of North Carolina, and developed a lure and a system to fish them. The system he calls Spoonplugging, and the lure is the Spoonplug. Buck himself has traveled the nation teaching his method of fishing. In the Chain-o-Lakes north of Chicago, for example, he found bass sanctuaries far out in the lake and caught trophy fish nobody knew were there.

Finding these deep-water concentrations, let me repeat, is not easy. It requires work on a particular lake for hours and days, but the rewards are great. A trip I made with Don Norton last summer is a good example of this method of getting bass.

Don lives in Clinton, Mississippi, where he manufactures his Johnny Reb line of lures, and has fished nearby Barnett Reservoir until he has located more than a score of sanctuaries. Using a map, a Fish Lo-K-Tor, and a notebook full of diagrams he had drawn, we fished one day from one of his hotspots to the next.

After five hours we didn't have a bass. Again and again we hit sanctuaries where nobody was at home. But finally—as usually happens if you are persistent—we found a good concentration. In two hours we landed twenty-seven good bass.

If you would like to catch bass in bunches, anywhere you fish, observe these facts:

1. Most bass are deep most of the time.
2. When bass are deep they are concentrated in schools.
3. When bass are deep they are on the bottom.
4. Lures must be fished on the bottom to take these fish.   ◉

Carl Rungius
A HUNTER'S ART

*No painter has
equaled him
in capturing the quality
of North American
big game and the majestic
wilderness
in which it lives.*

Bugling Elk

Caribou on the Smokey

Mule Deer (etching)

For fifty years his campfires blazed in remote regions teeming with game, for fifty years his rifle cracked and his portable easel unfolded. He lived in harmony with action and art, striking a balance between the two which won him more honors than any nature painter since Audubon.

Born in Berlin in 1869, Carl Clemens Moritz Rungius received his academic training there. He showed a perfectionist's interest in anatomical detail, and shot and skinned cats in order to study musculature.

In 1894, an American uncle invited him to hunt moose in Maine. Afterwards, he drifted West, hunting as he went, and when he reached the high-country wilderness he fell in love with it. Later trips took him into the Canadian Rockies and Alaska, where he painted and sketched

Lake Louise

Moose in Water

Dall's Sheep (etching)

beside smudge fires built to drive away monstrous summer mosquitoes.

Rungius was never injured while hunting. A short, wiry man with a cocky grin, great hardihood, and an undimming sense of humor, he was a tireless trail rider who seemed to be able to stay on a horse longer than the saddle. As a shot he was unerring, but he preferred to fire at close range, where his knowledge of vital organs could be used to best advantage. While no record was kept of his kills, his trophy elk, moose, bear, and sheep, like his paintings, numbered in the hundreds.

Rocky Mountain Goats

A Woodland Stag (etching)

Bear in Landscape

Rungius owed his success no more to rendering the actual animal than to his ability to capture landscape, wilderness atmosphere, and the excitement of that moment before a hunter squeezes off the decisive shot. Not long after he came to this country (he later became a citizen), Rungius drew illustrations for *Forest and Stream;* in 1907 he placed a wide range of animal oils at the Sportsmen's Show in Pittsburgh, and sold all of them. Shortly thereafter he was befriended by Dr. William Hornaday, president of the New York Zoological Society, who commissioned an extensive series of paintings. The New York

Museum of Natural History commissioned Rungius, during his heyday in the 1920's, to design dioramas of North American big game and to paint the backgrounds.

Rungius and his wife were as alike as day and night; she treasured the fireside, he the high wilderness. At home he played the quiet husband—mentally plotting his next pack trip. On one of the few trips Mrs. Rungius took with him into the wilds, she made up the sleeping bags with sheets.

Rungius eventually established a studio above Lake Louise at Banff, high in the Canadian Rockies. Here he and his wife summered with the great spaces and the great animals he loved near at hand.

Carl Rungius' recollections of big game hunting cast light on his personality as a sportsman: "Wyoming was a great game country in 1895," he is quoted as saying in William Schaldach's limited-edition biography. "Hunting antelope—a game on which I first started—was a difficult sport even then. The fleet little animals were very abundant between the Wind River and the Uinta Range, where I was located, but they were kept stirred up by the cowboys. . . .

"It was a country of long parallel hills, and I soon learned to ride in the valleys and occasionally creep cautiously up to the top of a rise for a look about. When I saw a bunch out of range I attracted their attention by rising a number of times and disappearing again. Antelope have a great bump of curiosity and anything unusual fascinates them. Returning to my horse I rode quickly to a spot within range, keeping concealed behind the hill. Dismounting and crawling up to look over the hill, I usually found the antelope at the place where I had last been. By using this ruse I would get an easy shot. With the buck tied across the saddle I would walk home happily smoking my pipe."

This is a casual picture of a man happy in the open spaces, a natural hunter. However, as artist and devotee of color he hunted on the whimsical side also—for butterflies, for instance, which he collected in every variety from every region in which he hunted and painted.

Among the big game, elk became his absorbing interest, for they reminded him of the great red deer of his native Europe.

Prominent and common citizens alike appreciated his art. Theodore Roosevelt called it, "The most spirited animal painting I have ever seen."

In his old age, Rungius returned permanently to New York, working in a studio apartment. He died there in 1959, at the age of ninety, a brush in his hand and a painting before him. Not long before, Rungius had made his last excursion to Alaska —where he had traveled across the countryside by helicopter and sketched the wildlife through plexiglass.

His wilderness studio at Banff, easily accessible today by superhighway, has been made a museum by the Glenbow Foundation. There, his sketches, paintings, palette, and dry brushes cast a poignant mood as one gazes into the mountainous distance where the sheep Rungius hunted still cling to the trails of the Rockies.

Rungius' art captures game's muscular dynamics.

THE PRAIRIE TRAVELLER

In 1849, Captain Randolph B. Marcy of the U.S. Army escorted a large company of emigrants heading for the California gold fields from Fort Smith, Arkansas, over rugged terrain and through hostile Indian country to Sante Fe, New Mexico, more than five hundred miles to the west. The expedition not only established a principal link in what was to become a major cross-country highway, it also established Marcy as a capable guide and explorer.

In nine years Marcy commanded five important exploring expeditions throughout the Southwest and the Rocky Mountain region, in many cases charting territory for the first time. On one of these he traced and mapped the Red River, a major tributary of the Mississippi, which Zebulon Pike had sought and failed to find some years earlier.

As a result of his explorations, Marcy became an authority on the geography, wildlife, and Indians of the Southwest and on the practical aspects of survival in the country beyond the frontier. To his consternation he often found that contemporary maps were inaccurate, information was erroneous, and settlers were ignorant about what they would face during a long overland journey.

To correct this he wrote *The Prairie Traveller, A Hand-Book for Overland Expeditions*. The book, much of which is printed here, was published in 1859; it sold for a dollar and remained in print for more than forty years.

It is a fascinating account of the logistics of one of the great symbols of American history—the covered-wagon train—and contains interesting details on the care and handling of firearms and of meat-hunting along the way.

by Randolph B. Marcy

Emigrants or others desiring to make the overland journey to the Pacific should bear in mind that there are several different routes which may be travelled with wagons, each having its advocates in persons directly or indirectly interested in attracting the tide of emigration and travel over them.

Information concerning these routes coming from strangers living or owning property near them, from agents of steam-boats or railways, or from other persons connected with transportation companies, should be received with great caution, and never without corroborating evidence from disinterested sources.

There is no doubt that each one of these roads has its advantages and disadvantages, but a judicious selection must depend chiefly upon the following considerations, namely, the locality from whence the individual is to take his departure, the season of the year when he desires to commence his journey, the character of his means of transportation, and the point upon the Pacific coast that he wishes to reach.

Persons living in the Northeastern States can, with about equal facility and dispatch, reach the eastern terminus of any one of the routes they may select by means of public transport. And, as animals are much cheaper upon the frontier than in the Eastern States, they should purchase their teams at or near the point where the overland journey is to commence.

Those living in the Northwestern States, having their own teams, and wishing to go to any point north of San Francisco, will of course make choice of the route which takes its departure from the Missouri River.

Those who live in the middle Western States, having their own means of transportation, and going to any point upon the Pacific coast, should take [a] middle route.

Others, who reside in the extreme Southwest, and whose destination is south of San Francisco, should travel the southern road running through Texas, which is the only one practicable for comfortable winter travel. The grass upon a great portion of this route is green during the entire winter, and snow seldom covers it. This road leaves the Gulf Coast at Powder-horn, on Matagorda Bay, which point is difficult of access by land from the north, but may be reached by steamers from New Orleans.

There are stores at Powder-horn and Indianola where the traveller can obtain most of the articles necessary for his journey, but I would recommend him to supply himself before leaving New Orleans with every thing he requires with the exception of animals, which he will find cheaper in Texas.

This road has received a large amount of travel since 1849, is well tracked and defined, and, excepting about twenty miles of "hog wallow prairie" near Powder-horn, it is an excellent road for carriages and wagons. It passes through a settled country for 250 miles, and within this section supplies can be had at reasonable rates.

The next route to the north is that over which the semi-weekly mail to California passes, and which, for a great portion of the way to New Mexico, I travelled and recommended in 1849. This road leaves the Arkansas River at Fort Smith, to which point steamers run during the seasons of high water in the winter and spring.

Supplies of all descriptions necessary for the overland journey may be procured at Fort Smith, or at Van Buren on the opposite side of the Arkansas. Horses and cattle are cheap here. The road, on leaving Fort Smith, passes through the Choctaw and Chickasaw country for 180 miles, then crosses Red River by ferry-boat at Preston, and runs through the border settlements of northern Texas for 150 miles, within which distances supplies may be procured at moderate prices.

This road [connects] with the San Antonio road at El Paso, and from that point they pass together over the mountains to Fort Yuma and to San Francisco in California.

Another road leaves Fort Smith and runs up the south side of the Canadian River to Santa Fé and Albuquerque in New Mexico.

This route is set down upon most of the maps of the present day as having been discovered and explored by various persons, but my own name seems to have been carefully excluded from the list. Whether this omission has been intentional or not, I leave for the authors to determine. I shall merely remark that I had the command and entire direction of an expedition which in 1849 discovered, explored, located, and marked out this identical wagon road from Fort Smith, Arkansas, to Santa Fé, New Mexico, and that this road, for the greater portion of the distance, is the same that has been since recommended for a Pacific railway.

The grass upon all the roads leaving Fort Smith is sufficiently advanced to afford sustenance to animals by the first of April, and from this time until winter sets in it is abundant. The next route on the north leaves the Missouri River at Westport, Leavenworth City, Atchison, or from other towns above, between either of which points and St. Louis steamers ply during the entire summer season.

This is the great emigrant route from Missouri to California and Oregon, over which so many thousands have travelled within the past few years. The track is broad, well worn, and can not be mistaken. It has received the major part of the Mormon emigration, and it was traversed by the U. S. Army in its march to Utah in 1857.

Many persons who have had much experience in prairie travelling prefer leaving the Missouri River in March or April, and feeding grain to their animals until the new grass appears. The roads become muddy and heavy after the spring rains set in, and by starting out early the worst part of the road will be passed over before the ground becomes wet and soft. This plan, however, should never be attempted unless the animals are well supplied with grain.

The grass, after the 1st of May, is good and abundant upon this road as far as the South Pass, from whence there is a section of about 50 miles where it is scarce; there is also a scarcity upon the desert beyond the sink of the Humboldt. As large numbers of cattle pass over the road annually, they soon consume all the grass in these barren localities, and such as pass late in the season are likely to suffer greatly, and oftentimes perish from starvation. When I came over the road in August, 1858, I seldom found myself out of sight of dead cattle for 500 miles along the road, and this was an unusually favorable year for grass, and before the main body of animals had passed for that season.

Upon the head of the Sweetwater River, and west of the South Pass, alkaline springs are met with, which are exceedingly poisonous to cattle and horses. They can readily be detected by the yellowish-red color of the grass growing around them. Animals should never be allowed to graze near them or to drink the water.

ORGANIZATION OF COMPANIES

After a particular route has been selected to make the journey across the plains, and the requisite number have arrived at the eastern terminus, their first business should be to organize themselves into a company and elect a commander. The company should be of sufficient magnitude to herd and guard animals, and for protection against Indians.

From 50 to 70 men, properly armed and equipped, will be enough for these purposes, and any greater number only makes the movements of the party more cumbersome.

In the selection of a captain, good judgment, integrity of purpose, and practical experience are the essential requisites, and these are indispensable to the harmony and consolidation of the association. His duty should be to direct the order of march, the time of starting and halting, to select the camps, detail and give orders to guards, and, indeed, to control and superintend all the movements of the company.

An obligation should then be drawn up and signed by all the members of the association, wherein each one should bind himself to abide in all cases by the orders and decisions of the captain, and to aid him by every means in his power in the execution of his duties; and they should also obligate themselves to aid each other.

On long and arduous expeditions men are apt to become irritable and ill-natured, and oftentimes fancy they have more labor imposed upon them than their comrades, and that the person who directs the march is partial toward his favorites, etc. That man who exercises the greatest forbearance under such circumstances, who is cheerful, slow to take up quarrels, and endeavors to reconcile difficulties among his companions, is deserving of all praise, and will, without doubt, contribute largely to the success and comfort of an expedition.

Unless a systematic organization be adopted, it is impossible for a party of any magnitude to travel in company for any great length of time, and for all the members to agree upon the same arrangements in marching, camping, etc. I have several times observed, where this has been attempted, that discords and dissensions sooner or later arose which invariably resulted in breaking up and separating the company.

When a captain has once been chosen, he should be sustained in all his decisions unless he commit some manifest outrage, when a majority of the company can always remove him, and put a more competent man in his place. Sometimes men may be selected who, upon trial, do not come up to the anticipations of those who have placed them in power, and other men will exhibit, during the course of the march, more capacity. Under these circumstances it will not be unwise to make a change.

WAGONS AND TEAMS

Wagons should be of the simplest possible construction: strong, light, and made of well-seasoned timber, especially the wheels, as the atmosphere, in the elevated and arid region over which they have to pass, is so exceedingly dry during the summer months that, unless the wood-work is thoroughly seasoned, they will require constant repairs to prevent them from falling to pieces.

Wheels made of the bois-d'arc, or Osage orangewood, are the best for the plains, as they shrink but little, and seldom want repairing. As, however, this wood is not easily procured in the Northern States, white oak answers a very good purpose if well seasoned.

Spring wagons made in Concord, New Hampshire, are used to transport passengers and the mails upon some of the routes across the plains, and they are said, by those who have used them, to be much superior to any others. They are made of the close-grained oak that grows in a high northern latitude, and well seasoned.

Wagons with six mules should never, on a long journey over the prairies, be loaded with over 2000 pounds, unless grain is transported, when an additional thousand pounds may be taken, provided it is fed out daily to the team. When grass constitutes the only forage, 2000 pounds is deemed a sufficient load.

There has been much discussion regarding the relative merits of mules and oxen for prairie travelling, and the question is yet far from being settled. Upon good firm roads, in a populated country, where grain can be procured, I should unquestionably give the preference to mules, as they travel faster, and endure the heat of summer much better than oxen; and if the journey be not over 1000 miles, and the grass abundant, even without grain, I think mules would be preferable. But when the march is to extend 1500 to 2000 miles, or over a rough sandy or muddy road, I believe young oxen will endure better than mules; they will, if properly managed, keep in better condition, and perform the journey in an equally brief space of time. Besides, they are much more economical, a team of six mules costing six hundred dollars, while an eight-ox team only costs upon the frontier about two hundred dollars. Oxen are much less liable to be stampeded and driven off by Indians, and can be pursued and overtaken by horsemen; and, finally, they can, if necessary, be used for beef.

Cows will be found very useful upon long journeys when the rate of travel is slow, as they furnish milk, and in emergencies they may be worked in wagons. I once saw a small cow yoked beside a large ox, and driven about six hundred miles attached to a loaded wagon, and she performed her part equally well with the ox.

STORES AND PROVISIONS

Supplies for a march should be put up in the most secure, compact, and portable shape.

Bacon should be packed in strong sacks of a hundred pounds to each; or, in very hot climates, put in boxes and surrounded with bran, which in a great measure prevents the fat from melting away.

If pork be used, in order to avoid transporting about forty per cent of useless weight, it should be taken out of the barrels and packed like the bacon; then so placed in the bottom of the wagons as to keep it cool. The pork, if well cured, will keep several months, but bacon is preferable.

Flour should be packed in stout double canvas sacks well sewed.

Butter may be preserved by boiling it thoroughly, and skimming off the scum as it rises to the top until it is quite clear like oil. It is then placed in tin canisters and soldered up.

Sugar may be well secured in India-rubber or gutta percha sacks, or so placed in the wagon as not to risk getting wet.

Desiccated or dried vegetables are almost equal to the fresh, and are put up in such a compact and portable form as easily to be transported over the plains. They have been extensively used in the Crimean war, and by our own army in Utah, and have been very generally approved. They are prepared by cutting the fresh vegetables into thin slices and subjecting them to a very powerful press, which removes the juice and leaves a solid cake, which, after having been thoroughly dried in an oven, becomes almost as hard as a rock. A small piece of this, about half the size of a man's hand, when boiled, swells up so as to fill a vegetable dish, and is sufficient for four men. It is believed that the antiscorbutic properties of vegetables are not impaired by desiccation, and they will keep for years.

The allowance of provisions for each grown person, to make the journey from the Missouri River to California, should suffice for 110 days. The following is deemed requisite, viz.: 150 lbs. of flour, or its equivalent in hard bread; 25 lbs. of bacon or pork, and enough fresh beef to be driven on the hoof to make up the meat component of the ration; 15 lbs. of coffee, and 25 lbs. of sugar; also a quantity of saleratus [baking powder] or yeast powders for making bread, and salt and pepper.

CLOTHING

A suitable dress for prairie travelling is of great import to health and comfort. Cotton or linen fabrics do not sufficiently protect the body against the direct rays of the sun at midday, nor against rains or sudden changes of temperature. Wool, being a non-conductor, is the best material for this mode of locomotion, and should always be adopted for the plains. The coat should be short and stout, the shirt of red or blue flannel, such as can be found in almost all the shops on the frontier: this, in warm weather, answers for an outside garment. The pants should be of thick and soft woolen material, and it is well to have them re-enforced on the inside, where they come in contact with the saddle, with soft buckskin, which makes them more durable and comfortable.

Woolen socks and stout boots, coming up well at the knees, and made large, so as to admit the pants, will be found the best for horsemen, and they guard against rattlesnake bites.

In travelling through deep snow during very cold weather in winter, moccasins are preferable to boots or shoes, as being more pliable, and allowing a freer circulation of the blood. In crossing the Rocky Mountains in the winter, the weather being intensely cold, I wore two pairs of woolen socks, and a square piece of thick blanket sufficient to cover the feet and ankles, over which were drawn a pair of thick buckskin moccasins, and the whole enveloped in a pair of buffalo-skin boots with the hair inside, made open in the front and tied with buckskin strings. At the same time I wore a pair of elkskin pants, which most effectually prevented the air from penetrating to the skin, and made an excellent defense against brush.

In the summer season shoes are much better for footmen than boots, as they are lighter, and do not cramp the ankles; the soles should be broad, so as to allow a square, firm tread, without pinching the feet.

The following list of articles is deemed a sufficient outfit for one man upon a three months' expedition, viz.:

---

2 blue or red flannel overshirts, open in front, with buttons.
2 woolen undershirts.
2 pairs thick cotton drawers.
4 pairs woolen socks.
2 pairs cotton socks.
4 colored silk handkerchiefs.
2 pairs stout shoes, for footmen.
1 pair boots, for horsemen.
1 pair shoes, for horsemen.
3 towels.
1 gutta percha poncho.
1 broad-brimmed hat of soft felt.
1 comb and brush.
2 tooth-brushes.
1 pound Castile soap.
3 pounds bar soap for washing clothes.
1 belt-knife and small whetstone.
& Stout linen thread, large needles, a bit of beeswax, a few buttons, paper of pins, and a thimble, all contained in a small buckskin or stout cloth bag.

The foregoing articles, with the coat and the overcoat, complete the wardrobe.

CAMP EQUIPAGE

The bedding for each person should consist of two blankets, a comforter, and a pillow, and a gutta percha or painted canvas cloth to spread beneath the bed upon the ground, and to contain it when rolled up.

Every mess of six or eight persons will require a wrought-iron camp kettle, large enough for boiling meat and making soup; a coffee-pot and cups of heavy tin, with the

242

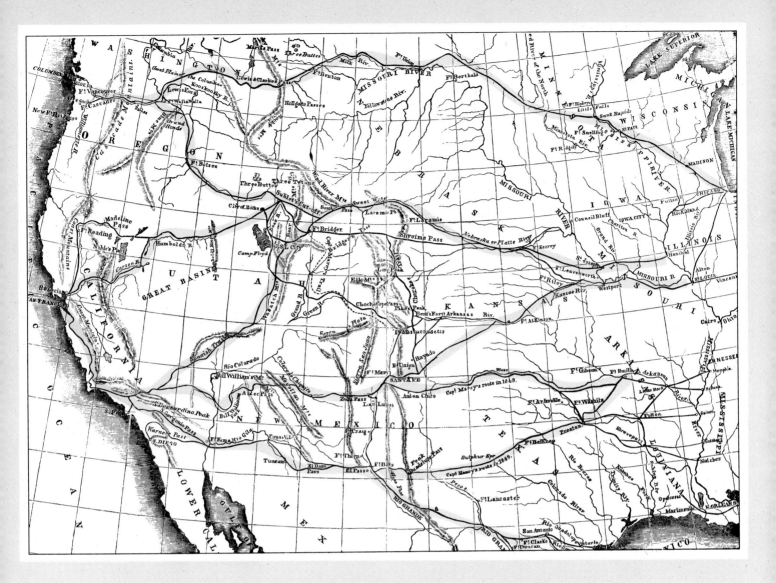

Darkened lines on Traveller *map show routes west in 1850's. Northern trail generally followed Lewis and Clark's expedition. Oregon Trail began at Hannibal; Santa Fe at St. Louis. Marcy's two 1849 routes originated at Ft. Smith; one joined Santa Fe Trail, other San Antonio Trail.*

handles riveted on; tin plates, frying and bake pans of wrought iron, the latter for baking bread and roasting coffee. Also a mess pan of heavy tin or wrought iron for mixing bread and other culinary purposes; knives, forks, and spoons; an extra camp kettle; tin or gutta percha bucket for water; an axe, hatchet, and spade will also be needed, with a mallet for driving picket-pins. Matches should be carried in bottles and corked tight, so as to exclude the moisture.

A little blue mass [cathartic pill containing mercury], quinine, opium, and some cathartic medicine, put up in doses for adults, will suffice for the medicine-chest.

ARMS

Every man who goes into the Indian country should be armed with a rifle and revolver, and he should never, either in camp or out of it, lose sight of them. When not on the march, they should be placed in such a position that they can be seized at an instant's warning; and when moving about outside the camp, the revolver should invariably be worn in the belt.

A great diversity of opinion obtains regarding the kind of rifle that is the most efficient and best adapted to Indian warfare, and the question is perhaps as yet very far from being settled to the satisfaction of all. A large majority of men prefer the breech-loading arm, but there are those who still adhere tenaciously to the old-fashioned muzzle-loading rifle as preferable to any of the modern inventions. Among these may be mentioned the border hunters and mountaineers, who can not be persuaded to use any other than the Hawkins [Hawken] rifle, for the reason that they know nothing about the merits of any others. My own experience has forced me to the conclusion that the breech-loading arm possesses great advantages over the muzzle-loading, for the reason that it can be charged and fired with much greater rapidity.

Colt's revolving pistol is very generally admitted, both in Europe and America, to be the most efficient arm of its kind known at the present day. As the same principles are involved in the fabrication of his breech-loading rifle as are found in the pistol, the conviction to me is irresistible that, if one arm is worthy of consideration, the other is equally so. For my own part, I look upon Colt's new patent rifle as a most excellent arm for border service. It gives six shots in more rapid succession than any other rifle I know of, and these, if properly expended, are oftentimes sufficient to decide a contest; moreover, it is the most reliable and certain weapon to fire that I have ever used, and I can not resist the force of my conviction that, if I were alone upon the prairies, and expected an attack from a body of Indians, I am not acquainted with any arm I would as soon have in my hands as this.

WATER

In mountainous districts water can generally be found either in springs, the dry beds of streams, or in holes in the rocks.

During a season of the year when there are occasional showers, water will generally be found in low places where there is a sub-

Sentinels guard wagon train fording river; Captain Marcy stressed constant vigilance en route.

stratum of clay, but after the dry season has set in these pools evaporate, and it is necessary to dig wells. The lowest spots should be selected for this purpose when the grass is green and the surface earth moist.

There are many indications of water known to old campaigners, although none of them are absolutely infallible. The most certain of them are deep green cottonwood or willow trees growing in depressed localities; also flags, water-rushes, tall green grass, etc.

The fresh tracks and trails of animals converging toward a common centre, and the flight of birds and waterfowl toward the same points, will also lead to water. In a section frequented by deer or mustangs, it may be certain that water is not far distant, as these animals drink daily, and they will not remain long in a locality after the water has dried up. Deer generally go to water during the middle of the day, but birds toward evening.

Water taken from stagnant pools, charged with putrid vegetable matter and animalculæ, would be very likely to generate fevers and dysenteries if taken into the stomach without purification. It should therefore be thoroughly boiled, and all the scum removed from the surface as it rises; this clarifies it, and by mixing powdered charcoal with it the disinfecting process is perfected.

JOURNADAS

In some localities 50 or 60 miles, and even greater distances, are frequently traversed without water; these long stretches are called by the Mexicans "journadas," or day's journeys. There is one in New Mexico called Journada del Muerto, which is 78½ miles in length, where, in a dry season, there is not a drop of water; yet, with proper care, this drive can be made with ox or mule teams, and without loss of animals.

On arriving at the last camping-ground before entering upon the journada, all the animals should be as well rested and refreshed as possible. To insure this, they must be turned out upon the best grass that can be found, and allowed to eat and drink as much as they desire during the entire halt. Should the weather be very warm, and the teams composed of oxen, the march should not be resumed until it begins to cool in the afternoon. They should be carefully watered just previous to being hitched up and started out upon the journada, the water-kegs having been previously filled. The drive is then commenced, and continued during the entire night, with 10 or 15 minutes rest every two hours. About daylight a halt should be made, and the animals immediately turned out to graze for two hours, during which time, especially if there is dew upon the grass, they will have become considerably refreshed, and may be put to the wagons again and driven until the heat becomes oppressive toward noon, when they are again turned out upon a spot where the grass is good, and, if possible, where there are shade trees. About four o'clock P.M. they are again started, and the march continued into the night, and as long as they can be driven without suffering.

ADVANCE AND REAR GUARDS

A few men, well mounted, should constitute the advance and rear guards for each train of wagons passing through the Indian country. Their duty will be to keep a vigilant look-out in all directions, and to reconnoitre places where Indians would be likely to lie in ambush. Should hostile Indians be discovered, the fact should be at once reported to the commander, who (if he anticipates an attack) will rapidly form his wagons into a circle or "corral," with the animals toward the centre, and the men on the inside, with their arms in readiness to repel an attack from without. If these arrangements be properly attended to, few parties of Indians will venture to make an attack, as they are well aware that some of their warriors might pay with their lives the forfeit of such indiscretion.

SELECTION OF CAMPS

One of the most important considerations that should influence the choice of a locality is its capability for defense. If the camp be pitched beside a stream, a concave bend, where the water is deep, with a soft alluvial bed inclosed by high and abrupt banks, [it] will be the most defensible, and all the more should the concavity form a peninsula. The advantages of such a position are obvious to a soldier's eye, as that part of the encampment inclosed by the stream is naturally secure, and leaves only one side to be defended. The concavity of the bend will enable the defending party to cross its fire in case of attack from the exposed side.

When a halt is made the wagons are "corraled," as it is called, by bringing the two front ones near and parallel to each other. The two next are then driven up on the outside of these, with the front wheels of the former touching the rear wheels of the latter, the rear of the wagons turned out upon the circumference of the circle that is being formed, and so on until one half of the circle is made, when the rear of the wagons are turned in to complete the circle. An opening of about twenty yards should be left between the last two wagons for animals to pass in and out of the corral, and this may be closed with two ropes stretched between the wagons. Such a corral forms an excellent and secure barricade against Indian attacks, and a good inclosure for cattle while they are being yoked; indeed, it is indispensable.

The mountaineers and trappers exercise a very wise precaution, on laying down for the night, by placing their arms and ammunition by their sides, where they can be seized at a moment's notice. They are therefore seldom liable to be surprised.

The chief causes of accidents from the use of fire-arms arise from carelessness, and I have always observed that those persons who are most familiar with their use are invariably the most careful. Many accidents have happened from carrying guns with the cock down upon the cap. When in this position, a blow upon the cock, and sometimes the concussion produced by the falling of the gun, will explode the cap; and, occasionally, when the cock catches a twig, or in the clothes, and lifts it from the cap, it will explode. With a gun at half-cock there is but little danger of such accidents; for, when the cock is drawn back, it either comes to the full-cock, and remains, or it returns to the half-cock, but does not go down upon the cone. Another source of very many sad and fatal accidents resulting from the most stupid and culpable carelessness is in persons standing before the muzzles of guns and attempting to pull them out of wagons, or to draw them through a fence or brush in the same position. If the cock encounters an obstacle in its passage, it will, of course, be drawn back and fall upon the cap. These accidents are of frequent occurrence, and the cause is well understood by all, yet men continue to disregard it, and their lives pay the penalty of their indiscretion. It is a wise maxim, which applies with especial force in campaigning on the prairies, "Always look to your gun, never let your gun look at you."

An equally important maxim might be added to this: *Never to point your gun at another, whether charged or uncharged, and never allow another to point his gun at you.*

I know of nothing in the woodman's education of so much importance, or so difficult to acquire, as the art of trailing or tracking men and animals. To become an adept in this art requires the constant practice of years, and with some men a lifetime does not suffice to learn it.

A party of Indians, for example, starting out upon a war excursion, leave their families behind, and never transport their lodges; whereas, when they move with their families, they carry their lodges and other effects. If, therefore, an Indian trail is discovered with the marks of the lodge-poles upon it, it has certainly not been made by a war-party; but if the tracks do not show the trace of lodge-poles, it will be equally certain that a war or hunting party has passed that way, and if it is not desired to come in conflict with them, their direction may be avoided. Mustangs or wild horses, when moving from place to place, leave a trail which is sometimes difficult to distinguish from that made by a mounted party of Indians, especially if the mustangs do not stop to graze. This may be determined by following upon the trail until some dung is found, and if this should lie in a single pile, it is a sure indication that a herd of mustangs has passed, as they always stop to relieve themselves, while a party of Indians would keep their horses in motion, and the ordure would be scattered along the road. If the trail pass through woodland, the mustangs will occasionally go under the limbs of trees too low to admit the passage of a man on horseback.

I remember, upon one occasion, as I was riding with a Delaware upon the prairies, we crossed the trail of a large party of Indians travelling with lodges. The tracks appeared to me quite fresh, and I remarked to the Indian that we must be near the party.

"Oh no," said he, "the trail was made two days before, in the morning," at the same time pointing with his finger to where the sun would be at about 8 o'clock. Then, seeing that my curiosity was excited to know by what means he arrived at this conclusion, he called my attention to the fact that there had been no dew for the last two nights, but that on the previous morning it had been heavy. He then pointed out to me some spears of grass that had been pressed down into the earth by the horses' hoofs, upon which the sand still adhered, having dried on, thus clearly showing that the grass was wet when the tracks were made.

Fresh tracks generally show moisture where the earth has been turned up, but after a short exposure to the sun they become dry. If the tracks be very recent, the sand may sometimes, where it is very loose and dry, be seen running back into the tracks, and by following them to a place where they cross water, the earth will be wet for some distance after they leave it. The droppings of the dung from animals are also good indications of the age of a trail. It is well to remember whether there have been any rains within a few days, as the age of a trail may sometimes be conjectured in this way. It is very easy to tell whether tracks have been made before or after a rain, as the water washes off all the sharp edges.

It is not a difficult matter to distinguish the tracks of American horses from those of Indian horses, as the latter are never shod; moreover, they are much smaller.

In trailing horses, there will be no trouble while the ground is soft, as the impressions they leave will then be deep and distinct; but when they pass over hard or rocky ground, it is sometimes a very slow and troublesome process to follow them. Where there is grass, the trace can be seen for a considerable time, as the grass will be trodden down and bent in the direction the party has moved; should the grass have returned to its upright position, the trail can often be distinguished by standing upon it and looking ahead for some distance in the direction it has been pursuing; the grass that has been turned over will show a different shade of green from that around it, and this often marks a trail for a long time.

INDIAN FIGHTING

No people probably on the face of the earth are more ambitious of martial fame, or entertain a higher appreciation for the deeds of a daring and successful warrior, than the North American savages. The attainment of such reputation is the paramount and absorbing object of their lives. A young man is never considered worthy to occupy a seat in council until he has encountered an enemy in battle; and he who can count the greatest number of scalps is the most highly honored by his tribe.

It is not surprising, therefore, that the young man who has gained no renown as a warrior, should be less discriminate in his attacks than older men who have already acquired a name. The young braves should, therefore, be closely watched when encountered on the Plains.

The prairie tribes are seldom at peace with all their neighbors, and some of the young braves of a tribe are almost always absent upon a war excursion. The objects of these forays are to steal horses and mules, and to take prisoners; and if it so happens that a war-party has been unsuccessful in the accomplishment of these ends, or has had the misfortune to lose some of its number in battle, they become reckless, and will often attack a small party with whom they are not at war, provided they hope to escape detection. The disgrace attendant upon a return to their friends without some tro-

phies as an offset to the loss of their comrades is a powerful incentive to action, and they extend but little mercy to defenseless travellers who have the misfortune to encounter them at such a conjuncture.

The prairie warrior is occasionally seen with the rifle in his hand, but his favorite arm is the bow, the use of which is taught him at an early age. By constant practice he acquires a skill in archery that renders him no less formidable in war than successful in the chase.

The Comanches, Sioux, and other prairie tribes make their attacks upon the open prairies. Trusting to their wonderful skill in equitation and horsemanship, they ride around their enemies with their bodies thrown upon the opposite side of the horse, and discharge their arrows in rapid succession while at full speed; they will not, however, often venture near an enemy who occupies a defensive position. If, therefore, a small party be in danger of an attack from a large force of Indians, they should seek the cover of timber or a park of wagons, or, in the absence of these, rocks or holes in the prairie which afford good cover.

HUNTING

I know of no better school of practice for perfecting men in target-firing, and the use of fire-arms generally, than that in which the frontier hunter receives his education. One of the first and most important lessons that he is taught impresses him with the conviction that, unless his gun is in good order and steadily directed upon the game, he must go without his supper; and if ambition does not stimulate his efforts, his appetite will, and ultimately lead to success and confidence in his own powers.

The man who is afraid to place the butt of his piece firmly against his shoulder, or who turns away his head at the instant of

Indians attack. Marcy respected Indians' fighting ability, urged classic wagon circle for defense.

pulling trigger (as soldiers often do before they have been drilled at target-practice), will not be likely to bag much game or to contribute materially toward the result of a battle. The successful hunter, as a general rule, is a good shot, will always charge his gun properly, and may be relied upon in action.

Although I would always encourage men in hunting when permanently located, yet, unless they are good woodsmen, it is not safe to permit them to go out alone in marching through the Indian country, as, aside from the danger of encountering Indians, they would be liable to become bewildered and perhaps lost, and this might detain the entire party in searching for them. The better plan upon a march is for three or four to go out together, accompanied by a good woodsman, who will be able with certainty to lead them back to camp.

THE BUFFALO

The largest and most useful animal that roams over the prairies is the buffalo. It provides food, clothing, and shelter to thousands of natives whose means of livelihood depend almost exclusively upon this gigantic monarch of the prairies.

Not many years since they thronged in countless multitudes over all that vast area lying between Mexico and the British possessions, but now their range is confined within very narrow limits, and a few more years will probably witness the extinction of the species.

There are two methods generally practiced in hunting the buffalo, viz.: running them on horseback, and stalking, or still-hunting. The first method requires a sure-footed and tolerably fleet horse that is not easily frightened. The buffalo cow, which makes much better beef than the bull, when pursued by the hunter runs rapidly, and, unless the horse be fleet, it requires a long and exhausting chase to overtake her.

When the buffalo are discovered, and the hunter intends to give chase, he should first dismount, arrange his saddle-blanket and saddle, buckle the girth tight, and make every thing about his horse furniture snug and secure. He should then put his arms in good firing order, and, taking the lee side of the herd, so that they may not get "the wind" of him, he should approach in a walk as close as possible, taking advantage of any cover that may offer. His horse then, being cool and fresh, will be able to dash into the herd, and probably carry his rider very near the animal he has selected before he becomes alarmed.

If the hunter be right-handed, he should approach upon the left side, and when nearly opposite and close upon the buffalo, deliver his shot, taking aim a little below the centre of the body, and about eight inches back of the shoulder. This will strike the vitals, and generally render another shot unnecessary.

When a rifle or shot-gun is used the hunter rides up on the right side, keeping his horse well in band, so as to be able to turn off if the beast charges upon him; this, however, never happens except with a buffalo that is wounded, when it is advisable to keep out of his reach.

When the animal is upon a hill, or in any other position where he can not be approached without danger of disturbing him, the hunter should wait until he moves off to more favorable ground, and this will not generally require much time, as they wander about a great deal when not grazing; he then pickets his horse, and approaches cautiously, seeking to screen himself as much as possible by the undulations in the surface, or behind such other objects as may present themselves; but if the surface should offer no cover, he must crawl upon his hands and knees when near the game, and in this way he can generally get within rifle range.

The tongues, humps, and marrow-bones are regarded as the choice parts of the animal. The tongue is taken out by ripping open the skin between the prongs of the lower jaw-bone and pulling it out through the orifice. The hump may be taken off by skinning down on each side of the shoulders and cutting away the meat, after which the hump-ribs can be unjointed where they unite with the spine. The marrow, when roasted in the bones, is delicious.

THE DEER

Of all game quadrupeds indigenous to this continent, the common red deer is probably more widely dispersed from north to south and from east to west over our vast possessions than any other.

Besides the common red deer of the Eastern States, two other varieties are found in the Rocky Mountains, viz., the "black-tailed deer," which takes its name from the fact of its having a small tuft of black hair upon the end of its tail, and the long-tailed species. The former of these is considerably larger than the eastern deer, and is much darker, being of a very deep-yellowish iron-gray, with a yellowish red upon the belly. It frequents the mountains, and is never seen far away from them. Its habits are similar to those of the red deer, and it is hunted in the same way. The only difference I have been able to discern between the long-haired variety and the common deer is in the length of the tail and body. I have seen this animal only in the neighborhood of the Rocky Mountains.

Twenty years' experience in deer-hunting has taught me several facts relative to the habits of the animal which, when well understood, will be found of much service to the inexperienced hunter, and greatly contribute to his success. The best target-shots are not necessarily the most skillful deer-stalkers. One of the great secrets of this art is in knowing how to approach the game without giving alarm, and this can not easily be done unless the hunter sees it before he is himself discovered. There are so many objects in the woods resembling the deer in color that none but a practiced eye can often detect the difference.

When the deer is reposing he generally turns his head from the wind, in which position he can see an enemy approaching from that direction, and his nose will apprise him of the presence of danger from the opposite side. The best method of hunting deer, therefore, is *across the wind.*

While the deer are feeding, early in the morning and a short time before dark in the evening are the best times to stalk them, as they are then busily occupied and less on the alert. When a deer is espied with his head down, cropping the grass, the hunter advances cautiously, keeping his eyes constantly directed upon him, and screening himself behind intervening objects, or, in the absence of other cover, crawls along upon his hands and knees in the grass, until the deer hears his steps and raises his head, when he must instantly stop and remain in an attitude fixed and motionless as a statue, for the animal's vision is his keenest sense.

Many men, when they suddenly encounter a deer, are seized with nervous excitement, called in sporting parlance the "buck fever," which causes them to fire at random. Notwithstanding I have had much experience in hunting, I must confess that I am never entirely free from some of the symptoms of this malady when firing at large game, and I believe that in four out of five cases where I have missed the game my balls have passed too high. I have en-deavored to obviate this by sighting my rifle low, and it has been attended with more successful results. The same remarks apply to most other men I have met with. They fire too high when excited.

THE ANTELOPE

This animal frequents the most elevated bleak and naked prairies in all latitudes from Mexico to Oregon, and constitutes an important item of subsistence with many of the Prairie Indians. It is the most wary, timid, and fleet animal that inhabits the Plains. It is about the size of a small deer, with a heavy coating of coarse, wiry hair, and its flesh is more tender and juicy than that of the deer. It seldom enters a timbered country, but seems to delight in cropping the grass from the elevated swells of the prairies. When disturbed by the traveller, it will circle around him with the speed of the wind, but does not stop until it reaches some prominent position whence it can survey the country on all sides, and nothing seems to escape its keen vision. They will sometimes stand for a long time and look at a man, provided he does not move or go out of sight; but if he goes behind a hill with the intention of passing around and getting nearer to them, he will never find them again in the same place. I have often tried the experiment, and invariably found that, as soon as I went where the antelope could not see me, he moved off. Their sense of hearing, as well as vision, is very acute, which renders it difficult to stalk them. By taking advantage of the cover afforded in broken ground, the hunter may, by moving slowly and cautiously over the crests of the irregularities in the surface, sometimes approach within rifle range.

The antelope possesses a greater degree of curiosity than any other animal I know of, and will often approach very near a strange object. The experienced hunter, taking advantage of this peculiarity, lies down and secretes himself in the grass, after which he raises his handkerchief, hand, or foot, so as to attract the attention of the animal, and thus often succeeds in beguiling him within shooting distance.

THE BEAR

Besides the common black bear of the Eastern States, several others are found in the mountains of California, Oregon, Utah, and New Mexico, viz., the grizzly, brown, and cinnamon varieties; all are hunted in the same manner.

From all I had heard of the grizzly bear, I was induced to believe him one of the most formidable and savage animals in the universe, and that the man who would deliberately encounter and kill one of these beasts had performed a signal feat of courage which entitled him to a lofty position among the votaries of Nimrod. So firmly had I become impressed with this conviction, that I should have been very reluctant to fire upon one had I met him when alone and on foot. The grizzly bear is assuredly the monarch of the American forests, and, so far as physical strength is concerned, he is perhaps without a rival in the world; but, after some experience in hunting, my opinions regarding his courage and his willingness to attack men have very materially changed.

It is possible that if a man came suddenly upon the beast in a thicket, where it could have no previous warning, he might be attacked; but it is my opinion that if the bear gets the wind or sight of a man at any considerable distance, it will endeavor to get away as soon as possible. I am so fully impressed with this idea that I shall hereafter hunt bear with a feeling of as much security as I would have in hunting the buffalo.

THE BIG-HORN

The big-horn or mountain sheep, which has a body like the deer, with the head of a sheep, surmounted by an enormous pair of short, heavy horns, is found throughout the Rocky Mountains, and resorts to the most inaccessible peaks and to the wildest and least-frequented glens. It clambers over almost perpendicular cliffs with the greatest ease and celerity, and skips from rock to rock, cropping the tender herbage that grows upon them.

It has been supposed by some that this animal leaps down from crag to crag, lighting upon his horns, as an evidence of which it has been advanced that the front part of the horns is often much battered. This I believe to be erroneous, as it is very common to see horns that have no bruises upon them.

The old mountaineers say they have often seen the bucks engaged in desperate encounters with their huge horns. This will account for the marks seen upon them.

The flesh of the big-horn, when fat, is more tender, juicy, and delicious than that of any other animal I know of.

In its habits the mountain sheep greatly resembles the chamois of Switzerland, and it is hunted in the same manner. The hunter traverses the most inaccessible and broken localities, moving along with great caution, as the least unusual noise causes them to flit away like a phantom, and they will be seen no more. The animal is gregarious, but it is seldom that more than eight or ten are found in a flock. When not grazing they seek sheltered sides of mountains, and repose among the rocks.

Randolph Marcy survived the dangers of Indians, starvation, stampeding buffalo, and Confederate guns (he was General McClellan's chief of staff) to die of natural causes in 1887, at the age of 75. ◉